THE SECRET LIFE
OF BUILDINGS

The Graham Foundation for Advanced
Studies in the Fine Arts
Chicago, Illinois

The MIT Press
Cambridge, Massachusetts
London, England

THE SECRET LIFE
OF BUILDINGS

An American
Mythology for
Modern Architecture

Gavin Macrae-Gibson

This book was set in Trump Medieval by
Achorn Graphics and printed and bound
by Halliday Lithograph in the United
States of America

Library of Congress Cataloging in
Publication Data

Macrae-Gibson, Gavin.
   The secret life of buildings.
   Bibliography: p.
   Includes index.
   1. Architecture, Modern—20th
century—Philosophy.   2. Architecture—
United States—Philosophy.   I. Title.
NA680.M23 1985   720'.973   84-28889
ISBN 0-262-13203-6

For Nonnie

CONTENTS

ACKNOWLEDGMENTS

I began this book in 1981, and I am much indebted to the Graham Foundation for its generous support. I am also indebted to the Paul Mellon Foundation for a fellowship that enabled me to study at the Yale School of Architecture from 1977 to 1979.

I am grateful to the many people who helped me: Vincent Scully inspired and encouraged me; Peter Eisenman asked the right questions at the right time; Philip Johnson gave concrete assistance; and Charles Warren discussed many difficult points with me. In addition, all the architects of this study cooperated fully over several years and made many useful comments. This book would not have been written, however, but for my father, whose views profoundly affect my thought, and for Anne Balcer, around whose continuing support and steadfastness the work took shape.

PREFACE

The influence of scientific method has increased rapidly since the end of the sixteenth century at the expense of other, less materialistic methods of knowing. It is only in this century, however, that it has been possible to extensively implement the intellectual revolution caused by scientific method and to actually inhabit a technological world. Until recently, what we have come to call modern architecture, the largest visible product of this implementation, was thought to be inevitable because it was believed to be based on function, technology, or a spirit of the times perceived in strictly material terms. These causes were seen as part of the fulfillment of scientific method, which in turn was thought to be a means of revealing universal truths. This provided the meaning of architecture.[1]

The world of the machine endures, if suspect now in subtle and tragic ways. We cannot relinquish its comforts, nor do we wish to. Yet a crisis in modern architecture has arisen from the disquieting realization that basing our architecture on a belief in materialistic causes was never a matter of fact but always a question of faith[2]—faith that because science had drastically altered the world, its method could be meaningfully applied in architecture. We continue to live in a world of machines, but now for the first time architectural culture seems capable of distinguishing between the methods of science and that form of knowledge necessary to successfully express the experience of life lived among machines. The rapidly declining power of the faith in an indissoluble relation between scientific method and architectural meaning has precipitated the present state of turmoil in theoretical discourse.

We now see that the faith in scientific method on which modern architecture was originally based was a *myth*, that is, a story told by architecture to explain man's relation to the world. This original myth gave the illusion of incontrovertible truth; modern architects did not therefore concern themselves with the poetic method of thinking, even though it was a poetic method they in fact used. The result was a myth of the end of myth, which continually impoverished their efforts and has brought us to our present impasse.

We have become increasingly aware of the necessity of a modernism that looks for causes beyond material ones. The challenge the architecture of the ongoing machine age now faces is to proceed from the observation of the diverse effects of industrial culture on man to the development of a new mythology for modern architecture—a body of stories that together convincingly elucidate the predicament of man in the late twentieth century. This can only be achieved through a poetic logic. The embodiment in architectural form of mythological knowledge having the power to address the ambiguity and mystery of human life is what I call the secret life of buildings and is the subject of this book.

I have written the book in the way in which I believe architecture should be made: that is, beginning with the observation of reality and culminating in the unified expression of experience. I have therefore chosen to make a close examination of seven recent buildings. Through forms which, collectively, are connected to the whole of history, these buildings embody distinctly different interpretations of the effects of late-twentieth-century culture on the human spirit and are symptomatic of a new period of modern architecture.

My discussion specifically excludes many important topics. I touch only briefly if at all, for example, on questions of function, physical structure, or politics as they relate to these buildings. Also, it is a disadvantage of my method that I cannot discuss other recent buildings of perhaps equal or greater merit. My goal, however, was to choose examples as different from one another in their secret lives as possible. I have done this because I believe that one can better understand the predicament of modern architecture by an intense concentration on the secret life of a few buildings of the most diverse sensibility than by any other means, whether by analyzing some other aspect of the same small group or by superficial characterization of a far larger group.

Observation of these seven buildings, then, provides my starting point. My aim, however, is unification of experience. For this reason my conclusion takes the form of an investigation of a conceptual city created when the secret lives revealed by my analyses are considered as a whole. This secret city is the habitat of an illusive subject who is present throughout the book. The subject is none other than ourselves, a presence I shall call the figure in the shadows; the city is a machine for thinking in. It is a place to construct the mythology by which we come to know the figure in the shadows and without which the modern city will continue as the lifeless container of merely material existence that it has sadly become.

INTRODUCTION
A Method of Criticism for
Modern Architecture

UTOPIAN MODERNISM

"The philosophers have only *interpreted* the world in various ways; the point, however, is to *change it*."

Karl Marx[1]

The original modern architecture of the machine age was founded on an ideology defined by Karl Popper as historicist. Historicism is not the application of stylistic motifs borrowed from history; it is a theory of history. It is the view that the principal aim of the social sciences should be historical prediction, along the lines developed so successfully by the physical sciences, achieved by discovering the trends that underlie the evolution of history, by laying bare the "spirit of the times." As elaborated by those architects of the 1920s whom Henry-Russell Hitchcock called the New Pioneers,[2] that doctrine engendered the view that because of the inexorable laws of historical development, every new period of architectural history should unfailingly produce a totally new and homogeneous expression of collective humanity, each one superior to the one before because closer to the perfect truth of unraveled time. As a result, architectural history was seen as consisting of discrete ages, each characterized by a different spirit that invalidated all previous traditions and cultural patterns. Architects were thus committed to the revelation of the essential spirit unique to their time, morally superior to all others, and tending toward ever more advanced development. This is the ideology of what we may justly call the Utopian period of modern architecture.

Three themes dominate this Utopian period: memory, expression, and morality.

Memory
The concept of a spirit that expresses the "essence" of a time and invalidates all previous traditions depends on a progressive view of history in which art, like science, is thought to improve incrementally. Le Corbusier expressed this view of the role of memory in *Towards a New Architecture* when he wrote, "The house has always been the indispensable and first tool that [man] has forged for himself . . . . Tools are the result of successive improvement . . . . We throw the out-of-date tool on the scrap heap."[3] Because this evolutionary argument regards the future as morally superior to the past, the forms of the past come to be regarded as contaminating. In *The International Style* Hitchcock and Johnson acknowledge that it is possible to learn the "healthiest lessons" from the past,[4] but such learning can be achieved only if the study is "scientific";[5] that is, if it is conducted according to a historicist view in which to go back to the visual attributes of past architectural forms or to acknowledge that such styles express sensibilities that may still be valid is to regress socially and morally. To the extent that the past is considered relevant at all, it is viewed competitively, as a catalogue of peaks to be equalled or surpassed—a rival, not a mentor. By these means "the great styles of the past" were to be emulated "*in their essence* without imitating their surface."[6]

This is an inversion of the preceding romantic view by which history contains periods in the distant past whose values are superior to those of the present and can be recalled by the use of styles. Instead, a teleological view prevailed, in which a superior force was thought to direct the present toward an incontrovertibly better future. The Utopian period could not model its forms on those of this favored period, as the romantics could by looking to Greece or Egypt, since the forms did not yet exist. Rather, it gave up the pursuit of form altogether by seeking refuge in the doctrine of functionalism.

Expression

Although the spirit of the age may have demanded such amnesia, the Utopian modernists recognized that a simple antihistorical functionalism, based on materials and program, was insufficient to generate expressive architecture.[7] Since they could not call upon the past as a source of formal inspiration, they were forced to resort instead to the designer's intuition to provide architecture with artistic power. "One may refuse to admit," as Hitchcock and Johnson put it, "that intentionally functionalist building is quite without a potential aesthetic element. Consciously or unconsciously the architect must make *free choices* before his design is completed."[8] These "free" choices were of course highly constrained because they were limited to a palette of novel forms endorsed by the historicist interpretation of history, with its suppression of memory. *Apparent* freedom came from the exercise of intuition in the pursuit of this very novelty. The expression of the Utopian building was therefore to be derived from that complex of superstitions and prejudices called the spirit of the age, which supposedly operated through the intuitive faculties of the designer like a weathervane recording the passing winds.

Morality

But the full strength of the Utopian period is incomprehensible without a third factor connecting the rivalry with history to the faith in intuition: the power accorded to morality as a justifying agent. In the historicist conception there could be only one style—the styleless style—since there was but one essence of the age. Historical types or styles were quite literally "a lie," in Le Corbusier's words,[9] because the essence of the age applied as much to conduct as to art and because an architecture of abstract expression could be justified by the conduct of modern people. Similarly, Adolf Loos could justify the "crime" of ornament by reference to the conduct of primitive people. Just as it was believed that these "good" people—those "in tune with the times" —would make "good" architecture, so it was believed that this architecture would, in its turn, make the people good. "Architecture," proclaimed Le Corbusier, is "a thing which in itself produces happy peoples."[10] Given the belief that the welfare of nations was at stake, it is understandable that the moral sanctioning of novel, abstract form could acquire such power at the expense of what now seem legitimate expressive impulses embodied in traditional forms. As Geoffrey Scott had rightly warned in *The Architecture of Humanism*, "the moral judgement, deceived by a false analogy with conduct, tends to intervene before the aesthetic purpose has been impartially discerned."[11]

The circle of historicism was thus complete: the moral analogy with conduct provided a justification for novel, abstract forms produced through the intuition of the utopianist; and their expressive capability was deprived of all memory connected with place or with artistic traditions by the "progressive" relation between history and morality. This triumvirate of themes made possible the central, most destructive characteristic of the Utopian period, the intuitive abstraction of so-called essence from form, and, in turn, the abstraction of essential form from place. As a result buildings became abstracted "essences" set down on little slices of utopia, like canapés for a feast at the end of the world.

The once powerful interaction of these themes has collapsed under the weight of its own logical and spiritual inadequacies. The failure shows all too clearly that the historicist underpinnings have collapsed as well. Modern architects have at last regained sovereignty over their experience of culture; the impartial discernment of aesthetic purpose is again possible.

LYRIC MODERNISM

How, dreamer,
            will fate mark you
in her index when she comes dressed
as a crystalographer
to religne the tumblers
inside your genetic padlock?

Edward Dorn, *Gunslinger*, Book II[12]

For the first time there is now a sufficient body of posthistoricist evidence available for detailed analysis. We are entering a new period of modern architecture, which recent buildings such as those examined in this study begin to create. This work is characterized by diversity of secret life rather than by universal commitment, however debased, to the expression of a single "correct" spirit of the times.

Simulation of the scientific logic that has produced our world no longer drives architecture vainly onward toward the one historicist utopia. Instead a poetic logic draws architecture inward in search of varied mythic resolution. It is not possible to replace the superhuman zeitgeist of the technological world with any singular force that will fill the emptiness we experience in our modern cities. This can be achieved only by songs sung in architecture about the search for value and meaning in a materialistic world. I therefore propose the term *lyric modernism* to describe the period we have reached.

To compare the Greek root of both my terms, we are no longer the inhabitants of an architecture of no real place, but characters in an architectural story about ourselves. Specifically, I use *lyric modernism* to describe a condition of mythological investigation through architectural form of the fact of life, sense of threat, and possibility of action that are the principal themes of life in industrial society as the century draws to a close.

The techniques appropriate to Utopian modernism and based on a historicist view of the concepts of memory, expression, and morality are no longer of any avail to either architect or critic. However, since our condition is marked by continuity and not by rupture, these concepts cannot be discarded, nor is that desirable. Rather, a reformulation of their relationship is needed before it is possible to penetrate the secret life of buildings and reveal the stories they tell.

Memory

If we free ourselves from the view that there is a single legitimate sensibility by which the uniqueness of our time can be revealed, we make history a repository of meanings relevant to the present. For the rejection of historicism also liberates us from the belief that whatever was meaningful in past ages is meaningful only to those ages and to no others, least of all our own. Thus history becomes transparent to the architect; it takes on a new reality as a mentor that can reveal to us aspects of ourselves we could not otherwise have known. It is no longer made opaque by antagonisms to a rival, who, though possibly admired, is not embraced. This attitude to history as a mentor makes available to us two fundamental concepts: type and style.

Type is that formal characteristic of any building or city that cannot be further reduced. It is, in Quatremère de Quincy's famous words, "not so much the image of a thing to be copied or perfectly imitated as the idea of an element that must serve itself as a rule for [a work of architecture] . . . . Type is an object according to which one can conceive works that do not resemble one another at all."[13] Different periods have produced different types, such as those of the centrally planned church or the Georgian townhouse. The Utopians rejected established types and the wealth of

meanings they carry in favor of novel ones with little cultural resonance, such as the German *siedlung*. The embrace of history makes this vast resource accessible to us once more.

Style is what must be fused with type to make designs. It is the means by which, from the same type, "one can conceive works that do not resemble one another at all." Just as there can be no styleless style, so in buildings there can be no type without style. The rejection of historicism makes the mysterious, complex means by which types have been transformed into artifacts accessible for the expression of contemporary culture.

Expression

The reawakened memory of the past permits two distinct vehicles of expression, both of which were denied by the ideology of the Utopian period. They derive from the simple fact that as human beings we have both physical and intellectual memory. From these two kinds of memory we may derive two kinds of expression in architecture: one that stems from an analogy with the physical memory of the effects of natural forces on the body and one derived from an analogy with the intellectual memory of places and events. We are here presented with the poles of post-Utopian expression: empathy and association. Both reject intuition as a basis for creation, for it is not intuition but precedent on which they depend. Empathy demands a constant reference to the human body; association finds its reference in human culture. Whereas the expressive inclinations of the Utopian period were supposedly intuitive and sought to fathom the mysteries of the zeitgeist, those of lyric modernism are based on inventive scholarship rather than on willful innovation and seek to turn precedent to creative ends by permitting and encouraging a diversity of secret life.

Morality
Obviously, therefore, we can no longer speak of a moral sanction for any single expression of "the times"; but neither may we speak of the representation of facets of cultural experience without considering how such expression gains architectural legitimacy.

Though ethical and aesthetic values may be related, we have learned from the failures of the Utopian period that there is not the slightest possibility that the moral instinct—that instinct by which we judge human behavior—can independently create or discern aesthetic value. We must ask, then, as Geoffrey Scott did in *The Architecture of Humanism*, about the extent to which an analogy exists between these realms.[14]

"The dignity of architecture," wrote Scott, "is the same 'dignity' that we recognise in character. Thus, when once we have discerned it aesthetically in architecture, there may arise in the mind its moral echo."[15] The aesthetic and ethical realms, to put it another way, are like two bells: when we strike one, the other may ring in harmony; but we can never strike one bell with the hammer of the other. This resonance is what Scott called "the true ethical analogy" and is what makes it possible for architecture to move us to the very core. "Morality," as Scott put it, "deepens the content of architectural experience."[16] This

deepening is in fact the role of morality in lyric modernism: it is no longer a justifying agent; it has become a deepening agent. It is exactly this deepening that legitimizes the secret life of buildings and prevents a spurious eclecticism or a dry and meaningless rationalism. For the deepening of architectural content by the true ethical analogy returns the diverse interpretations of culture to the moral world, the world of human conduct. This return of meaning from the aesthetic to the moral world, achieved through the resonance of the one with the other *when the first is sounded by its own means*, is what confers legitimacy on form.

We may now posit a reordering of the themes of Utopian modernism: the rejection of historicism makes history a mentor rather than a rival, permitting us through both style and type to see the meanings of all past forms as instructive and relevant to the present. This release of memory makes possible the expression of such meanings through empathy and association, whether separately or in combination. Finally, these meanings can be deepened by the true ethical analogy to produce diversity of secret life, which, returned to the moral world, is legitimized by the developed industrial culture it reflects, enhances, and ultimately helps create.

Our present modernism does not, therefore, seek the abstraction of essence from form but rather the representation of culture through form. In turn, it does not seek the abstraction of essential form from place but rather the urban discourse that is unique to architecture and that emanates from the secret life of buildings.

In the chapters that follow, a method of criticism based on the reordering I have described is applied to each of the seven examples. The structure of each chapter reflects the fundamental urbanistic change that derives from this reordering. In formal terms this structure telescopes inward from the city and landscape to the building and its details; but in terms of meaning it expands outward from the urban and architectural facts to the specific imagery of the building and then to the mythical expression which is the content of its secret life and by which the fullness of urban discourse is finally achieved.

THE SECRET LIFE
OF BUILDINGS

1 THE REPRESENTATION OF PERCEPTION

Gehry House
Santa Monica, California
Frank O. Gehry
Associates,
Architects (1978)

The Pacific Ocean is to Los Angeles what Europe is to New York. Perceived with the senses, it dissolves memories, just as Europe, perceived with the mind, creates them. The passing of time there does not confer upon history the same authority it has in other places, where it is treated with respect rather than with nostalgia. As a result, in Los Angeles the present instant has become a source of meanings that in other places would be supplied by history. This significance is registered through the senses, which bestow on perception the importance given elsewhere to memory. It is with the representation of this condition that Frank Gehry's own house in Santa Monica is concerned.

THE LOCATION OF THE HOUSE

The city of Santa Monica lies at the base of the expansive bay from which Los Angeles observes the ocean, equidistant from the two points, sensed as much as seen, that frame the infinite vista on a clear day (figure 1). The city is divided by the Santa Monica freeway, which disgorges traffic almost into the water, so great is its velocity from downtown Los Angeles to the beach (figure 2). The northern half of the city is a residential area whose rectangular blocks, aligned with the coast, carry the rhythm of the long waves of the Santa Monica beach straight back into the land from Ocean Avenue all the way to Twenty-sixth Street.

Frank Gehry's house is on Twenty-second Street at Washington Avenue, at the first place on Washington where there is a fracturing of the street pattern (figure 3). The house is on one of the few corners of the northern part of Santa Monica that is the end of a street rather than an intersection of continuing streets. Moreover, the house is at the edge of a zoning area, on the border between a zone of single-family residential units and a zone of multiple-family units. The lot on which Gehry's house is built is in fact the only lot in the neighborhood that is on the edge of an east-west zoning change and at the end of a noncontinuous north-south street. This circumstance, accidental or not, helps give the house its singular presence.

Adjustment to Place

As eccentric and out of place as the house at first appears in its prim, trim surroundings, it is in fact extraordinarily rooted to its site, although this is not by any means immediately obvious.

The house consists of a corrugated metal shell wrapped around three sides of an existing pretty, pink, shingled 1920s house in a way that creates new spaces between the shell and the old exterior walls (figure 4). The original dwelling was peculiar on Twenty-second Street in being a two-story house set among bungalows. It therefore already marked its corner location, and the eccentricity of Gehry's addition enhances its stance as a spatial marker. The corrugated metal planes, sharp-edged as knives, that face Twenty-second Street and Washington address the long suburban streets, with their lugubrious traffic and their unused pedestrian paths, directly in proportion to their importance. Thus the wider Washington Avenue, thirty blocks long and running to the ocean, is flanked by an imposing wall extended like a billboard toward the beach, brought close

1 Southern California, 1878

2 The road system of the
city of Santa Monica and the
location of the Gehry house

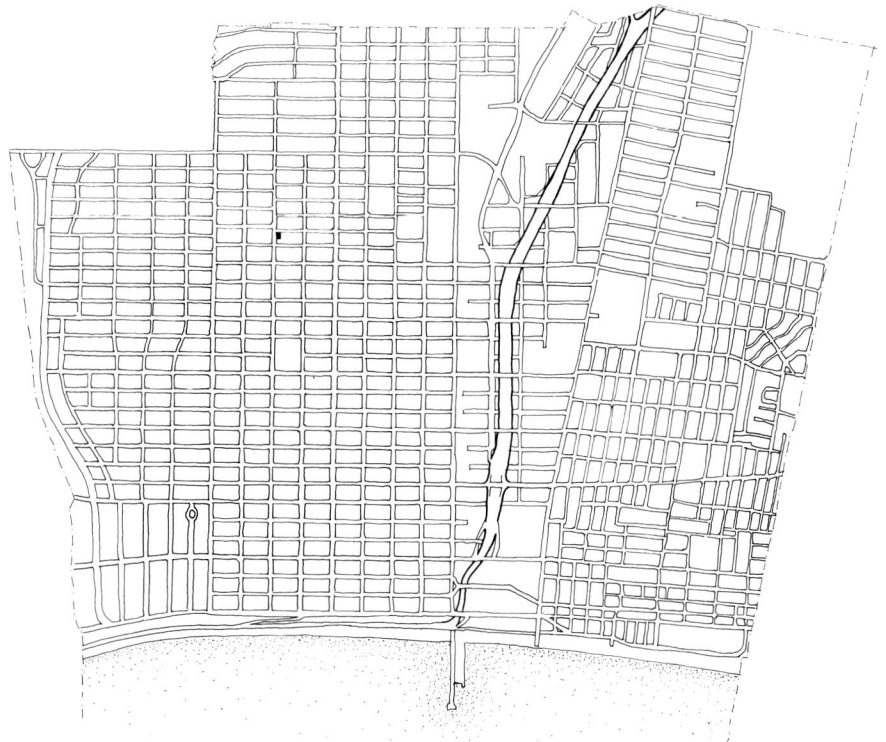

3 Gehry house, corner location at Washington Avenue and Twenty-second Street

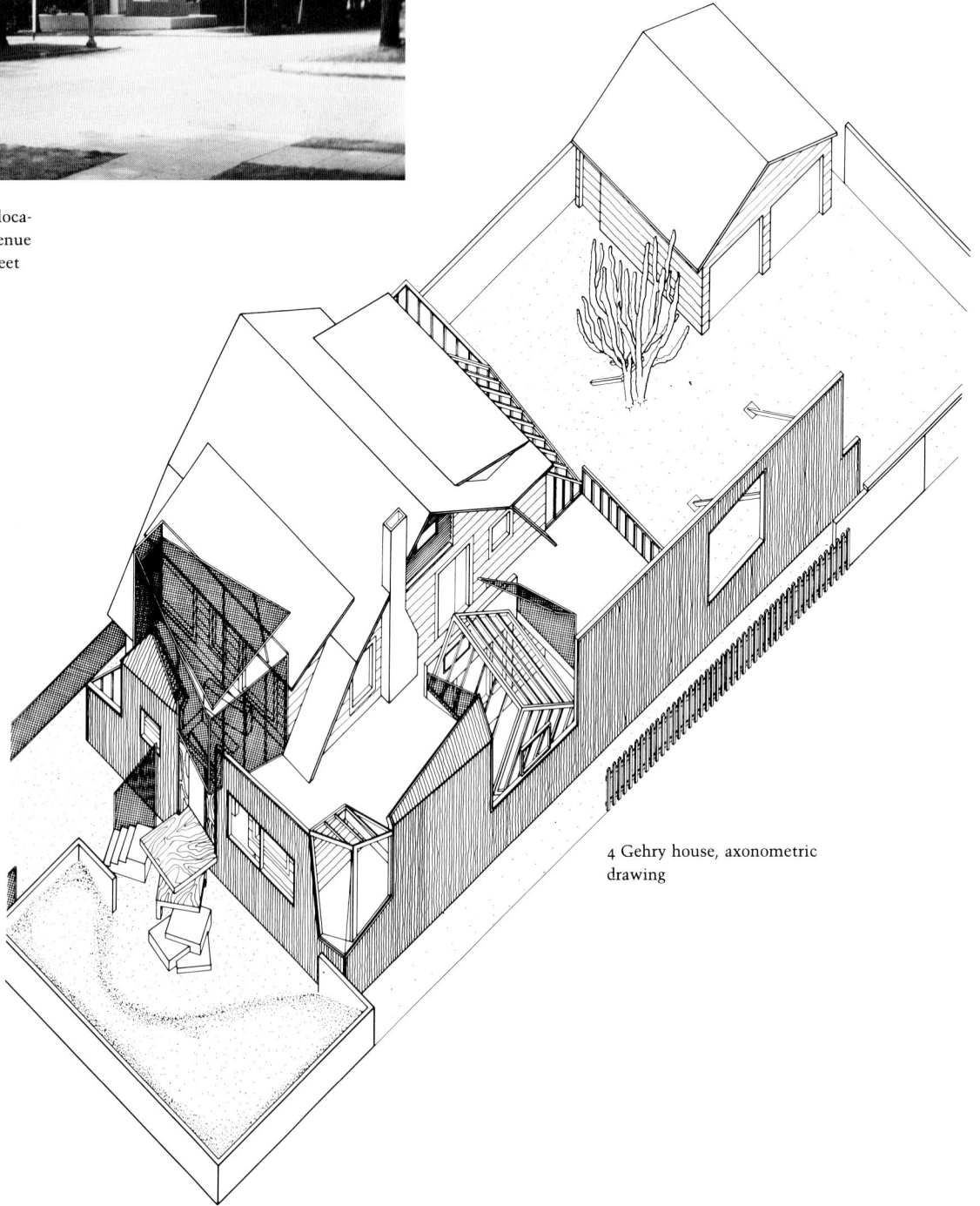

4 Gehry house, axonometric drawing

to the path, and given the most important visual events. The narrower
Twenty-second Street, only four
blocks long from the freeway to the
fracture at Washington, is acknowledged by a wall set back from the
street, severed in the middle, and
fenestrated with smaller scale windows. These two walls slide together
at the corner, with the corrugated
metal seeming to ripple under the
impact. Each wall builds up from its
extremity, where an L-shaped jog
mediates between it and the sidewalk,
through a series of acute angles in the
profiles of the tops of the walls, to a
collision in a sort of raised bay window. This window marks the junction
of the streets with what during the
day is a receding void and at night is
an advancing solid, like a beacon
(figure 5).

Just as the immediate context informs the new shell in this way, so
the literal structure of the existing
house informs the aesthetic of the
new interior. The old house is of
wood frame construction covered
with asbestos shingles over white
clapboard.[1] Because the shell advanced the threshold between the
dweller and the elements, the walls of
the old house were no longer required
as weatherproofing and the sheathing
material was selectively removed.
This has left the wooden framing
members exposed in places, thereby
creating a literal transparency between new and old spaces while re-
taining the ghost of old walls,
complete with phantom window
openings. In other places the old walls
remain intact. This process of literal
deconstruction gives great visual richness to the interior. The walls appear
at once ruined and half-finished, but
above all palpably sculptural.

5 Gehry house, front facade

It may be said of Gehry's house, therefore, that the new work enhances the original quality of the house as a spatial marker; that the shell is informed by its immediate context; and that the aesthetic of the new interior is informed by the literal structure of the existing house. Yet the house reflects the particular circumstances of Los Angeles in more complex and significant ways as well.

THE MARINE IMAGERY OF THE HOUSE

The front yard of the house contains a key to this deeper meaning. The yard is in two parts: to the left is a sand-covered area leading to a flight of steps and a plywood platform; to the right is a grassy area shaped into a rolling form (figure 6), which is surrounded by an aqua-colored wall of concrete block about two and a half feet high and which has random-looking concrete and plywood steps descending into it. Aqua is the color of the Pacific in shallow water when the sky is clear and the bottom is clean white sand; the form of the lawn is that of a gentle wave; the steps have the shape of flat rocks, water worn. This modest aqua wall, advancing toward the intersection and visible several blocks away, establishes the connection of the house to the general psychological condition of Los Angeles, which is bound up in its foremost symbol: the heaving Pacific, dissolver of memory.

Once this connection is understood, the meaning of certain elements of the house becomes clearer. Over the front door, rising above the flat plywood rocks, is a wild, trapezoidal chain-link fish tank with an off-center, pivoting chain-link lid hovering like a cirrus cloud (figure 7). Here

6 Gehry house, rolling form of the front yard

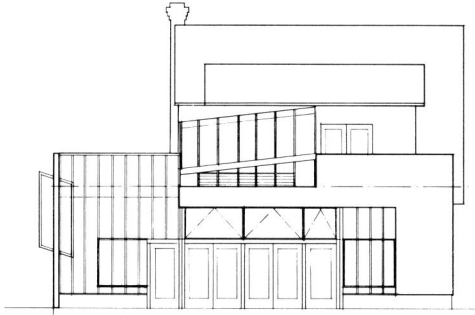

WEST ELEVATION

SOUTH ELEVATION

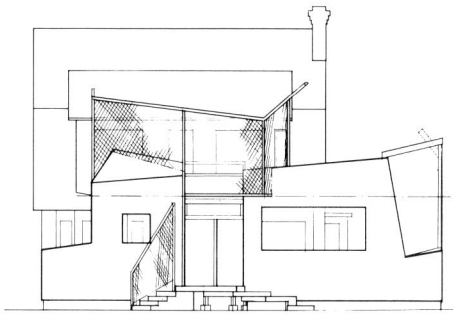

EAST ELEVATION

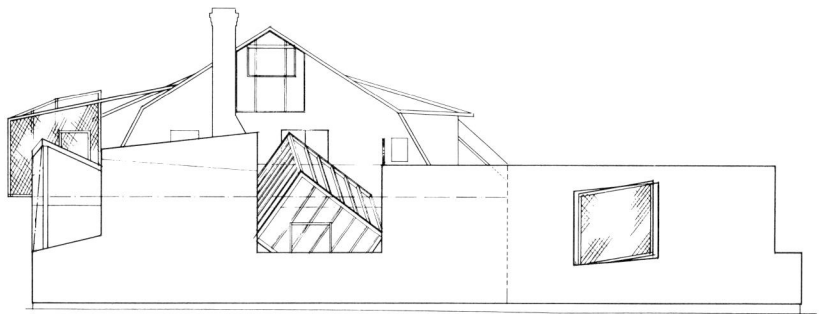

NORTH ELEVATION

7 Gehry house, four
elevations

Gehry has whimsically enclosed a small quantity of the ocean, as it were, and set it up, like a pediment, as a heraldic entrance symbol. Between the front door and this chain-link fish tank is a balcony around a small, flat, wired-glass skylight that lights the entrance hall inside. Seen from above, people entering the hall have the distinct look of submarine creatures: the sky is reflected in the glass and the sun sparkles on the crossed wires as on lightly rippling water, while the figures beneath, dimly visible, swim surrealistically in the watery depths. To ensure this effect even when there are no visitors, a superrealist sculpture of the painter Billy Al Bengston stands inside the front door, like the figurehead of some bizarre wreck.

Such sea imagery is ubiquitous in the house. Wherever two diagonal lines are contrived to overlap, they are arranged to give the impression of waves. This is noticeable whether in the kitchen, on the roof, or out in the garden. Under the kitchen skylights in particular there are unmistakable signs of a tumultuous sea (figure 8). But this imagery is certainly not limited to Gehry's own house. His Spiller house, for example, is organized along the same lines, with specially created views of crashing angles. The Cabrillo Marine Museum is no different, and it is here, perhaps, that these themes reach their utmost realization. People and real fish inhabit the same spaces, while outside chain link swirls into a misty collage of waves, clouds, masts, sails, and fins.

These marine images capture that quality of constant motion so important in detaching the instant of perception from memory. Yet, although they are images that concern percep-

8 Gehry house, kitchen interior

tion more than memory, they concern only the representation of waves or clouds and not the representation of perception itself.

To understand how in his house Gehry has passed from the formal pleasures of marine iconography to the complexities of secret life is to understand his methodology. To do this one must consider the use Gehry has made of the work of contemporary artists, for as he has said: "I search out the work of artists and use art as an inspiration. I try to rid myself . . . of the burden of culture and look for new ways to approach the work."[2]

GEHRY'S USE OF CONTEMPORARY ART

Revelation of Spontaneity
The literal deconstruction of buildings, which is so important in Gehry's work, is an idea that was developed into an art by the American sculptor Gordon Matta-Clark (1943–78). In New Jersey in 1973 he created *Splitting* (figure 9) out of an abandoned clapboard house, not unlike the original building incorporated by Gehry in his house. In this work Matta-Clark cut the two-story building down the middle, tilted one half back on its foundations, and then removed four corners from the building at its roof line.

The act of splitting seems to pervade Gehry's attitude to the taut frontal plane he uses to control plastic events. The split down the middle of the Loyola Law School facade shows this on a large scale. The door opening in his own house and the slots in the facade of the Spiller house show the same principle on a smaller scale.

In addition the corners removed by Matta-Clark in *Splitting* (figure 10) are close relatives of the glass corner of Gehry's house at Twenty-second and Washington (figure 11).

It is Matta-Clark's revelation of physical structure behind surface materials in found buildings, however, as in his *Bingo X Ninths* of 1973 (figure 12) or *Office Baroque* of 1977 (figure 13), that most clearly parallels Gehry's concerns. In these projects Matta-Clark put literal deconstruction at the service of architectural autobiography, calling attention to the act of creating new space as well as to the original act of construction involved in the buildings he used. This search for the revelation of spontaneity is one of the most important aspects of Gehry's representation of perception, since spontaneity, by definition, can exist only in the present, like perception itself. "I was interested in the unfinished," Gehry has said, "the quality that you find in paintings by Jackson Pollock, for instance, or de Kooning, or Cézanne, that looks like the paint was just applied. . . . I wanted to try that out in a building."[3] To Matta-Clark this quality was revealed "not [by] surface, but [by] the thin edge, the severed surface that reveals the . . . process of its making."[4] To Gehry also it is the edges of a surface, like those whose severance reveals the framing members of his interiors, rather than the surface itself that counts; the edge is not a container of memories but an event whose essence is of the present.

Of the many episodes in Gehry's house that occur arrestingly in the present, perhaps none evokes a greater sense of the spontaneous than the

9 Gordon Matta-Clark, *Splitting*, Englewood, New Jersey, 1973 (now destroyed)

10 Gordon Matta-Clark, *Splitting*, Englewood, New Jersey, 1973 (now destroyed), interior view

11 Gehry house, interior
view

12 Gordon Matta-Clark,
Bingo X Ninths, Niagara
Falls, New York, 1973 (now
destroyed)

13 Gordon Matta-Clark,
Office Baroque,
Antwerp, 1977

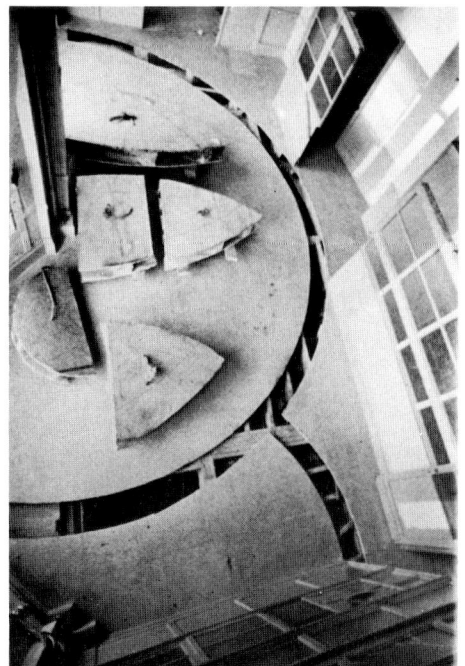

chain-link floor of the second-story passage between the roof of the dining room and the hot tub, which is enclosed by a forced perspective glass roof. At Kassel, Germany in 1977 Matta-Clark made a piece called *Jacob's Ladder*, which consisted of an enclosed, climbable rope-chain bridge hung off a seventy-five-meter smokestack. Gehry seems to have captured the immediacy of such a work and actually to have built what Aldo Rossi has described as the mysteriously threatening "room with the ten-meter drop."[5]

Contradictory Perspective
If the literal deconstructions of Matta-Clark have informed Gehry's attitude toward capturing the significance of the instant, the work of Chuck Arnoldi (whose studio adjoins Gehry's in Venice) has influenced the way the wooden studs, revealed by literal deconstruction, appear to have flown loose into a new composition.

Arnoldi is known for the overlapping, painted branches he forms into geometrical shapes. These branches are raw enough to leave knots and junctions clearly visible (though they are seldom forked) but refined to the extent that all the bark is removed. This closely parallels the kind of wood that Gehry uses. The framing members of Gehry's house are rough enough to look unfinished but never so raw that they look rustic.

A large-size Arnoldi hanging in Gehry's breakfast room (figure 14) exhibits a similarity to Gehry's sketch technique, which consists of mostly straightish, random-looking lines of varying sizes. Gehry has batteries of sketchbooks filled with these runic drawings. In these sketches, one sees the carefully strewn and artfully spontaneous converging and diverging lines that characterize Gehry's buildings, as in the masts of the Cabrillo Marine Museum or in the air-conditioning ducts of the Toyota offices of 1978 (figure 15), where the likeness to an Arnoldi is striking.

Like Gehry's sketches, however, the Arnoldi of the breakfast room is deceptively chaotic. This work is arranged so that the outer branches define a frame through which one can trace numerous contradictory perspective lines going to numerous vanishing points above and below a wide variety of horizons. Gehry achieves the same effect in his architecture.

Perspective illusion and perspective contradiction are used throughout Gehry's house, and many of his other projects, to prevent the formation of an intellectual picture that might destroy the continual immediacy of perceptual shock. When nothing is at right angles, nothing seems to vanish to the same point. This results in an ambiguous space that is enhanced by the reflections one sees at strange angles in tilted panes of glass, which create Arnoldi-like intersections. Such illusions and contradictions force one to continually question the nature of what one sees, to alter the definition of reality, in the end, from the *memory* of a thing to the *perception* of that thing.

Removal from the Ground Plane
The influence on Gehry of Arnoldi's use of lines in perspective is matched by the influence of the painter Ron Davis's use of planes in perspective. A rectangular plane in perspective

14 Gehry house, breakfast
room with Arnoldi artifact

15 Frank O. Gehry Associ-
ates, axonometric drawing of
the interior of Mid-Atlantic
Toyota Offices, Glen Burnie,
Maryland, 1978

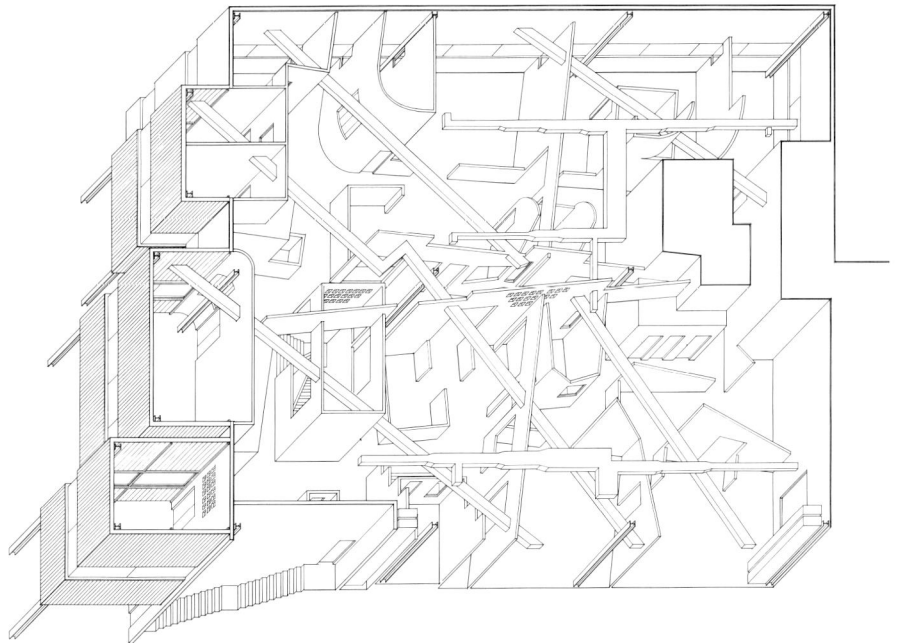

will assume the form of a trapezoid, a shape that first appeared in a major Gehry work in the windows and roof of the Ron Davis house of 1972,[6] where, as Gehry acknowledges, "the trapezoid grew out of his painting."[7]

Davis's work of the sixties, such as his illusionistic polyester resin and fiberglass slab *Six-Ninths Red* (figure 16), developed exactly the kind of ambiguous shapes that Gehry used so successfully in the Davis studio and, later, for the entrance pavilion to the Cabrillo Marine Museum (figure 17). The effect of these forms in Gehry's work is the same as in Davis's: "The beholder is not only suspended above the slab; he is simultaneously tilted towards it."[8]

16 Ronald Davis, *Six-Ninths Red*, 1966, polyester resin and fiberglass, 72 × 131 cm

Davis's works of the early 1970s continued the theme of perspective planes and apparently exerted a strong hold over Gehry, as one can see by comparing Davis's *Fan Rectangle V* (figure 18) to the chain-link "clouds" of Gehry's Toyota offices (figure 19). By the mid-1970s, however, Davis had abandoned the trapezoid form, turning instead to Vermeer-like grid systems, as in the *Checkerboard* series of 1978. These grids define the logic of perspective behind the earlier illusionistic forms. Architectonic structures from a make-believe world were projected onto a warped grid in the *Checkerboard* paintings, as in *Checkerboard Bridges* (figure 20).

What is important is the similarity between the presumed location of the viewer in Davis's *Checkerboard* paintings and the suggested location of an observer in Gehry's house. In Davis's early and recent works, the viewer is suspended above the warped

17 Frank O. Gehry Associates, Cabrillo Marine Museum, San Pedro, California, 1976, entrance pavilion

18 Ronald Davis, *Fan Rectangle V*, 1971, polyester
resin and fiberglass

19 Frank O. Gehry Associ-
ates, interior view of the
Mid-Atlantic Toyota Offices,
Glen Burnie, Maryland, 1978

20 Ronald Davis, *Checker-board Bridges*, 1978, acrylic on canvas, 198.1 × 251.4 cm

21 Jan Vermeer, *The Artist in His Studio*, c. 1670

perspective grids and tipped toward them. This can be clearly understood if *Checkerboard Bridges* is compared with a Vermeer like *The Artist in His Studio* (figure 21), in which the viewer is standing firmly on the ground. Gehry's distorted perspective planes and illusionistic use of framing members engender the same feeling in the beholder; the tilting of planes expected to be horizontal or vertical and the converging of studwork members cause one to feel suspended and tipped in various directions oneself.

Centrality

For Gehry the world vanishes to a multitude of points, and he does not presuppose that any are related to the standing human being. The human eye is still of critical importance in Gehry's world, but the sense of center no longer has its traditional symbolic value. Man no longer possesses the ground plane as he did in the Renaissance system of Vermeer's world. For the sense of center in Gehry's house is not universal as it is, for example, in a Renaissance church, but is instead entirely personal, having no point of contact with any force other than the perceptions recorded by the senses of the individual. The singular centrality of the plan of Gehry's house illustrates this fact.

The house can be divided into three parts (figures 22, 23). First, a group of small rooms at the back of the house on both floors consisting of stairs, bedrooms, bathrooms, and closets. Second, the major spaces of the old house, which have become the living room on the ground floor and the master bedroom on the first floor. Lastly, the complex attenuated spaces of the new spatial wrapper, consisting

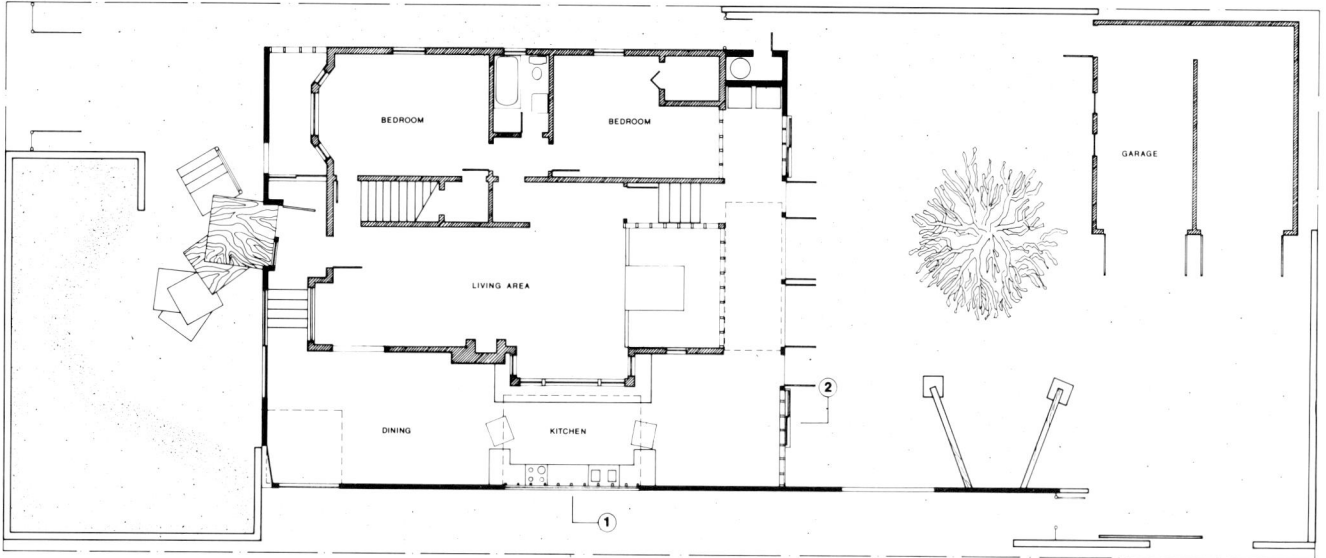

22 Gehry house, plan of first
floor

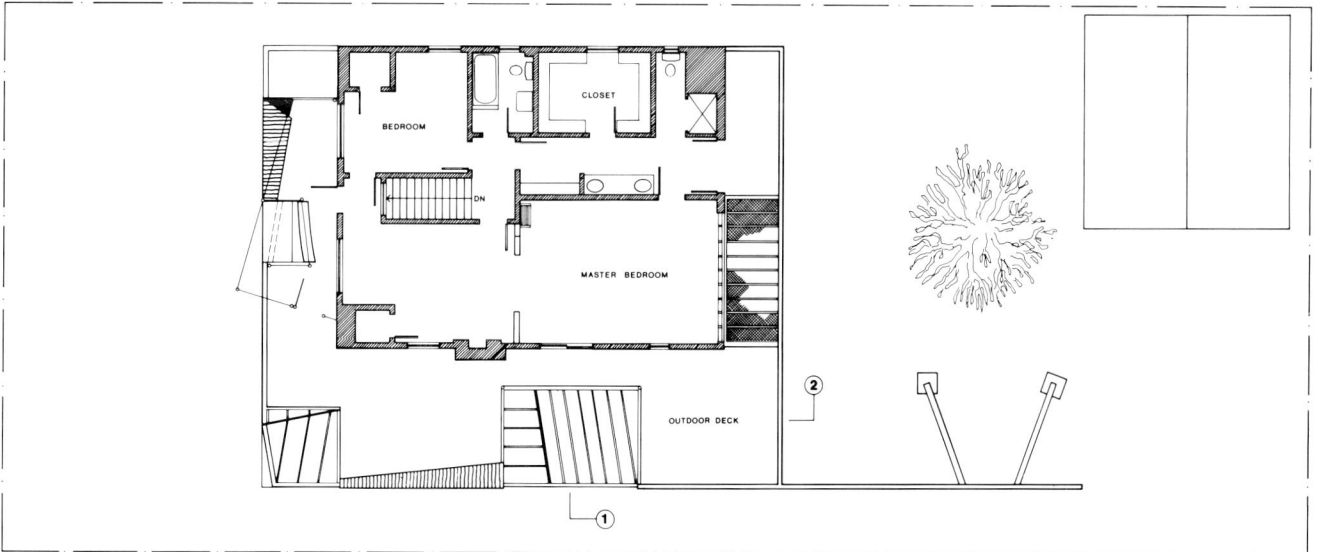

23 Gehry house, plan of
second floor

of the entry spaces, kitchen and dining areas, which are five steps below
the living room.

The part of the original house that
contains the new living room and
master bedroom has had much of its
old cladding material removed, while
the other half has not and remains by
comparison an ironic, superrealist
fragment of Californian banality,
turned by its new context from base
metal into gold. One can therefore
read the literally deconstructed part of
the original house as being surrounded on all sides by quite different
spaces, whether old or new, so that it
is a readily identifiable figure enclosed by a *poché* of space. The fact
that this figure is cruciform can
hardly escape attention, and it is in
fact very noticeable when one is in
the house because the living room has
an apse in which one can sit, tran-
septs and nave, and is approached
through a porch.

At the crossing of this cruciform
space stands a monumental, three-
sided glass sculpture on a six-foot-
square plan by Larry Bell—the arterial
pump of the life blood of Gehry's
house. The fourth side opens toward
Washington Avenue, denying the
thrust of the "nave." Its sides are
treated with varying degrees of reflec-
tive coatings, so that its optical qualities are profoundly ambiguous. One
can walk around it, but more importantly, one can stand inside it, in the
very soul of the house.

From inside, space in all directions
is rendered completely fluid; it extends and returns on itself as reflections, transparencies, literal deconstructions, and perspective distortions all interfere with one another.
Trees, lampposts, cacti—all seem to

be flying through the disjointed angles
of the house. There is no "real" space
and no "real" time; there is no reality
at all but what the senses register
from one moment to the next. The
observer is denied the relevance of
memory, for the space is a space of
pure perception. This is a space representing the centrality of the individual solely within his own perceptions,
not his centrality within a larger order, whether cosmic or technocratic.

THE INFLUENCE OF KASIMIR MALEVICH

The concept of a geometrical art
purely about perception and having
no reference to the memory of things
perceived is far from new, however;
the Suprematism of Kasimir Malevich
is its wellspring. If we are to fully
comprehend the secret life of Gehry's
house, we must examine that profound revision of seeing invented by
Malevich around 1913, for it is from
Malevich that Gehry's work on the
representation of perception can be
said to ultimately derive.

Suprematism has been traced to
Malevich's 1913 set design for scene
V of the opera *The Victory over the
Sun*, where a dominant quadrilateral
appears for the first time in his work
(figure 24).[9] This opera was an allegor-
ical drama extolling the triumph of
modern man's self-sustaining energy
sources. The sun was vanquished by
the men of the future, for whom it
was a symbol of the illusionary world
of the past. The sun represented the
figurative world, the world of objects
that could be destroyed by the darkness of an eclipse. Malevich's design
for scene V shows a quadrilateral

tending toward a square that is still a recognizably figurative image of a partial eclipse. Just before this scene the actors sing: "Our face is dark/ Our light is on the inside."[10]

"Total darkness" was achieved by Malevich in Suprematism. The figurative world of perspective, of possession of the ground plane, is completely eclipsed in his *Black Quadrilateral* (figure 25). Thereafter, as if one had passed through a tunnel connecting one world with another, the "light of the inside" is revealed by the shifting, psychologically active geometries of Malevich's Suprematist canvases.

The fundamental importance of *Black Quadrilateral* was demonstrated by the unique placement of the painting in Malevich's first exhibit of Suprematist works at the *0–10* show in 1915 in Petrograd. Gehry's affinity for the work of this period could not be better demonstrated than by his recreation of the *0–10* show in the 1980 exhibition at the Los Angeles County Museum of "The Avant-Garde in Russia 1910–1930: New Perspectives," and by the power of Gehry's sets for the reenacted *Victory over the Sun.* The peculiar, almost autobiographical hold that the work seems to have had on Gehry is one that he laconically admits: "I decided that work feels so much like home that maybe my Polish-Russian background is coming out."[11]

Gehry recreated the Malevich section of the *0–10* show to the extent available paintings allowed (figure 26). A substitute for *Black Quadrilateral* was hung high up in a corner of the gallery, just as the real *Black Quadrilateral* had been in the original show. It is in such a position, high in

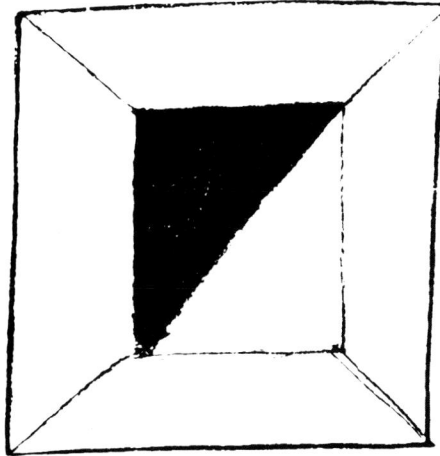

24 Kasimir Malevich, set design for scene V of *Victory over the Sun,* 1913

25 Kasimir Malevich, *Black Quadrilateral,* c. 1913

26 Frank O. Gehry Associates, installation of the 1980 Los Angeles County Museum of Art show *The Avant-Garde in Russia 1910–1930: New Perspectives*. Photograph of original Malevich display at *0–10* is at right.

the corner of the main room, span-
ning walls displaying other icons, that
the principal icon hangs in Russian
Orthodox homes. The believer, on entering the room, faces the icon and
crosses himself.[12] Malevich therefore
felt himself to have created a new
spiritual object, what he referred to as
"the face of the new art . . . a living,
royal infant," what he recognized as
"the icon of my time."[13]

Black Quadrilateral

To understand *Black Quadrilateral* is
to go a long way toward penetrating
the secret life of Gehry's house. If it
represents the eclipse of the sun, then
it is something in the sky at which
one looks. Such an eclipse would
plunge the world into total darkness,
however. *Black Quadrilateral* can
therefore be seen as an aerial perspective representing the surface of the
darkened earth,[14] and in this it is
quite different from Malevich's set for
scene V of *Victory over the Sun,*
which represents only the sun's partial eclipse as seen from the earth.
The sun, however, was not darkened
by lunar movement; it was darkened
by man with his self-sustaining energy sources, as, in his new-found
power, he seized the reins of Apollo's
sun chariot, like the mortal Phaeton.
It was from this lofty vantage point
that Malevich observed the modern
world, now illuminated by a new
light, the "light of the inside," by the
instant of perception rather than by
memory of the external world. In so
doing Malevich exchanged the earth-
bound vanishing point of the Renaissance for an aerial perspective and the
representation of earthly things for
the representation of perception itself.

But this is not the only reading of
Black Quadrilateral. When Malevich
turned away from Suprematist painting after his *White on White* of 1918,
he became preoccupied with the for-
mulation of a volumetric Suprematism, a subject that fascinated him
until his death in 1935. The basic
idea for this three-dimensional Suprematism was very simple and is
shown in Malevich's sketch for its in-
tended development (figure 27).

The equivalent of *Black Quadrilateral* in the new system was to be
the black cube. The development of
the "Suprematist spatial volume" was
to proceed with the disintegration of
the cube into pieces, at first into a
few simple blocks and finally into a
nonrectilinear, diagonally overlapping
collection of Suprematist volumes.
"In this manner," wrote Malevich,
"one could obtain a new architectural
approach. A purely artistic approach,
outside all practical use, for architecture can be so called only in as much
as this is so."[15] Unfortunately Malevich never progressed beyond the extended, rectilinear stage, beyond his
rigid "architectons." The only
volumetric Suprematist work realized
in other than model form was his
tombstone (figure 28).

Erected in 1935, this cubic monument embodied his earlier proclama-
tion, "From this basic shape, the
volumetric side of Suprematism must
proceed."[16] *Black Quadrilateral* can
be understood in this sense as an aerial view of Malevich's own tombstone, as its plan, and as his "plan of
battle," to use Le Corbusier's words.[17]
For Malevich may have returned to
Earth to develop his "cities for Earth

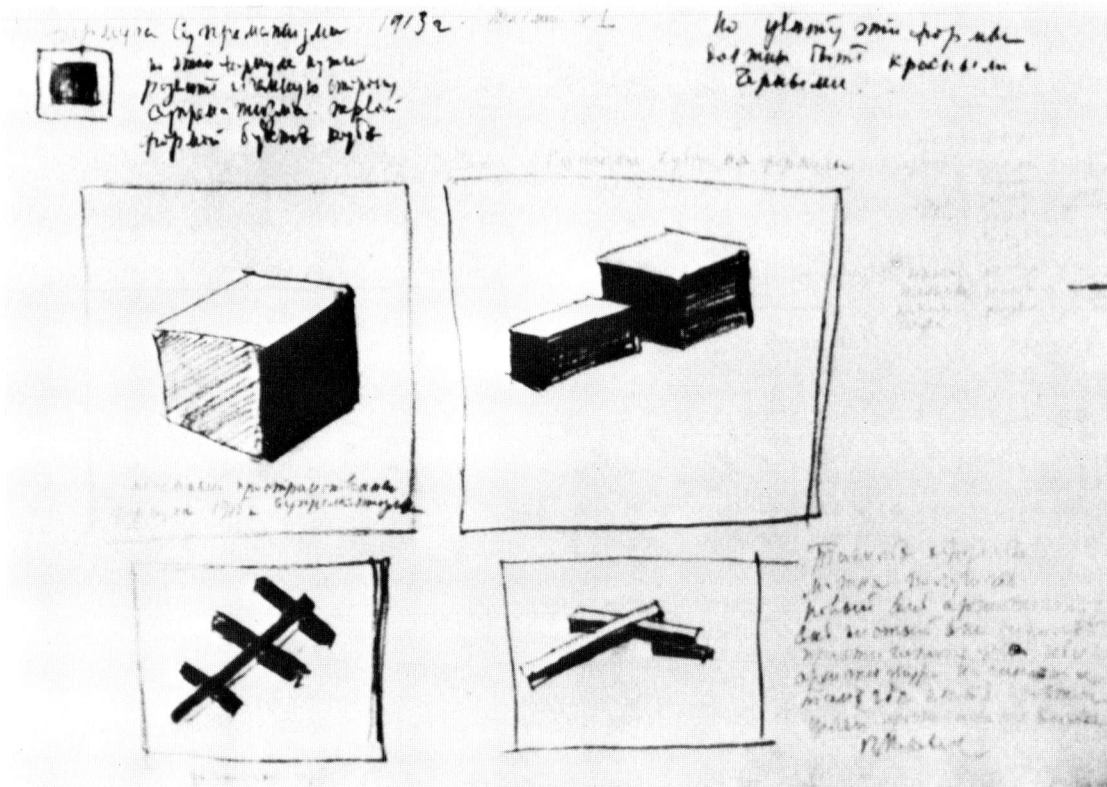

27 Kasimir Malevich, "Diagram for the development of volumetric Suprematism," from an unpublished manuscript, after 1923

28 Kasimir Malevich, tombstone 1935

dwellers," as he called his volumetric
exercises, but he brought with him
the secrets of ideal worlds and a Utopian modernism for such a world.

Finally, therefore, we can comprehend *Black Quadrilateral* as the
plan of battle for an architecture that
would exchange the light of the sun, a
cosmic phenomenon, for the light of
the inside, an individual phenomenon; that would exchange the representation of figurative reality for the
representation of perception, but that
would express this representation in
utopian terms.

The Influence of Suprematism

Gehry's house is a direct descendant
of *Black Quadrilateral*. With its illusionistic and contradictory perspectives of crashing diagonals, it is the
incarnation of Malevich's final, un-
realized stage of volumetric Suprematism. It is the architectural
equivalent of the psychologically active geometry of Malevich's mature
Suprematist canvases, which, late in
life, Malevich saw as aerial views of
urban configurations (figure 29).

While Gehry's works may be the
progeny of Malevich's "light of the inside," this light has been refracted
through the distant lens of Californian culture, and through the individ-
ualism of Wright (figure 30) and
Schindler (figure 31) in particular, into
a spectrum that reveals a sensibility
derived from the mortality, not the
god-like glory, of Phaeton. That sensibility is now eccentrically and
definitively personal, drained of
Malevich's universal techno-
mysticism.

29 Kasimir Malevich,
*Suprematist Composition
(Aerial View)*

30 Frank Lloyd Wright,
Arizona desert camp,
Ocatillo, 1927. "The buildings will look something
like ships coming down
from the mesa, rigged like
ships balanced in the
breeze."

31 Rudolph M. Schindler,
House for Ellen Janson,
Hollywood, 1949

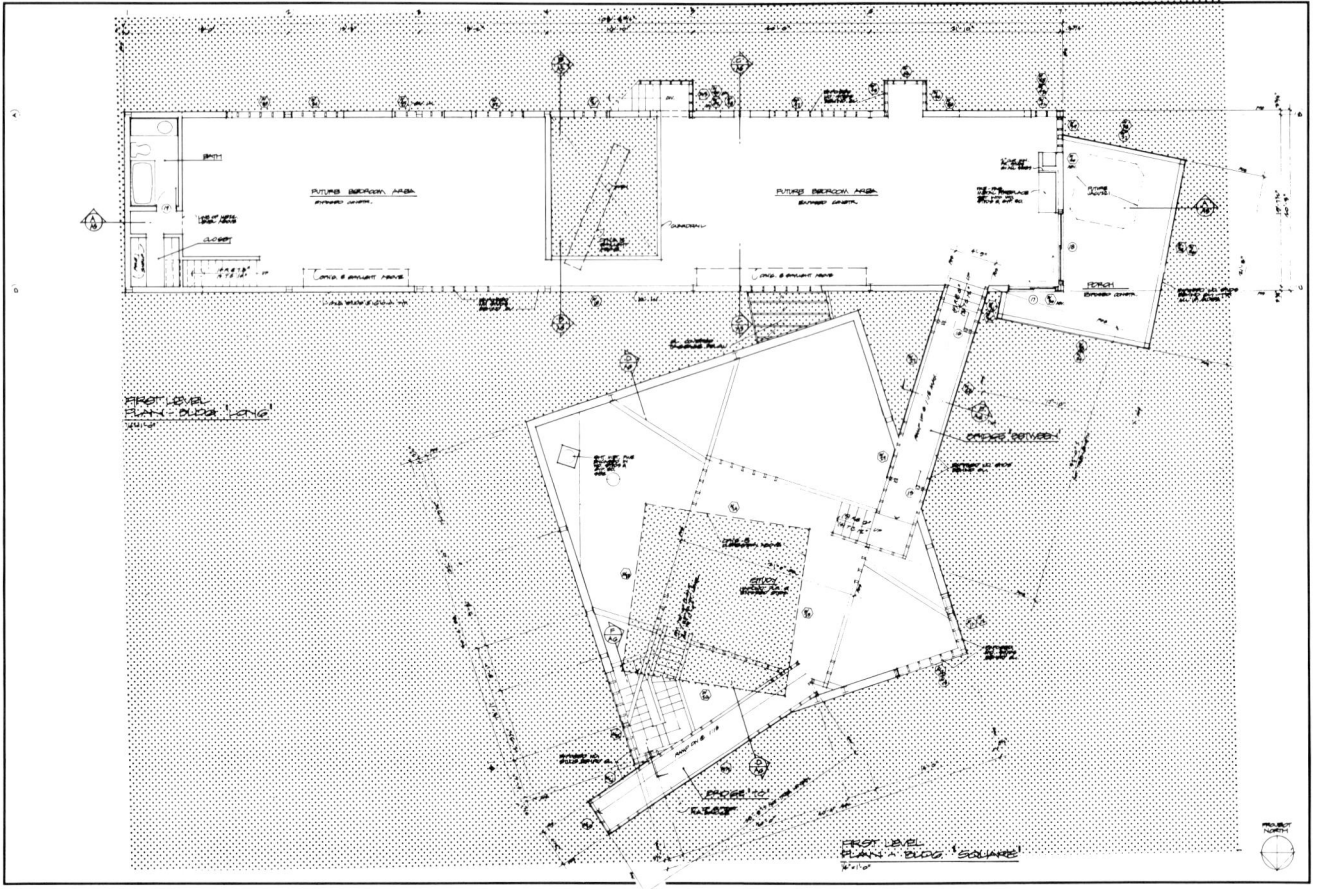

32 Frank O. Gehry Associates, plan of the Familian residence, Santa Monica, California, 1977–78

33 Kasimir Malevich, *Suprematist Composition: Red Square and Black Square,* 1914 or 1915(?), oil on canvas, 28 × 17½ in. Collection of the Museum of Modern Art, New York

In Gehry's Familian residence project of 1977–78 (figure 32), for example, the main masses form a clearly Suprematist grouping, recalling Malevich's *Red Square and Black Square* (figure 33); and the beam-shaped private areas conform to a typically Suprematist format. The shapes are connected by bridges (figure 34), like those of a Constructivist stage set such as Lyubov Popova's design for *The Magnanimous Cuckold* (figure 35). The two forms of the Familian residence have a balanced tension: "One main structure, forty feet by forty feet in plan, is basically one volume reserved for public gatherings. The second main structure is twenty by one hundred and ten feet in plan, and houses private functions on the second floor."[18] The structures are invested with emotional qualities by the relationship of the forms. Thus the public area of confrontation is kinetic; a cube erupts through the roof, the bridges gouge the walls on two sides, and the corner is stripped bare. The long form is reserved, calmer; it receives the impact of the bridge at one end only, holding the other form at bay. Malevich has attempted the same relationship between his red form—angled out of true, not quite square, smaller and more kinetic—and the more stable, cooler black square (also not a square, but only barely so). Gehry has elaborated in particular and idiosyncratic terms what Malevich stated in general and idealized ones.

Again, in the Wagner residence, 1977–78 (figure 36), Gehry has produced a major form sheared into a parallelogram and surrounded by

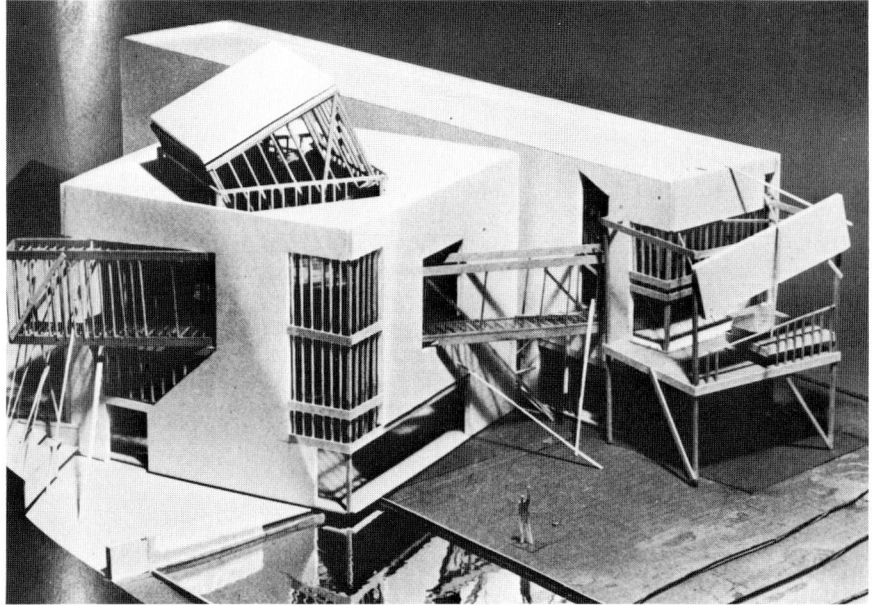

34 Frank O. Gehry Associates, model of the Familian residence, Santa Monica, California, 1977–78. "I believe we pay too slight attention to making slight buildings beautiful or beautiful buildings slight." (Frank Lloyd Wright, *An American Architecture*, 1955)

35 Lyubov Popova, set design for *The Magnanimous Cuckold*, 1922

"bedrooms and decks which appear as floating satellites in orbit, with a mother ship, bumping into each other, not quite touching."[19] Here we have a more introspective scheme, where the relationship of forms is less aggressive and more interdependent. The forms proceed from inside the larger form out, as in Malevich's *Football Match* (figure 37) or in the second painting hanging to the left of *Black Quadrilateral*'s lower left corner in the *0–10* show (see figure 26). Once again Gehry transforms Malevich's abstract idealism into concrete forms that are eccentric and individualistic.

THE TUMBLING CUBE

It is in Gehry's own house, however, and especially in the Washington Avenue facade that the legacy of Malevich's "royal infant" is most evident. This facade is a corrugated metal plane stretched as tight as canvas and interrupted only by three painterly "events": a skewed rectangular void to the garden; a distorted cubic, wood-framed skylight covered with wired glass over the kitchen; and the large, angled sheets of glass that turn the corner to Twenty-second Street, forming a kind of bay window to the dining room. The void to the garden (figure 38) is a standard Suprematist shape, often employed by Malevich to generate energy between the corners of the enclosed form and the edge of the canvas (figure 39). The bay window spans its corner, high up like the traditional Russian icon whose position on the wall *Black Quadrilateral* claimed in the *0–10*

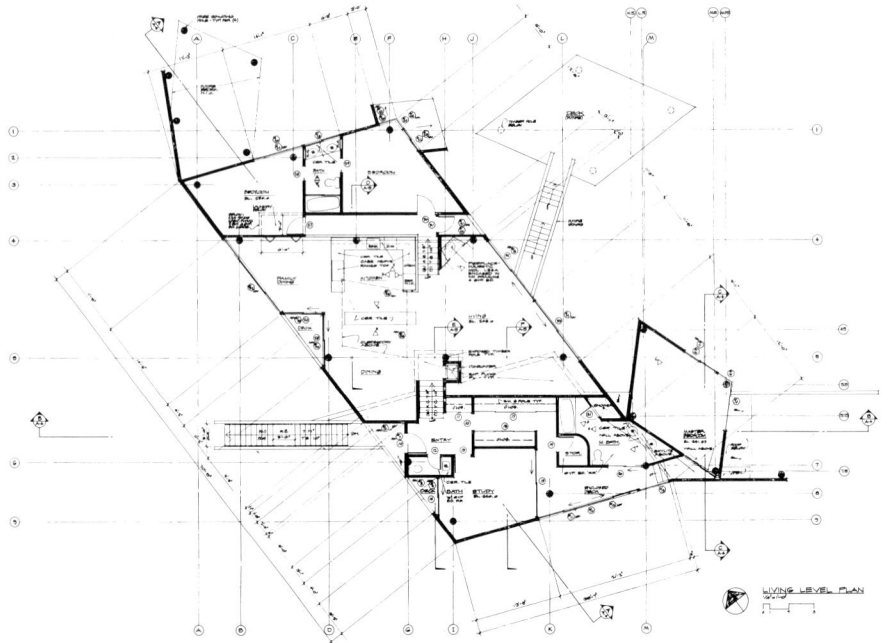

36 Frank O. Gehry Associates, plan of the Wagner residence, Malibu, California, 1977–78

37 Kasimir Malevich, *Football Match*, 1915

38 Gehry house, detail of
Washington Avenue facade

39 Kasimir Malevich, *Small
Trapezoid*, 1920, lithograph

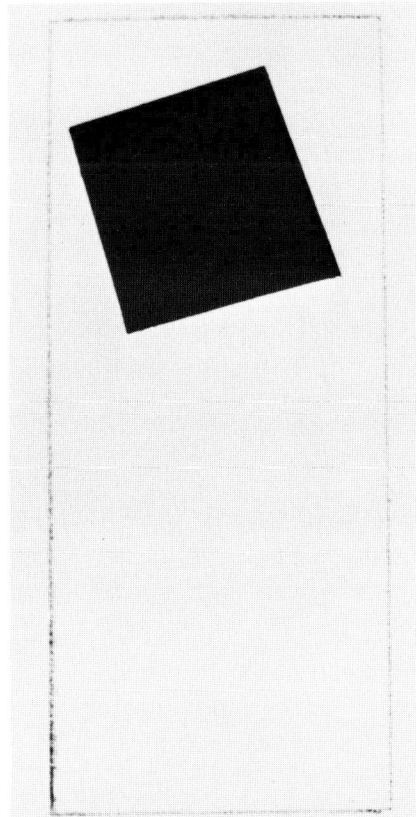

show. Between these windows is the
most important form in the house—
what Gehry calls the "tumbling
cube" but which seems rather to rise
out of the ground like the breath of a
giant subterranean diver breaking
through a broth of scrap metal
(figure 40).

What looks like a cube could hardly
be more deceptive. The surface that is
squashed up against the plane of the
exterior wall is rectangular rather
than square, and the back face of the
cube has been pushed sideways and
sheared upwards so that no framing
member forms a right angle with any
other, except in the front plane. As
a result, while the panels of glass
in the front plane may be rectangular,
those on the other faces are all
parallelograms.

Here is Malevich's idealized black
cube, rendered in glass, ambiguous
and distorted.[20] Visually it is anchored by an axis running through an
operable window in its front plane,
through the central section of the bay
window between old and new construction, and into the very center of
the house through the open fourth
side of the Larry Bell sculpture that
stands at the crossing of the cross.

It is here, on the axis joining the
cube with the central void, that the
Utopian and the humanist traditions
cancel one another and produce a
lyric modernism. The house crosses
itself, acknowledging its icon (figure
41). For man in Gehry's house is no
longer a divine droplet, sparkling in
the center of a perspective web, nor is
he any longer a god-like charioteer
arcing heroically over the world; he is
an individual adrift in an ocean of being. It is not the material nature of

the world as revealed by perspective but the nature of our perception of the world that is represented here; it is not the artifacts of past realities but the fact of the present instant that is represented; it is not the representation of things perceived with which Gehry is concerned in his house, but the representation of perception as a centering force that motivates the work.

40 Gehry house, detail of "tumbling cube" on Washington Avenue facade

41 Diagram showing cruciform void in the center of the Gehry house

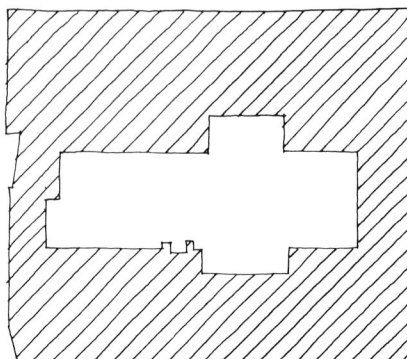

Ronald Davis, *Asterisk
Nebula*, 1981, acrylic on
canvas, 48 × 60 in. Cour-
tesy of Blum Helman
Gallery, New York

Kasimir Malevich, *Suprematist painting*, c. 1913. Collection of Stedelijk Museum,
Amsterdam

Kasimir Malevich, "Suprematist composition conveying
the feeling of a mystic
'wave' from outer space,
1917," from *The Non-Objective World*, p. 35

2

THE ANXIETY OF
THE SECOND FALL
House El Even Odd
Peter Eisenman,
Architect (1980)

House El Even Odd has no physical context, and the model of the house (figure 42), a few dollars worth of cardboard, is its sole three-dimensional manifestation. This model is the representation of another reality, however, the reality of a Manhattan state of mind. Buried, caged, and overwrought, House El Even Odd half strains against its self-inflicted imprisonment and half revels in the convolutions of its introspective world. It is a house haunted by ghosts, as Manhattan is itself haunted by its peoples' pasts; and like the recollection of a house we might have known but cannot now inhabit, House El Even Odd is haunted by memories it wishes to forget but cannot help remembering.

THE CONCEPTUAL CONTEXT

It is impossible to understand House El Even Odd without considering the series of houses of which it is a part and without considering the ideas these houses put forward, for they form the context of House El Even Odd in the same way the urban fabric or rural landscape forms the context of a normal building.

This series of houses, numbered mostly in Roman numerals, have been Eisenman's ongoing project since the 1960s. The series demonstrates one fundamental shift: a shift from the process of making form to the cultural implications of form. Eisenman has developed a vocabulary of forms and terms with which to describe this shift, and House El Even Odd cannot be usefully discussed without reference to them.

The early houses, numbers I through IV (figures 43–46), make up a group concerned entirely with processes of formal transformation, with the inherent logic by which cubic form can be transformed according to dualities such as flat space and deep space, central or peripheral energy, compression or tension, and so on. These projects focus singlemindedly on the possibility of formal transformation from a single, simple solid to a more complex state.

House VI: Centrality as a Metaphor
House VI of 1972 is quite different, however (figure 47). Where the earlier houses are simply formal manipulations of the cube, House VI begins with a more complex figure, the crossing of two planes. Where Houses I–IV express neither interest nor lack of interest in centrality as a metaphor, House VI has a void center that is explicitly metaphorical. The two planes are split apart to make four walls,[1] and these walls are then turned inside out. The pairs of walls are at right angles to one another and leave a space in the middle that is a void, created out of the substance of the wall itself as it was divided. This central void is a place derived from and beholden to nothing but the architectural object. It is not a space that can be commanded by man or woman.

This change was a significant one for Eisenman. If Houses I–IV represent nothing but the process of their own formation, House VI strives to represent a cultural condition. This is the condition Eisenman has identified with a sense of man's loss of control over those things, both material and

42 House El Even Odd,
model showing the house
set into the earth

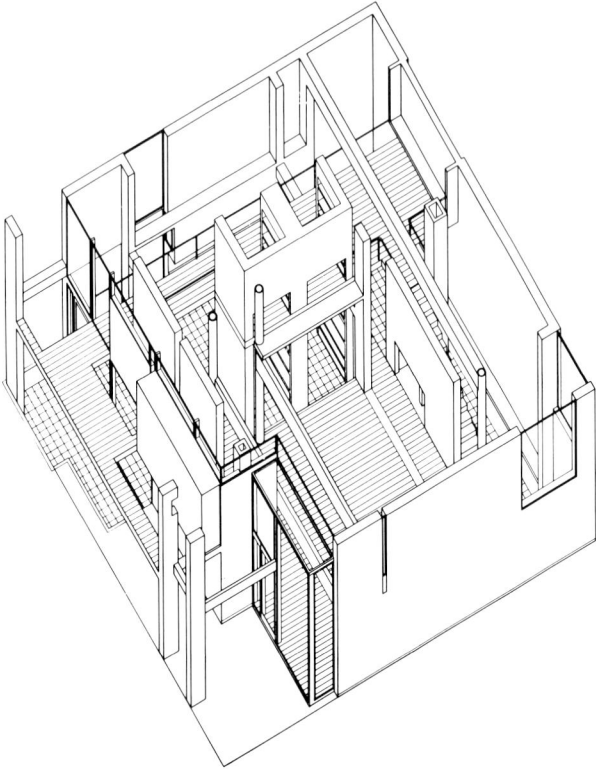

43 House I, 1967–68

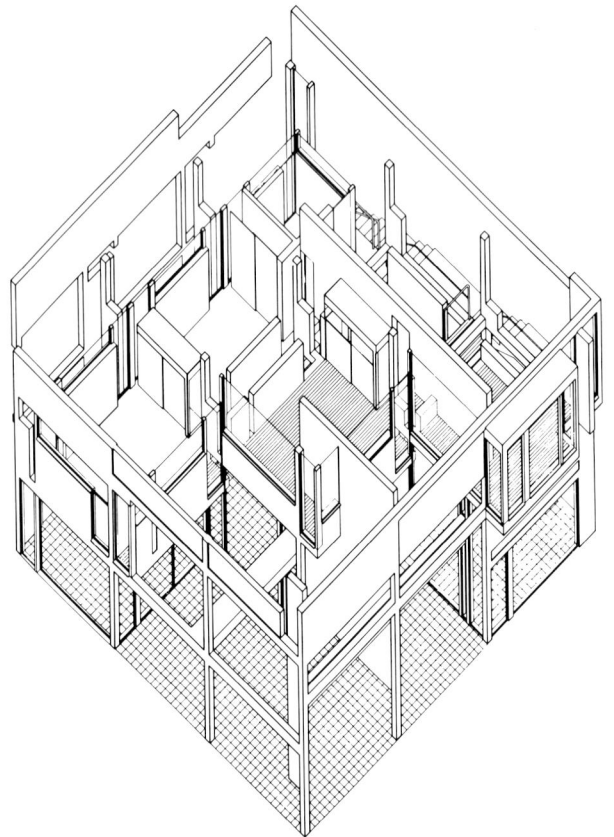

44 House II, 1969–70

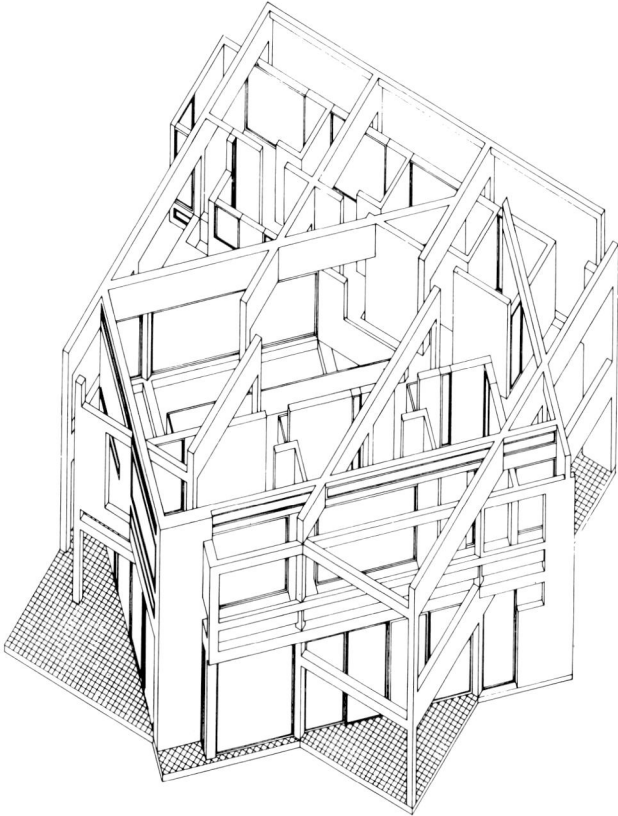

45 House III, 1969–71

46 House IV, 1971. "The
process becomes the object."

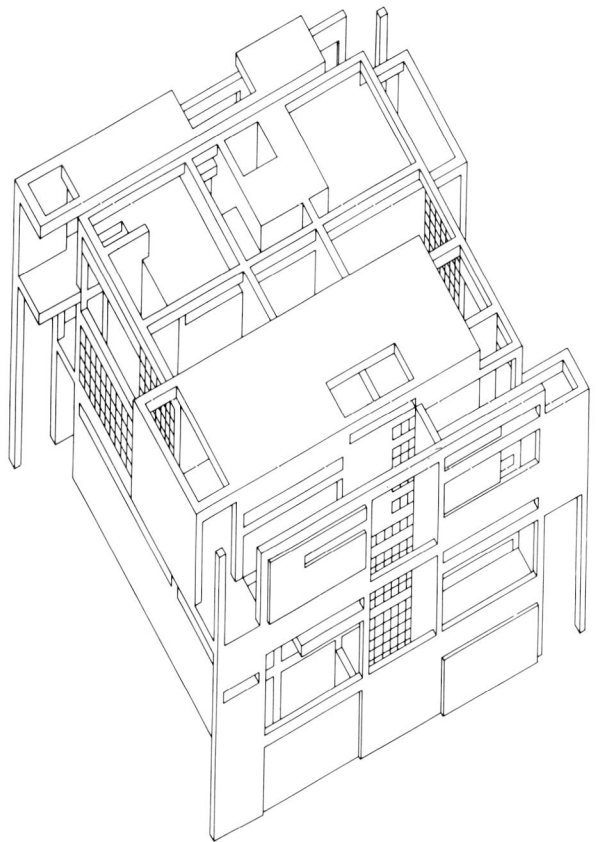

47 House VI, 1972–76, analytical drawing showing a diagonal cut through an axonometric view of the crossed, doubled walls of the house

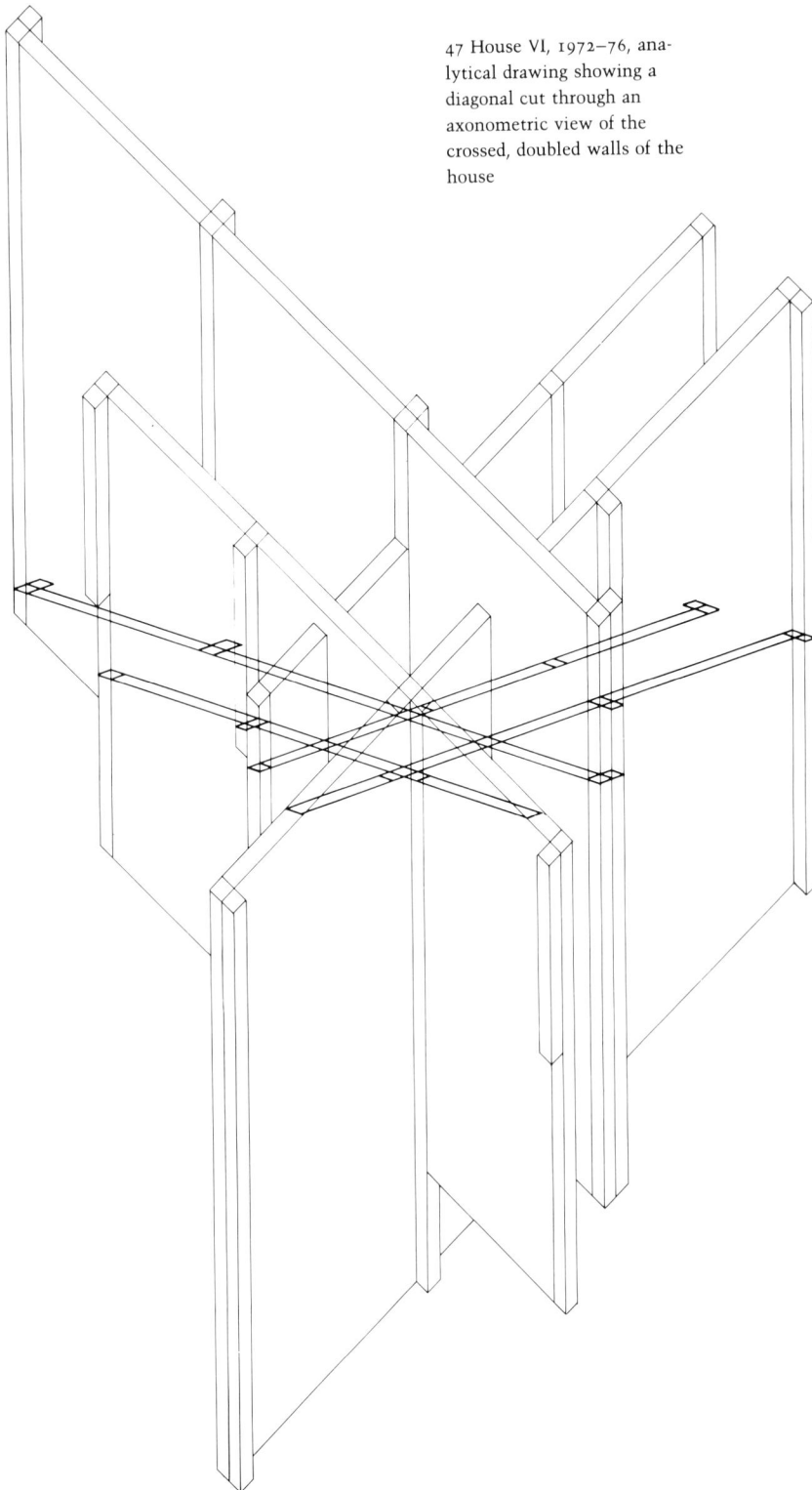

conceptual, to which he has given rise and with the impossibility of sustaining an idealized attitude toward these artifacts and mental constructs. This loss is symbolized in House VI by the loss of a center through which man can become a dominant force. What is important in House VI is not so much the self-closing process by which objecthood is attained, where "the process becomes the object,"[2] but rather the cultural implications of a perceived rupture in the relationship between man and object.

House X: A Machine for Thinking in

The development of this sensibility reaches ideological fruition in House X and its accompanying text (figure 48). Eisenman could now claim:

The imagery . . . is rooted in a pervasive and explicit ideological concern with a cultural condition, namely the apparent inability of modern man to sustain any longer a belief in his own rationality and perfectibility . . . . It is precisely this concern with a broader cultural condition which . . . distinguishes House X from [the] earlier houses.[3]

The mechanism for representing this "broad cultural condition" is what Eisenman calls "decomposition,"[4] which is in some ways the reverse of the earlier "transformational" method of Houses I–IV. For where "transformation" was the manipulation in logical stages of a simple geometrical solid into a more complex state, "decomposition" is the attempt to distill the wider cultural context of dissonant relations between man and object, the "pre-existing condition"[5] as Eisenman calls it, into an intelligible, and therefore simpler, order within

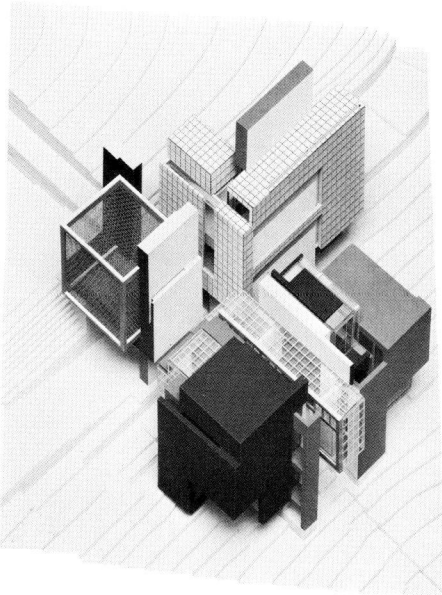

48 House X, 1975–77,
axonometric model. "The
precise aspect of an
axonometric drawing."

the architectural object itself. Where transformation works out from a supposedly cultureless object, decomposition works in from an acknowledged object culture.

The "pre-existing condition" presupposed by decomposition is one in which man and object can no longer act instructively toward each other but are driven to act competitively with one another. It is a condition in which intellectual systems and physical artifacts are incapable of being comprehended from some central place, either conceptual or tangible. They must therefore be unredeemably fragmentary to human beings, be simply "approximations of absent wholes."[6]

In the attempt to represent this perceived condition, House X develops the cross configuration of House VI. It turns the negative spaces of its quadrants into positive masses, masses that are not simple cubes, however, as one might have expected from the transformational method of the first houses; rather, they are "three-dimensional els."

The Three-Dimensional El

The three-dimensional el (figure 49), a cube with a "bite" taken out of one corner, is a transformational form inasmuch as it is a more complex version of a cube. More importantly, however, it is also a "decompositional" form because it represents in a simple geometrical configuration the complex cultural condition of an "age of partial objects." As a result, says Eisenman, it is "both a fragment in itself and the sign of a fragment."[7]

Because the three-dimensional el can be seen "as a fragmentary reduction of the cube" and because in addi-

tion "the cube can be seen as an expansion of the el," it therefore follows that "the el is [either] moving towards completion as a single cube, or else incompletion (non-existence) as a single void."[8] In this sense the three-dimensional el represents the displacement suffered by man in the universe perceived by Eisenman, for in this universe man no longer commands the center (the cube) but is instead a fragment threatened by the possibility of no longer existing in it at all (the void). The three-dimensional el is the sign of this displacement, halfway between nostalgia for the idealism of the past, expressed by the centrality of a Platonic solid, and fear of an uncertain future, expressed by the void.

The Axonometric Model

While Houses I–IV and VI were all built, neither House X nor its heirs, which include House El Even Odd, have been. What then does it mean to call them houses at all? Perhaps it would be accurate to say that since House X, Eisenman's houses have been conceived not as houses for the body, but as houses for the brain, betraying Eisenman's impulse, to use Manfredo Tafuri's words, toward an "Icarus-like" state,[9] the impulse toward escape from all that is corporeal. These houses are not meant to provide shelter from rain, cold, and so on, things that are unpleasant for the body; they are meant to provide shelter from narrow-mindedness and slick formulas, from "the arbitrary disorder that is indifferent to order, a kind of moral obtuseness, complacent well-being, forgetfulness,"[10] things that are

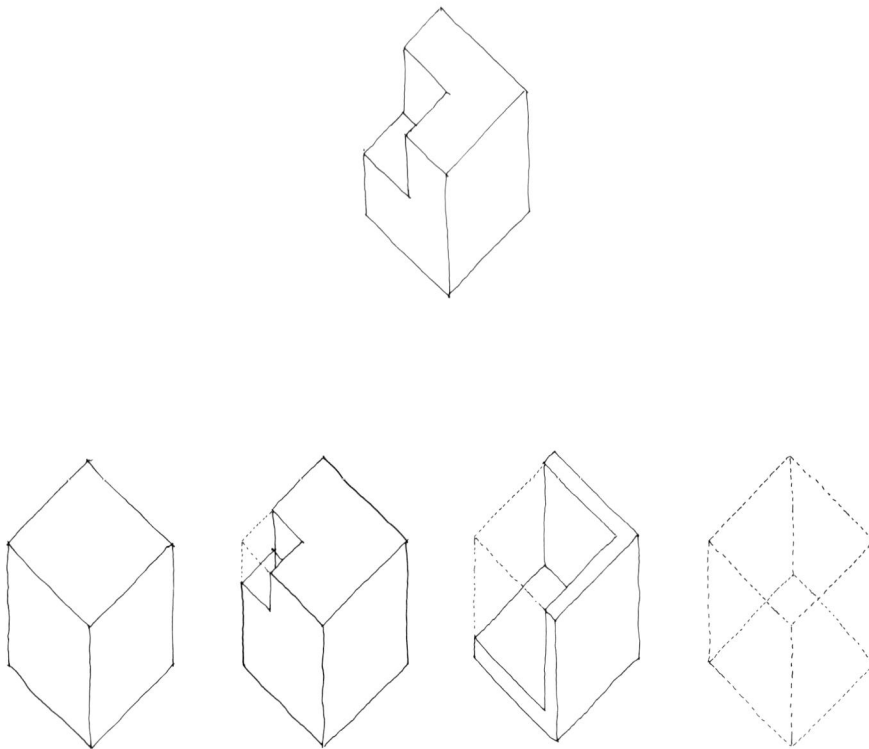

49 Diagram showing the
three-dimensional el as a
form oscillating between a
Platonic solid and the void

unpleasant for the mind. They do this
by challenging our understanding of
what architecture is.

For this reason the definitive representation of House X is not a building
at all, nor a normal model, but an axonometric model. As Eisenman says:

Usually a model is stationary, and the
viewer moves around, above or even
below it to understand its reality;
there is no fixed viewpoint. An axonometric drawing, on the other
hand, is based on a fixed, usually
frontal viewpoint. The information it
conveys does not change from different viewpoints. The axonometric
model, in contrast, changes depending
on the position of viewing. From the
side and from eye level it is seen as
raking in different directions. Then
from a slightly raised angle on the
oblique it is seen as a conventional
orthogonal model. Finally, when
viewed from the oblique at a 45 degree angle with one eye closed, it appears to flatten out and assume the
precise aspect of an axonometric
drawing: the viewer, forced into a
frontal and monocular view, sees the
building as through a camera.[11]

The axonometric model (figure 50),
then, by evoking an image of the
"real" and then nullifying its substan-
tiality, by calling into question the
authority of sight, and by frustrating
visual interpretation, is the declaration of the true nature of the house itself: a machine for thinking in.

If Le Corbusier's famous declaration
about the house being "a machine for
living in"[12] cast the architectural object as an obedient servant to man,
the house as a machine for thinking
in emancipates the object. The object
is now cast as its own master, and
man's mind inhabits what it finds,

infinitely adjusting itself to the
vagaries of the object. Like Beckett,
therefore, Eisenman can proclaim,
"The kind of work I do is one in
which I'm not master of my material."[13] Like Alice, we have entered a
world in which man has lost control
over the things that surround him.

When one compares the axonometric drawing of House X (figure 51)
to its axonometric model twin, there
is a point at which the model resolves
itself into the appearance of the drawing. It is like the looking glass,
through which one enters a separate
reality where every point obeys a different logic dictated by the object.
The looking-glass is a Checkpoint
Charlie between the realms of man
and object. What we "know" about
House X from the axonometric drawing is but a fragment of what axonometric modeling can reveal about
it.[14] And so the axonometric model is
a further stage of "decomposition," a
further iteration in the aesthetic cal-
culus by which man's displacement
from the center in a world now composed of partial structures can be represented. Vitruvian man, for
Eisenman, has been ripped from his
Platonic frame and flung headlong
into a world of indifferent and uncon-
trollable objects.

This is a condition of profound anxiety, and one which could perhaps
have been distilled only in the al-
chemical, intellectual alembics of
Manhattan. It is this condition that
House El Even Odd takes as its point
of departure.

50 House X, axonometric
model shown raking

51 House X, axonometric
drawing

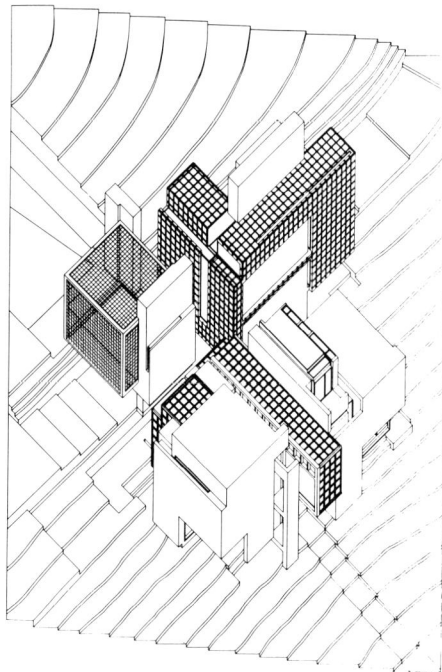

HOUSE EL EVEN ODD: REBIRTH FROM THE DEATH OF HUMANISM

The house occurs entirely below ground, as though it were a coffin (figure 52). It can be analyzed in terms of two basic principles, centrality and transformation, each of which has been imbued with specific cultural resonances.

Centrality

The loss of center is as crucial to the meaning of House El Even Odd as to Houses VI and X, but now this loss is more acute. If in House X the center was implied by the intersection of four volumes but denied by its void condition, in House El Even Odd the center is implied by the superimposition of three progressively smaller three-dimensional els (figure 53). The "bite" from the largest three-dimensional el is displaced and comes to rest in the center of the form from which it was bitten. This el-cube is then itself bitten and that smaller cube displaced to the center of the second form. Finally this smallest cube is diminished by the same amount, so that there is a ratio of volumes 1:8:64:512, a sequence implicitly without limit, a chain reaction of el-cubes, as if the house were an atom without a smallest particle.

While centrality is suggested in this manner, there is no center, as in a cube. The form of the el-cube is, furthermore, itself a metaphor for the loss of center, is "both a fragment in itself and the sign of a fragment." House El Even Odd subverts the traditional centrality of, say, Frank Lloyd Wright's prairie houses, which stretch and flex into the landscape and are anchored by a massive central hearth. The memory of such a centrality was definitely retained in House X, if only by inversion. In House El Even Odd there is even a rejection of the inversion of the traditional center; there is instead a parody of centrality through which Eisenman can deliver a more severe critique of center than ever before. For while the center is made to continually recede, the centrality of the house is reinforced by this very process. The observer looking for a center is led on and on in an endless search, getting nearer and nearer, but never arriving. As Eisenman says: "My houses are ideological in the sense that they deny the anthropocentricity of man . . . My houses make a commentary on the loss of center . . . Man's conception of the world is no longer anthropocentric just as it is no longer theocentric."[15]

Transformation

In addition to being in a process of contraction within itself toward a center that does not exist, however, the el-cube coffin is also engaged in a process of transformation. In House El Even Odd the el-cube "collapses" upward, as if drawn by a force from above. By this inversion, the normal process of decay one would expect in a coffin is replaced by a process derived from the world that survives above. The flat surface of the upwardly collapsed el-cube is flush with the ground, and nothing projects above this plane. Like a time-lapse photograph, the axonometric model preserves an intermediate stage of forty-five degree distortion. The model therefore creates an oscillation between cube and flattened surface—much like that in the el-cube itself,

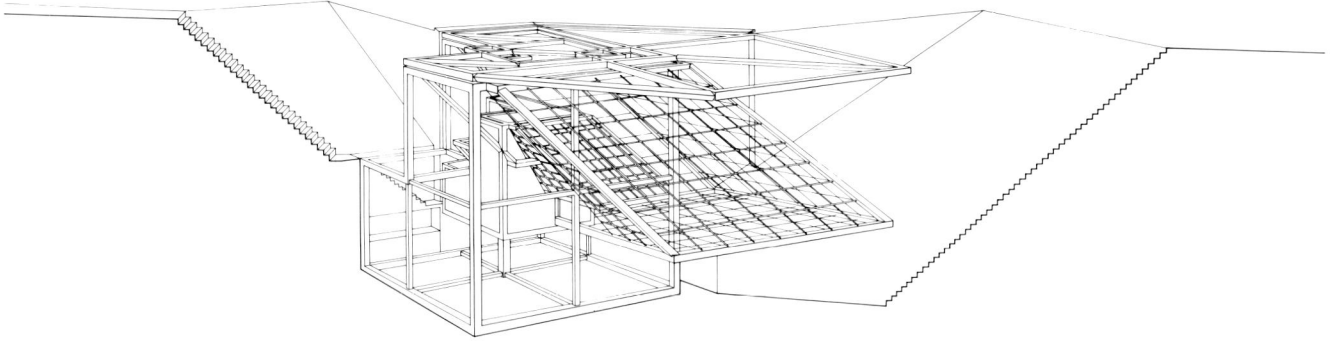

52 House El Even Odd, perspective drawing showing the house set into the earth

53 House El Even Odd, transformational drawings showing its generation. Drawing at lower right shows the superimposition of two axonometric states of the three-dimensional el on the el itself and the placement of the three three-dimensional els inside each other.

which tends alternately toward completion and the void. It creates a pulse, as if the house were a giant crystal measuring out some unspecified quantity of time, full of foreboding, the mechanism of some vast pacemaker to which human life is inescapably tied.[16]

The house therefore has two clearly differentiated parts: the coffin-cube, with its maze of coffins within coffins, with no final resting place, no center, describing a kind of nightmarish living death; and the pulsating axonometric forms with their implications of life, however threatened, of escape from the grave, and of upward movement.

If the parody of traditional humanist centrality can be interpreted as a critique of idealist notions of perfectibility, the "rebirth" from this exhausted condition, as it is portrayed in House El Even Odd, can be seen as a manifesto of the anti-idealism of the cultural condition Eisenman perceives. This can be discerned in the three states of the el-cube.

In the first state the form is a black, orthogonal representation of the el-cube. In the second state it is a gray, cage-like axonometric model of the cube. In the third state it is a white, open, flat "double axonometric"[17] of the form. The house is therefore at once "a three-dimensional object, an axonometric projection and a plan."[18] Any of these three states can be derived from any other, so the process of transformation is not a linear one. Nevertheless, while it is not linear in the transformational sense of Houses I–IV, it is clear that the double axonometric surface, or "plan," is a further decomposition of the original

el-cube, beyond the "last decomposition" of House X, which was the axonometric model.

The Double Axonometric Model
This "plan" is no longer the generator, the instrument of man's control, the "plan of battle" heroically wielded as it was for Palladio or Le Corbusier.[19] Instead it has been generated, metaphorically at least, by the forces of decomposition acting on the object, forces that have "collapsed" the orthogonal model of the el-cube upward. This further decompositional operation therefore makes the house for thinking in no more than a thought lacking all corporeality and makes the self-reproducing object a sign of its independence from man's originating influence.

The double axonometric, however, is not only a plan. Because it is the only element in the house directly and fully in contact with the world, it is also the principal facade. It can be considered the element that proclaims the true nature of the house; namely, the representation of man's loss of center in his object world.

The memory of this loss haunts House El Even Odd; this ghost blows through its intricate physical and conceptual membrane. The anxiety of this loss provokes the desire to forget that a loss has been sustained, but it is a memory too strong to remain for long suppressed.

The historical instant of this loss is of crucial importance in the secret life of House El Even Odd, and the most incisive tool for analyzing this moment is the history of perspective, which reveals to us the changing meaning of centrality since the Renaissance.

CENTRALITY AND PERSPECTIVE

Construzione Legittima

At the inception of the Renaissance, Filippo Brunelleschi painted a picture of the Baptistry in Florence viewed from inside the central door of the Duomo. This painting was done in perspective and may have been the first perspective image in history to be properly constructed. It had a hole drilled through it at the vanishing point. The viewer held a mirror at arm's length and looked into it from the back of the painting through the hole (figure 54). No distortion could enter in because the viewer's gaze was fixed and monocular.[20] A condition of identity was thus established between the eye and the vanishing point, with no conceptual difference between the two. The human eye became the center of the world shown in the image, just as man became the center of the world shown in the Vitruvian figure. Both symbolized the cosmic balance existing in the mind of the Renaissance humanist between the microcosm of man and his works and the macrocosm of God and his works.

Alberti codified this principle of perspective, calling it the *Construzione Legittima* in his *Della Pittura* of 1435. The method held sway as the orthodox means of constructing perspective illusion for over two hundred years.

The strength of the humanist assumptions behind the *Construzione Legittima* can be grasped by the inability of Vignola in his influential later treatise on perspective to depart from them. This text, *Le Due Regole della Prospettiva Pratica*[21] of 1583,

54 Reconstruction of Brunelleschi's perspective experiment, c. 1425

describes two methods of constructing perspective. The first *regola* was
derived directly from Alberti and restated his single-point method, although with some ingenious technical
changes. The second *regola*, however,
discussed the distinctly non-Albertian
"distance-point" method of construction, which had been developed in
northern Europe.

**The Distance-Point Method of
Perspective Construction**
In Alberti's method, as in Vignola's
prima regola, the eye point and the
vanishing point, coincident in Brunelleschi's experiment, are separated, but
only for convenience (figure 55). Both
points are still defined in terms of
sight, in terms of man, not the object
represented. Everything vanishes to a
single point. In the distance-point
method, however, the eye point is
projected onto the picture plane at an
angle of forty-five degrees from the
actual position of the eye. This point
is the "distance point," so called because it represents the distance the
real eye would be away from the object depicted. The vanishing point and
the distance point are no longer
defined in terms of sight but in terms
of an abstract, geometrical system.
Because of this conceptual displacement of the eye, the method is a two-
point one, no longer converging at a
single point as before.

The inescapable fact presented by
the second method—two vanishing
points instead of one—left Vignola
with a philosophical problem, which
can be seen in his diagram for the perspective construction of a cube placed
at an angle (figure 56). Here Vignola
draws the plan of the cube according
to the distance-point method, show-

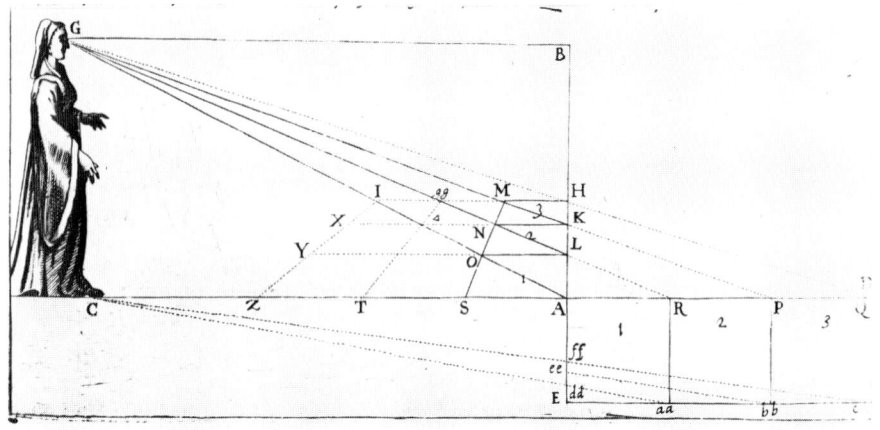

55 Squares in perspective
according to Vignola's first
regola

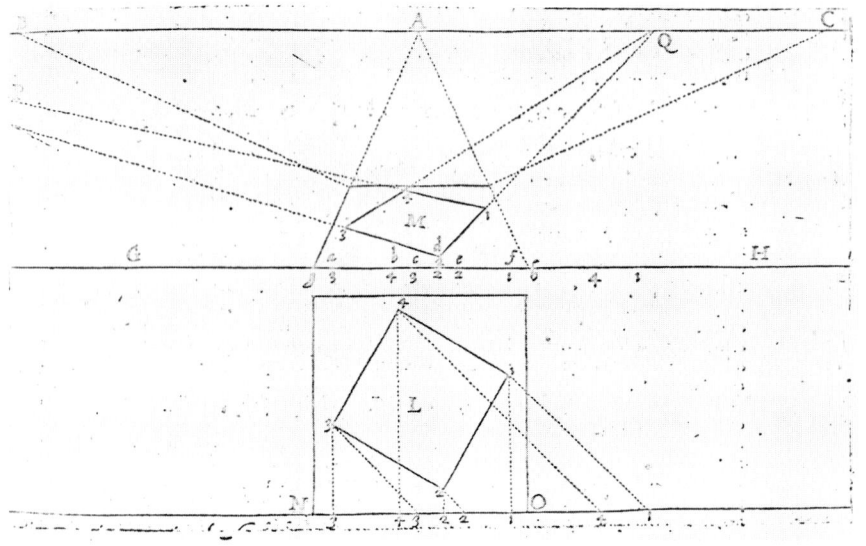

56 Perspective of a square at
an angle according to Vignola's second *regola*

ing a number of vanishing points, but he also shows the object on a continuous field that is itself vanishing to a single central point. In the discussion of the procedure, he says:

It has been said in . . . La Prima Regola that all visible things terminate at a single point in man's sight. This is, in effect, so. Thus even though in this demonstration it may appear that there are more points in operation, still it is not true that one is not supposed to use primarily the point of sight as the principle—without which point . . . one cannot find the first four points which establish a layout for the process. These other points are added here for brevity's sake because one could still proceed without them, only it would take longer.[22]

The method of the second *regola* therefore cannot be for Vignola anything but a one-point system.

Development of the Second *Regola*
The prejudice demonstrated by Vignola in his treatise retarded for over a century the exploitation of the second method. As late as 1693 the virtuoso vault painter and stage designer Andrea Pozzo was still arguing unequivocally for the Albertian system.[23] By the eighteenth century, however, the second *regola* was gaining ground. It was explicitly acknowledged as a starting point by the Venetian scenographer Ferdinando Galli de Bibiena for his *L'Architettura Civile* of 1711.[24] He wrote: "[We begin] our demonstration in perspective with the form that Vignola teaches as the second manner in his book on perspective."[25] What Ferdinando did in this book was to legitimize the method of the second *regola*. He ignored the central stage perspective of the Renaissance theatre and tilted

everything at an angle in plan to generate diagonal views, creating the so-called *Scena per Angolo* (figure 57). This method was developed to great effect by other members of the extensive Bibiena family (figure 58).

The new rococo stage invention acted in turn as an influence on the young Giovanni Battista Piranesi. Whereas the Bibienas used the second *regola* for purely visual effect, as a delightful way to amuse their court audiences, Piranesi endowed the rejection of the central Renaissance vanishing point with intellectual force. Where Vignola had been unable to accept the conceptual framework of the two-point method because of his inability to conceive of man as anything but a microcosmic representation of macrocosmic harmony, Piranesi seized the new possibilities. He condemned the eye to wander forever between alternative resting places, thereby destroying the humanist balance and imbuing the playfulness of the Bibienas' scenes with a new darkness, with a loneliness and an anxiety that were wholly new.

Piranesi and the Critique of Center
The result of Piranesi's acceptance of ambiguity was a critique of humanist centrality. Informing that critique was his rejection of the continuous field upon which the square at an angle had existed in Vignola's universe. In Piranesi's most provocative work, the *Invenzioni Capric di Carceri* series,[26] or *Prisons*, each object exists separately and competes with every other object; and the field that joins the separated elements is an endless patchwork space of contradiction, compromise, and uncertainty. The

57 Ferdinando Galli de
Bibiena, stage design showing a *scena par angolo*, 1711

58 Giuseppe Galli de
Bibiena, stage design, 1740

modern theme of fragmentation has
irrevocably entered.[27] The eye is no
longer at the center and is no longer
trusted as an instrument of truth. A
fundamental change in the perception
of man's place in the world has oc-
curred: in Piranesi's *Prisons*, man has
lost his centrality in the universe.

The axonometric model of House X
and the "real" house shown in the axonometric drawing differ for the same
reason that Piranesi's space subverts
spaces created by the "real" laws of
Renaissance perspective: hierarchical
centrality has been relinquished for a
universe of fragments. In both cases
the space of the flesh is transformed
into a space of the mind.

In plate VII, for example (figure 59),
the defying of traditional perspective
leads to confusing optical effects and
makes it virtually impossible to follow any axis across the space on the
same plane. The right portion of the
drawbridge and the bridge that appears below it seem at first to be in
the same plane, as they both intersect
the tower on the right edge of the
drawing. But the right portion of the
drawbridge is impossibly angled for
that to be true. The "lower" bridge,
moreover, also intersects the tower to
the left in the drawing, while the
drawbridge is forward of that tower.
In that case, the "lower" bridge is
really a more distant bridge, though of
course its junction at the right tower
makes that impossible. The left portion of the drawbridge is properly angled to be in the same plane as the
other bridge, which it must be because it is in front of the left tower.
Furthermore, the figures on the left
part of the drawbridge are three-
fourths the size of the two figures at

59 Giovanni Battista Piranesi, *Invenzione Capric di Carceri*, plate VII, second state, c. 1760; first state, 1745. "A colossal pointlessness [that] goes on indefinitely, and is co-extensive with the universe." (Aldous Huxley, *Prisons*, 1949)

the springing point on the right, which, when added to their differing angles and proportions, puts the two halves of the bridge in different planes and makes it impossible for the two parts to meet when lowered.[28]

This space of fragmentation rejects the centrality of man in a Renaissance humanist world and transfers attention instead to objects, casting man as an indifferent item within an object order. In plate VII the spiral stairs rotate like the threads of a gargantuan screw and force the upper walkways to turn like blades, creating around the vast spindle of the tower an endless motion of conveyor belts and pulley systems and producing clouds of steam and smoke. The people who are trapped in this metropolis machine seem at once its helpless, amnesiac operatives and its mass-produced products, as they are carried along the apparent escalators and moving walkways not against their will, for they have none, but by the accidental linking of autonomous power centers. The inhabitants of Piranesi's world, are, in fact, not governed by any human order, but are adrift in a world whose law is fashioned and implemented only by objects. The last vestige of the natural order, the inhabitants are deprived of freedom, enslaved, and have become objects themselves, mere fragments of Eisenman's "world of partial objects" in which, to quote Colin Rowe, "there is nothing final about any of their possible relationships."[29]

THE MYTH OF THE CUBE

In the *Prisons* the humanist tradition is spurned, jettisoned for the first time. It is this impulse that Eisenman turns upon the pure geometry of the cube through the process of decomposition. But the Platonic geometry of the cube did not lose its attractiveness for architects just because the Renaissance humanist system of perspective and all it stood for broke down. As Rowe has shown in *The Mathematics of the Ideal Villa*, the "natural" beauty of the cube, with its claim to universal, ideal beauty founded on absolute value, was as appealing to Le Corbusier as to Palladio, as powerful within a functionalist ideology as within a Renaissance humanist one. The Villa Malcontenta and the Villa Stein are both cubic blocks; both are mathematically determined, one by humanist harmonics, the other by *tracés régulateurs.* In both, "the realization of an idea which is represented by the house as a cube could also be presumed to lend itself very readily to the purposes of Virgilian dreaming."[30] It is this idealism, whether deriving from a religious absolute or the absolutes of technological paradise, that Eisenman condemns in the three-dimensional el.

Piranesi's *Prisons* are no more Virgilian dreams than Eisenman's own postfunctionalist *capriccio*, his House El Even Odd. Far from embodying an Arcadian utopia, Piranesi's etchings present us with a *negative* utopia[31]; and his geometry, like Eisenman's, is anxious and fragmentary, even paranoid. Le Corbusier may embrace a technological world unknown to Palladio, but he maintains the same idealism, and it is this idealism that we see rejected in the *Prisons*, just as surely as it is scorned in House El Even Odd. It is for this reason that Eisenman has called the func-

tionalism of Utopian modernism no more than a late phase of humanism,[32] meaning that for him true modernism must be, in essence, anti-idealistic, deprived of any external, centering force.

House El Even Odd pursues this Piranesian theme but couched in late-twentieth-century terms. The Platonic grandeur of Palladio's Malcontenta (figure 60); the noble idealism of Ledoux's unsullied, spherical Shelter for the Rural Guards, resting gently in a dip in the landscape (figure 61); Le Corbusier's "Primary Solids"; and finally Philip Johnson's Glass House, prophetic for Eisenman of the "modernist dialectic,"[33] differ in the most fundamental way from the black cube with a bite taken out of it that lies at the heart of House El Even Odd. In the 1550s Palladio's villa was the representation of a cosmic ideal; in the 1780s Ledoux's landscape was a Garden of Enlightened Eden, the sun shown rising to bless an endless summer of plentiful and well-guarded harvest; in 1922 Le Corbusier's Ozenfant house (figure 62) was a great volume of centralized space in wonderful technological balance between heaven and earth; and Johnson's glass prism (figure 63) is "the last pure form, the final gesture of a belief in humanism so debilitated by the events of 1945."[34]

The cube that is interred and altered so significantly in House El Even Odd is the Platonic form of all these predecessors, but Eisenman rejects the external centering force these forms embody by burying the cube, blackening it, and stripping it of its innocence and purity. For Eisenman, in the changed relationship of man and object prophesied by Piranesi

60 Andrea Palladio, Villa
Malcontenta, Mira, c. 1550–
60, front facade

61 Claude-Nicolas Ledoux,
Shelter for the Rural Guards,
c. 1780, plan and section

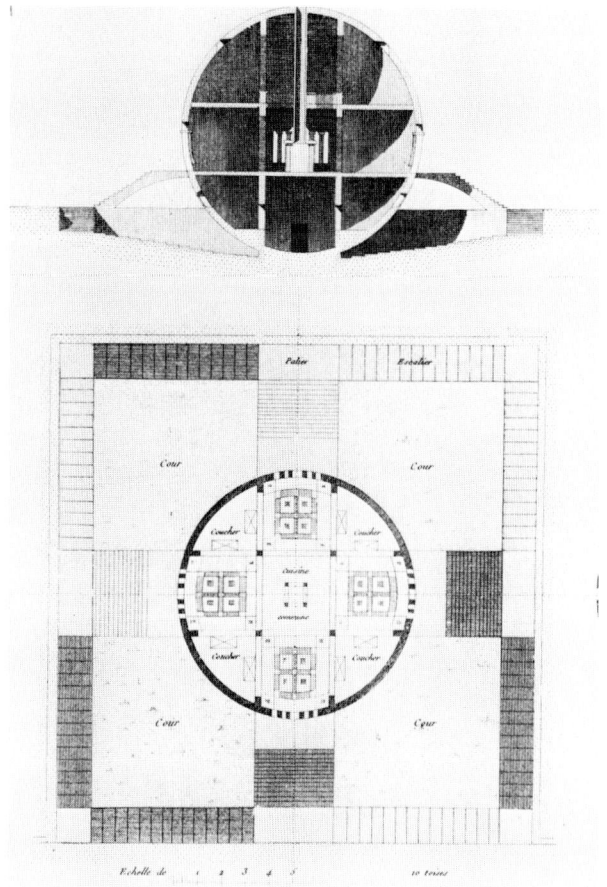

62 Le Corbusier, Ozenfant house, 1922, interior view

63 Philip Johnson, Glass House, New Canaan, Connecticut, 1949

and brought on by the nuclear age
with its threat and history of mass
death, "we are all in the situation of
being survivors rather than heroes."[35]

Man has fallen from a state of innocence in House El Even Odd, and, as
in the primal myth of man's Fall,
Eisenman has taken a Platonic solid
to represent an innocence that has
vanished with the ripening of the industrial world. It is from the Tree of
Knowledge that man has eaten once
again, but of a different fruit. Like the
apple offered Eve in Dürer's *Adam
and Eve* (figure 64), House El Even
Odd represents the knowledge of our
new weakness; the fatal bite is now a
cube, not a sphere. This image of the
second Fall, of a loss no less certain
than the loss of Eden, lies at the heart
of House El Even Odd's secret life
(figure 65).

It is appropriate and telling, therefore, that the main entrance to the
house occurs in the plane of the double axonometric, which, because it
has no thickness, is plan and elevation as well as section and thus contains the essential nature of the
house. The entrance is directly under
the "bite" that has been taken out of
the facade corresponding to the missing corner of the three-dimensional
el (figure 66). One therefore enters
through the very bite that represents
the second Fall. To have such knowledge is to confront responsibility and
to be familiar with the cares of a
greater state of complexity. The
facade is full of the poignancy of this
situation. It is strained against the
plane of the earth as if it wanted to
open up into a real building above
ground, but it is given a tension by
the force preventing it from doing so.

64 Albrecht Dürer, *Adam
and Eve*. Collection of the
Cooper-Hewitt Museum.
Gift of Mrs. Leo Wallerstein.

65 Diagram showing the
three-dimensional el as a
representation of the myth
of man's Fall

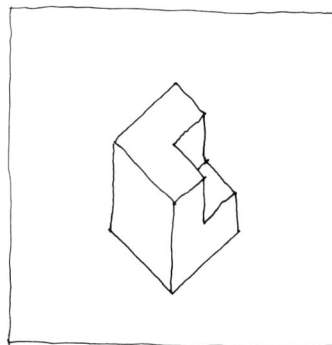

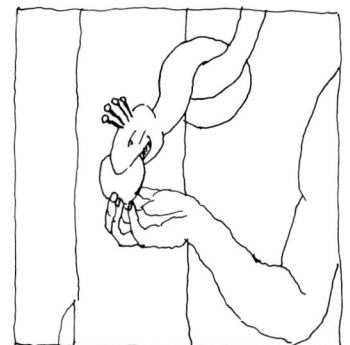

At the same time, however, precisely because it is a plan, the facade implies a blueprint for action, even if man's control has been thrown into doubt. And so from the depths of House El Even Odd the flattened form of the double axonometric rises up. Icarus-like in its escape from the memory of loss, it is doubly distant from the Renaissance, an order of the object not the eye and of the object's sign and not its substance, scoured to a new whiteness by experience of a changed world. Flattened into a huge map, divided and gridded not according to human laws but to the laws of the object world, it is the chart of unexplored territory on which man must find his way as best he may.

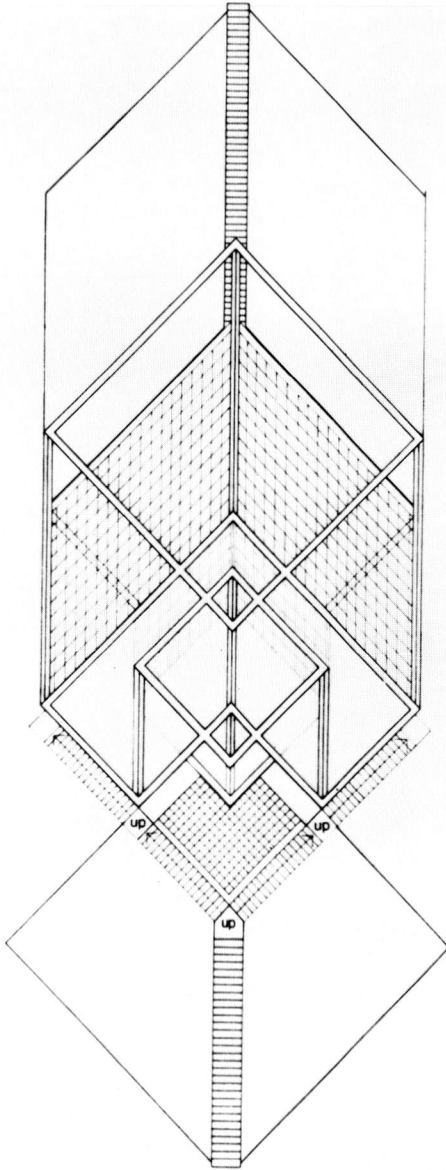

66 House El Even Odd, roof plan and principal facade

3

THE SENSIBILITY
OF SILENCE
Four Leaf Towers
Houston, Texas
Cesar Pelli
and Associates,
Architects (1982)

DIFFUSE URBANISM

Downtown Houston is a burst of towers in an utterly flat landscape. It stands in the center of the enormous ring of the Loop freeway, which is fringed with rival centers of enterprise. The most vital of these is the development just off the West Loop along South Post Oak Road (figure 67).

South Post Oak Road is intersected at its north end by San Felipe and at its south end by Westheimer (figure 68). North of San Felipe are the postwar ranch houses of Tanglewood and, further east, the older mansions of River Oaks. South of Westheimer are the Southwest freeway and the tracks of the Southern Pacific Railroad. Between and around Westheimer and San Felipe on South Post Oak Road are the towers of the Post Oak section. At the south end is the Galleria shopping center and Johnson and Burgee's Transco tower. At the north end are Cesar Pelli and Associates Four Leaf Towers apartments and their adjacent office development of Four Oaks Place. In the middle stand Johnson and Burgee's Post Oak Central office buildings. Scattered all around are dozens of other towers and mid-rise buildings, participating in a form of urbanism barely ten years old (figure 69).

The Dynamic and the Static Tower
The typical architectural forms of this urbanism are dynamic. The dynamic tower requires movement on the part of the observer to yield its expressive potential. This principle was first realized on a large scale in Mies van der Rohe's 1949–51 Lake Shore Drive apartments in Chicago (figure 70).

The masses of these buildings create what Sigfried Giedion described as "relational space,"[1] a phenomenon in which space is channeled in such a way that the masses appear to slide weightlessly past one another as the viewer moves around them (figure 71).

Houston's most accomplished example of this phenomenon is Johnson and Burgee's Penzoil Place in the downtown core. The two parts of Penzoil Place are arranged so that they enter into a relationship with the driver on the freeway; they reveal their nature as dynamic objects as the observer moves over large distances. This is the same principle Johnson incorporated in the diagonal approach to his Glass House of 1949, but blown up from pedestrian to freeway scale. Post Oak Central demonstrates the same principle, as do most other buildings in the Post Oak section, although these others are all too often diluted to a vernacular and banal level.

Four Leaf Towers were the first tall buildings in the Post Oak section to break with the dynamic form of the Lake Shore Drive apartments (figure 72). They are static as forms. They express no horizontal movement because of their perfectly square plans (figure 73). They *mark* space rather than *channel* it. Movement around the towers is not required on the part of the observer to comprehend the towers' meaning. To emphasize this marking of space, Four Leaf Towers have clearly defined volumetric tops.

The Carved Crown
Utopian modernism demanded at all costs a flat roof on tall buildings. Since the flat roof can cover any

67 Houston road system,
showing the Loop and the
location of Four Leaf Towers

68 Aerial photograph of the Post Oak section. Note the axis running down South Post Oak Road, connecting Pelli's Four Oaks Place and Johnson's Transco tower, and the axis formed between the point where San Felipe Road crosses the west Loop and the Four Leaf Towers.

69 Figure-ground diagram of the Post Oak section. Diffuse urbanism. Four Leaf Towers circled.

70 Mies van der Rohe, Lake
Shore Drive apartments,
Chicago, 1949–51

71 Mies van der Rohe, Lake
Shore Drive apartments,
Chicago, 1949–51, plan

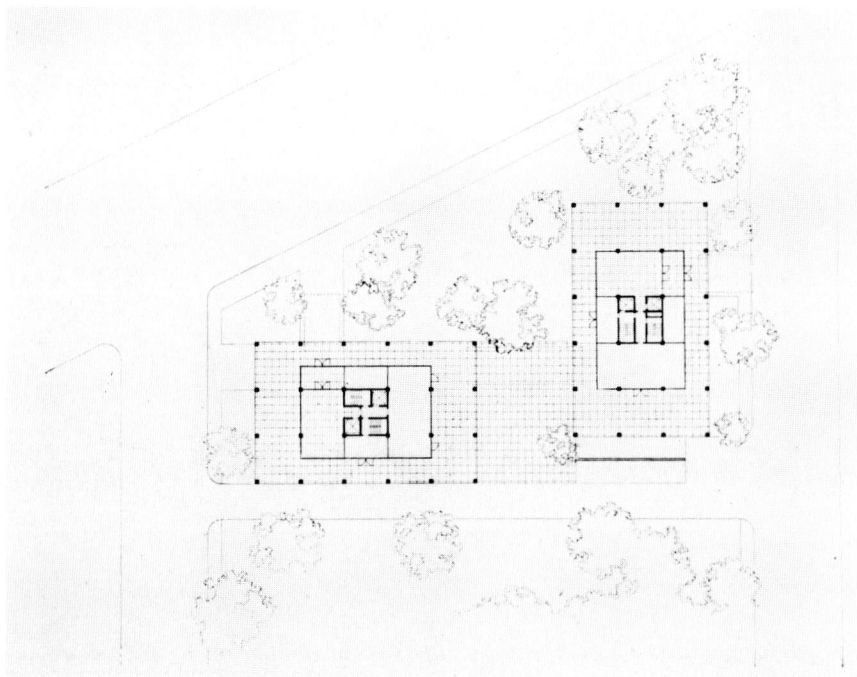

72 Four Leaf Towers from San Felipe Road. The static towers are flanked by vernacular examples of the dynamic tower.

73 Four Leaf Towers, plan

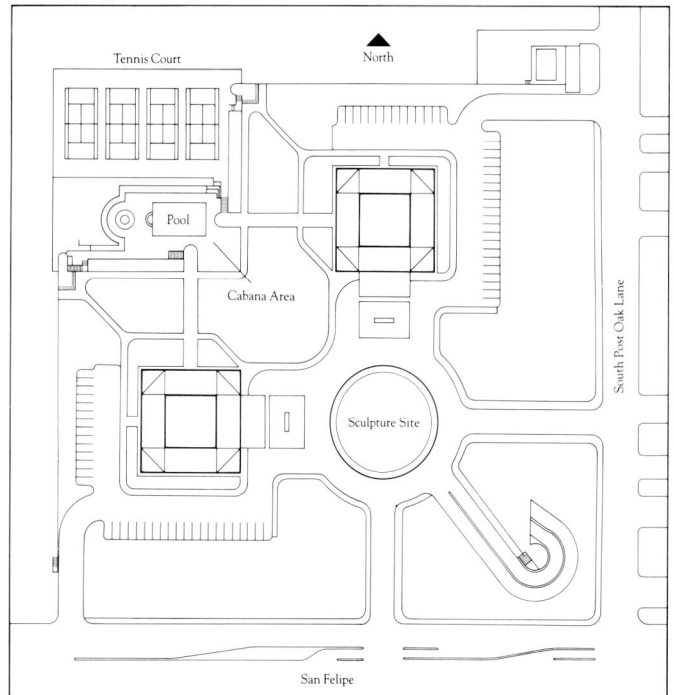

configuration, the top of a Miesian building does not convey anything about its plan. In Mies's towers the flat roof is, rather, the consequence of an idealized geometry, which can itself be seen as symbolizing the "construction" of a technological future whose potential for perfectibility is without limit. In many cases this original meaning is, of course, reduced to no more than a fashionable motif.

Four Leaf Towers, on the other hand, appear as two boxes of Utopian modernism whose flat tops have been cut up into symmetrical crowns as if by the precise strokes of a gigantic scalpel (figure 74). Their forms are no longer potentially limitless in the vertical dimension but are palpably limited. These forms embody not the Miesian process of construction but rather the massive quality of a solid object carved rather than constructed (figure 75). Unlike the flat Miesian top, these crowns can spring from only one plan. The crowns can therefore be seen as signs of the centralized, symmetrical plan. They are signs, that is, of the condition of marking space rather than the condition of channeling space—signs of a condition indifferent to the movement of the observer. The crowns are signs, one can conclude, of an autonomous condition of the object rather than an idealized condition of society.

MONUMENTAL FORM

Additive and Subtractive Form Making

Because of the static quality embodied in the plan and signified by the tops, Four Leaf Towers are like obelisks and have the same purpose:

74 Four Leaf Towers, the "carved" tops

75 Four Leaf Towers, carved form

to mark urban space. This is an attitude made clear by Pelli in his entry to the Chicago Tribune Tower competition (figure 76). There Pelli used a form similar to that employed in the Four Leaf Towers project. In both cases the towers appear to be cut from a block (although the Chicago Tribune Tower is without a top). As Pelli says: "The aesthetic intentions are to develop a recognizable urban icon. An archetypal office building . . . it is an obelisk or pylon."[2]

The rootedness that characterizes both obelisks and Four Leaf Towers as seen from a distance is a product of their symmetrical, carved quality. Carving is a subtractive approach to form making, whereas Miesian construction is additive. They are alternative compositional techniques of the immediately premodern era and correspond to the Romantic classicism of a Ledoux, on the one hand, and the rationalism of a Durand on the other.

Durand's method of horizontal and vertical combination is relentlessly additive: structure is emphasized, corners are articulated with pilasters, and the impression is all frame and lightness. Ledoux, on the other hand, considers his forms as solid geometries: surface is emphasized, openings are carved out, the corners are sharp, and the impression is all volume and heaviness.

Durand's towered development of the square building type (figure 77) and Ledoux's prison at Aix (figure 78) have similar forms. Both are square in plan, two storied, and have towers at each corner. Yet these elements are treated quite differently in each scheme. Durand's towers are vertical

76 Cesar Pelli and Associates, late entry to the Chicago Tribune Tower competition, 1980

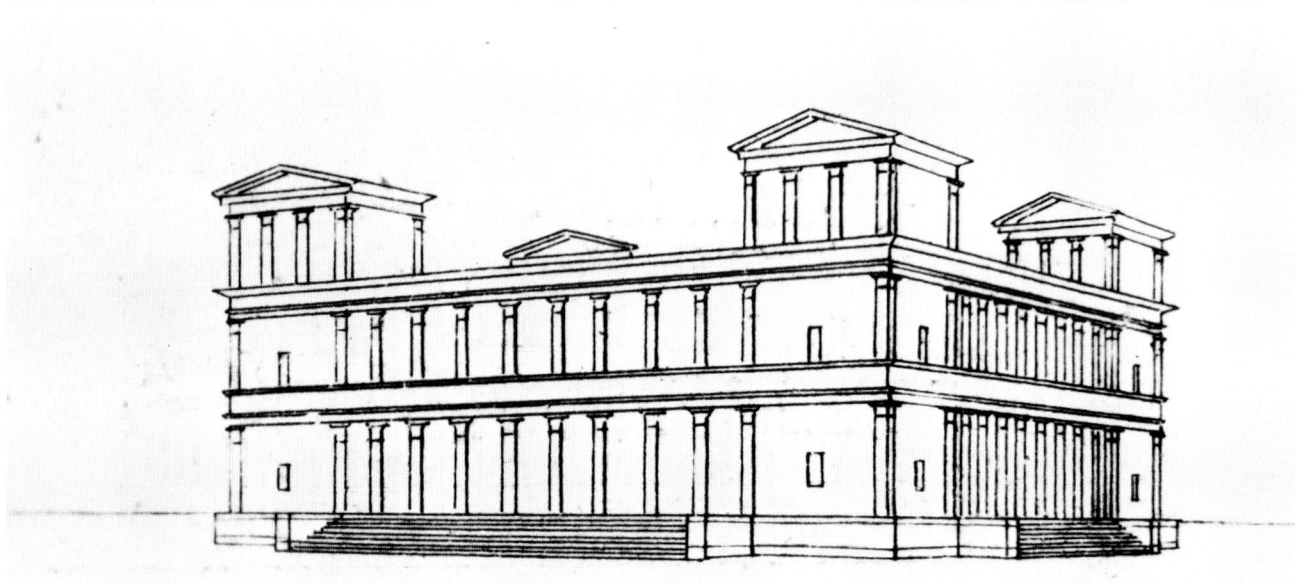

77 Jean-Nicolas-Louis
Durand, the development of
the square building type
with towers

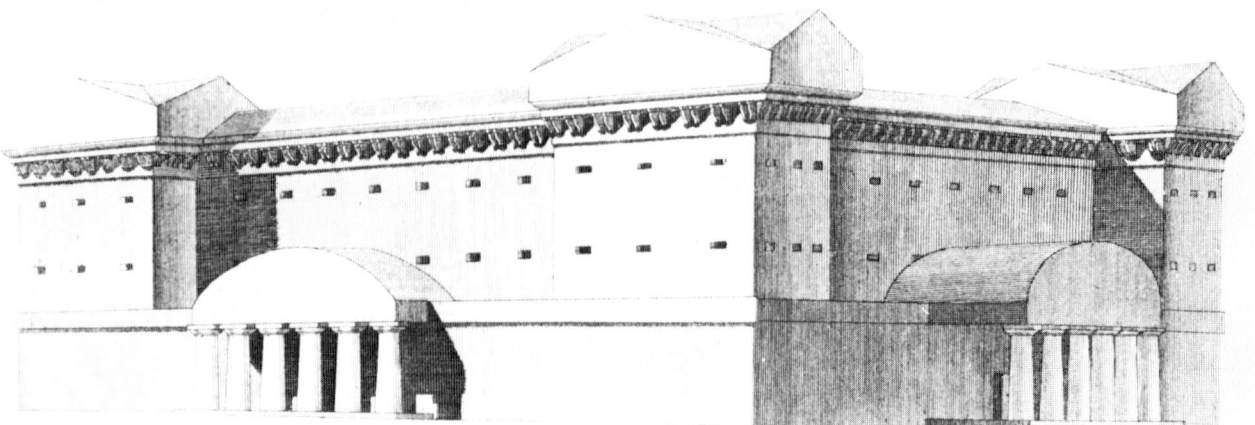

78 Claude-Nicolas Ledoux,
Prison at Aix-en-Provence,
c. 1787

extensions of the plan grid, the intermediate wall sections are coplanar
with the towers, the grid is articulated with pilasters, the towers
are capped with simple pitches, which
are themselves unobtrusive extensions of the grid, and the whole is
hooped round with cornices to emphasize the grid from which it pro-
ceeds. Ledoux's towers, on the other
hand, are massive volumetric forms.
The intermediate wall sections are
cut back, the surfaces smoothly
sliced, the towers' tops precisely
carved, and the whole mass gives the
impression of an object hewn as if by
giants from an outcrop of rock.

Pelli's method is subtractive. The
tops of the Four Leaf Towers are
carved like the towers of Ledoux's
prison. The stepped wrappers of the
Battery Park City towers in New
York (figure 79) or the Humana project in Louisville (figure 80) are carved
like the gigantic stepping in Schinkel's Schloss Orianda (figure 81).
From a distance the Four Leaf Towers
are as rooted as Ledoux's prison and
seem as massive. Yet the scale of
Four Leaf Towers dwarfs Ledoux's
prison; and while Boullée's projects
may approach the towers in size, they
are always single objects that presuppose a hierarchical order of large to
small buildings in the city. Pelli's
towers are part of an urbanism of
other large objects. It is not hierarchy
of size but symmetrical, carved shape
that makes forms monumental in this
urbanism (figures 82, 83). Furthermore, the monumentality of buildings
in diffuse urbanism is not related to
function.

In *The Architecture of the City*
Aldo Rossi stressed that the tradi-

79 Cesar Pelli and Asso-
ciates, Battery Park City,
New York, 1985

80 Cesar Pelli and Asso-
ciates, Humana building
project, Louisville, Ken-
tucky, 1982

81 Karl Friedrich Schinkel,
Schloss Orianda, the Crimea,
central temple on "carved"
base containing the museum
room

82 Cesar Pelli and Associates, Four Oaks Place, 1983,
from South Post Oak Road

83 Four Leaf Towers from
San Felipe Road

tional monument has a quality of permanence in the city that is related to the adaptability of such monuments to multiple functions over time.[3] This adaptability corresponds in turn to "an extreme precision of form."[4] There is no reason to suppose that Four Leaf Towers will be preserved longer than other buildings in Houston, yet as static forms they appear as fixed points in a flux of dynamic buildings of the same size but without monumentality. This monumentality differs from that found in the traditional city because it does not ultimately derive from adaptability to human use but from the condition of the city as an object: the carved tower operates axially, depending on the city's primary physical structure of roads, rather than in "relational space" as a dynamic tower does, depending on the constant movement of the city's inhabitants.

The Distortion of Romantic Classicism

Like Bruno Taut's expressionist carving of mountain ranges (figure 84), Pelli's carved peak is monumental among other peaks in Houston. This monumentality gives the impression of permanence lacking in the "uncarved" peaks, as though, in the utter flatness of Houston, Pelli's towers had acquired a topographical quality to compensate for the absence of natural features. This is the scale at which Four Leaf Towers operate: the scale of Loos's Chicago Tribune Tower competition entry of 1921 (figure 85), which, as Aldo Rossi has observed, was the Viennese master's "synthesis of the distortions created in America by an extensive application of style in a new context."[5]

84 Bruno Taut, *Alpine Architecture*, 1913, plate VII. "The rock above the treeline is hewn away and smoothed into many-faceted crystalline forms." "Nature is great!"

85 Adolf Loos, entry to the
Chicago Tribune Tower
competition, 1921–22

Four Leaf Towers demonstrate the same distortion, but of Romantic classicism rather than Greek Revival, of "natural" formation rather than artificial construction. For the towers' form is the result of the subtractive compositional method of Romantic classicism distorted through the modern urban scale of Four Leaf Towers' fundamental ancestor—the expressionist Friedrichstrasse project of 1919 by Mies van der Rohe, the first glass-skin skyscraper ever conceived (figure 86).

In the Friedrichstrasse project, form is still more carved than constructed, the last frenzied scream of nineteenth-century Romanticism before the triumph of the International style. It is to this crucial stepping stone into the past that Pelli returns, but with a wholly different sensibility. For the Four Leaf Towers do not embody a sensibility of revolutionary action through technology but rather the numbing effects that technology has produced. The sound and the fury of Friedrichstrasse is in Four Leaf Towers drained away to the absolute silence of an inverse expressionism.

THE CODED SKIN

Accommodation

The sense of the monumental in the Four Leaf Towers, however, is qualified by an inseparable relationship with a spatial parameter, which is of crucial importance. It is only from a distance that the towers assume their monumental "carved" mode; from less than a quarter of a mile away, the whole character of the towers changes from a solid, rooted one, which appears irreducible, to an ephemeral but accommodating one (figure 87).

86 Mies van der Rohe, *Fried-richstrasse Office Building,* Berlin Project, 1921, perspective. Charcoal and pencil on brown paper mounted on board, 68¼ × 48 in. Collection, Mies van der Rohe Archive, The Museum of Modern Art, New York. Gift of Ludwig Mies van der Rohe.

87 Four Leaf Towers, the skin from San Felipe Road

The desire to make a tall building that is both a "recognizable urban icon" from a distance yet accommodating at close range is an overriding concern in Pelli's recent work, and the consequent adjustment to nearness involves two things: the physical manipulation of the base and the perceptual qualities of the skin.

When the urbanism is dense, the physical distortion of the base is great. In Pelli's Battery Park City project or the Humana project, for example, the sense of the towers as pure objects is almost completely lost below the twentieth story. This is a principle already convincingly demonstrated by Loos's Chicago Tribune project. When the urbanism is as diffuse as it is in Houston, however, the towers are hardly distorted at all and the shafts are barely altered by any form of physical accommodation. Little physical distortion is required in Four Leaf Towers because in the automobile urbanism of Houston, there are no buildings to define the streets in the traditional way. The only distortion in Four Leaf Towers, in fact, is in the first two stories, which accommodate the perspective of the viewer in a car as it turns off the road, and during the subsequent brief walk from car to building. As a result the principle of accommodation is carried out almost entirely by the skin in Four Leaf Towers; that is, by symbolic rather than physical means.

Many buildings during the seventies sought to reduce the glass skin to as smooth a surface as possible, following the experiments in the fifties of Bunshaft at Lever House and Saarinen at the Bell Laboratories. In his Medical Center in Century City of

1966, Pelli brought the theme of the self-referential skin to a conclusion. Thereafter he turned to the use of colored glass, as in the San Bernadino City Hall (brown glass, 1964) and the Pacific Design Center (blue glass, 1971), and then to patterns of colored glass, as in the Museum of Modern Art tower. In this process of development, the skin, rather than speaking only of itself, began to speak of "ideas about scale, pattern and expression"[6]; that is, it changed from a self-referential element to an extra-referential one—a shift similar to the one in Eisenman's work. Pelli's transformation of the literal nature of the glass skin, however, embodies a rupture of the idea of the skin as it was used in the Utopian period of modern architecture. For the polychromed curtain wall in Pelli's work can be seen as a sign of accommodation to the diverse urbanism of the American city, not as a sign (as expressed in the applied I-beams and idealized order of the Utopian period) of indifference to or contempt for this diversity.

The Readings of the Skin

It is possible to separate out four major patterns in the glass skin of the towers (figure 88), whose facades are identical. The patterns exist at different perceptual depths: the lighter colors advance and the darker colors recede, until they finally achieve the real depth of transparency in the vision glass and the deep space of the reflections.

The foremost perceptual surface is the horizontal banding of the white spandrel panels held in place by white mullions, which recall the piling of floor on floor and underscore the technological aspects of the buildings.

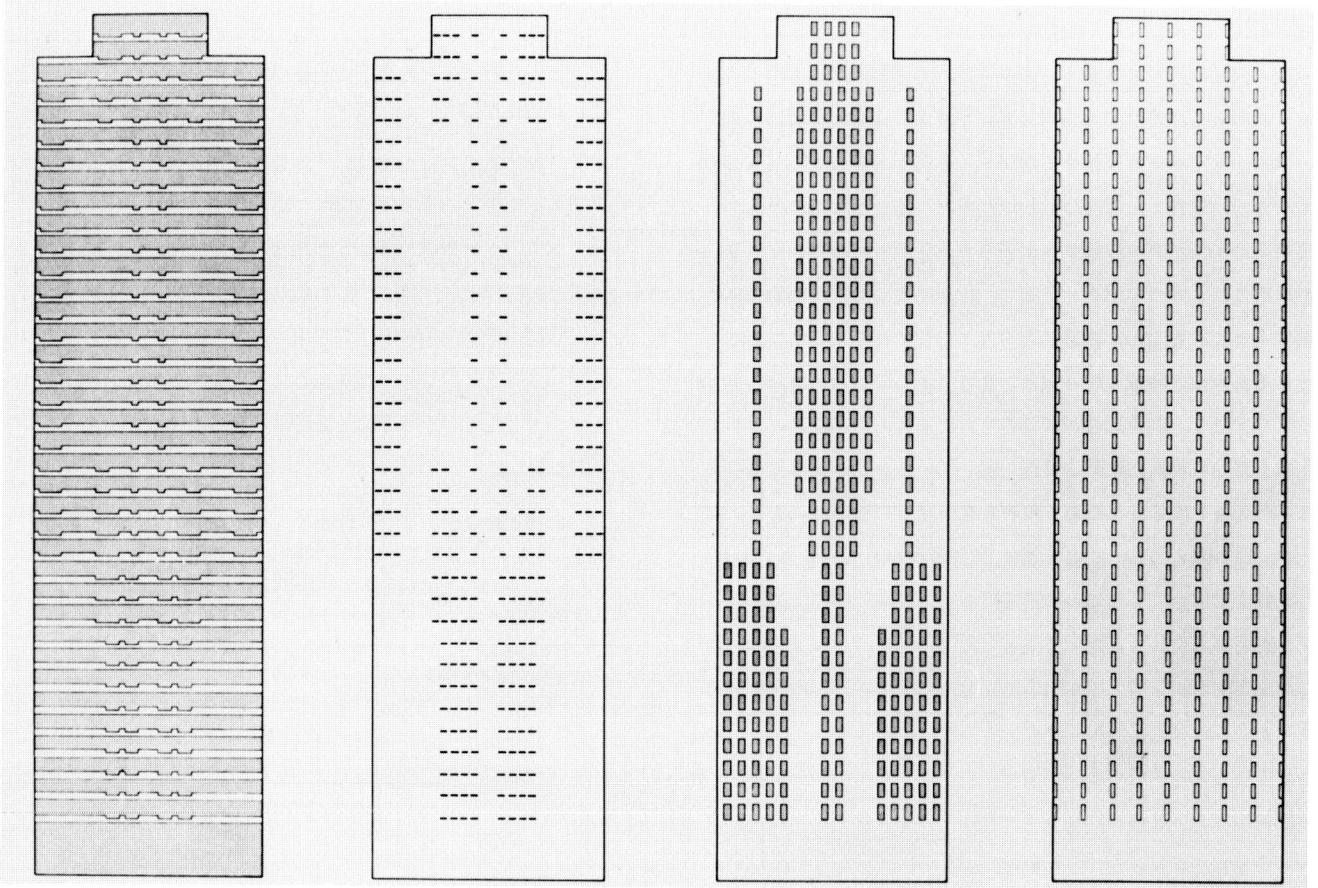

88 Four Leaf Towers, the separate patterns of the major components of the skin. *Left to right:* white spandrel panels, openings in the spandrel panels, pink panels, red panels.

This reading is particularly strong on the oblique, where it is emphasized by the acute angle of vision. From a distance, however, this pattern blurs into a hazy background because the bands are relatively thin and can no longer be perceived individually.

On the next surface back is the pattern established by the openings in the spandrel panels, which allow floor-to-ceiling glazing on the interior where they occur. These openings are identifiable only from very close up because the openings in the spandrel panels are small. They describe an anthropomorphic figure, which materializes behind the rows of spandrels as one approaches an angle where the luminosity of the sky makes the vision glass read more strongly.

At the third level is the pattern of the pink panels held in place by black mullions. These describe a complex interplay of empathetic forces rising and falling within the surface of the building, expressively addressing the earth and sky. These read very strongly from a distance because they are grouped in wide, solid bands and because at a distance the angle of vision is such that in most lights the vision glass reads less strongly than the opaque glass.

At the fourth level are the red panels, which like the pink panels are held in place by black mullions. These mullions crisply differentiate the deeper perceptual planes from the topmost one of white spandrel panels and their white mullions. These red panels cover the frame of the building and can be seen as a memory of the Miesian grid of applied framing members, as representing the idealized or-

der of a Miesian tower. The red panels are only visible at close range but gain in strength the closer one gets because of the clues given to their location by the piers at ground level. It is only at close range that the eye is able to separate the dark color from the vision glass as the vision glass becomes lighter with the changing angle of vision.

Four specific readings corresponding to each of these perceptual levels can therefore be discerned in the skin: technological, anthropomorphic, empathetic, and idealistic. The skin of Four Leaf Towers has become articulate in a way that the skin of the Miesian tower was not. It expresses a diversity analogous to that of the urbanism of which it is itself a part and to the society of which this urbanism is the concrete representation. The skin of the Four Leaf Towers, in other words, is a sign of a nonutopian condition.

In short, therefore, where the tops of the towers are signs of a "silent," autonomous, monumental condition symbolically related to the time scale of the city as an object, the skin of the towers is apparently the sign of a "noisy," accommodating, chameleonic condition, whose symbolic structure reflects the diversity of the lives of men and women in the present. A more detailed examination of the skin reveals, however, that it is in fact part of the same phenomenon of monumentality: the draining from the building's secret life of all scenographic impulses to create a sensibility of silence.

EPHEMERAL SKIN

The Importance of the Frame

One can divide the four readings of the skin into two groups: technological/idealistic and empathetic/anthropomorphic. These two groups correspond to the two roles the *frame* has played in tall buildings: the frame as idea and the frame as fact. The two masters of these approaches in the tall building in America were Mies van der Rohe and Louis Sullivan.

Frame as Idea

The Dom-ino diagram that Le Corbusier drew in 1914 (figure 89) shows in the clearest possible way the iconic character of the reinforced concrete frame of the Utopian period of modern architecture. The traditional anthropomorphic significance of the vertical facade has been replaced by the new and insistently nonanthropomorphic horizontality. In Mies's Friedrichstrasse scheme, this revolutionary horizontality is juxtaposed with reflections of the old vertical buildings of medieval German urbanism, so that the concrete floor slabs would have appeared, if built, to lacerate the offending images of the past.

In his later German work, such as the Reichsbank project of 1933 (figure 90), Mies eschewed his earlier expressionism; the skin is now considered opaque, but the same horizontal lines are still expressed in the skin. The role of the skin in these later German works is to express the iconic significance of the frame.

In his American work Mies sought to regain the verticality that the frame destroyed when it made the load-bearing wall obsolete. He did this

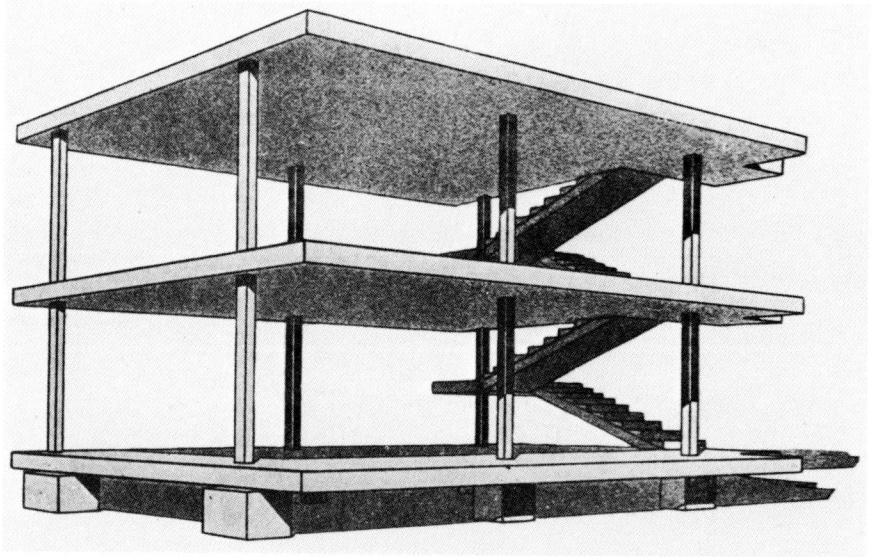

89 Le Corbusier, Dom-ino Diagram, 1914

90 Mies van der Rohe,
*Reichsbank Competition
Project*, Berlin, 1933, eleva-
tion of main facade. Print,
61.8 × 102.2 cm. Collection,
Mies van der Rohe Archive,
The Museum of Modern Art,
New York. Gift of Ludwig
Mies van der Rohe.

91 Cesar Pelli and Asso-
ciates, United States
Embassy, Tokyo, 1972

through a conceptual displacement of
the actual framed structure onto the
exterior surface in the form of a decorative grid of vertical framing members. In this way Mies reduced the
significance of the glass skin still further, from a representation of the
horizontal planes of the frame to a
neutral background for the decorative
application of vertical, steel framing
members.

Pelli's iconographic, coded use of
the glass skin derives from Mies's
German exercises with the vertical
membrane. The similarity of approach
can be observed in a comparison of
Mies's Reichsbank project with Pelli's
United States Embassy in Tokyo
(figure 91). By turning the Reichsbank
project on its end (ignoring for a moment the curvature of the facade in
plan), one can see the strategy Pelli
adopted toward the expression of the
structural frame in Four Leaf Towers.
The bands in the skin of the upended
Reichsbank do not now represent the
horizontal planes of the frame. The
vertical bands are instead representations of the applied, vertical framing
members that conveyed the sensibility of ideal order in Mies's American
buildings. The spandrels of the upended Reichsbank are therefore analogous to the regular rhythm of the
dark red panels hiding the real columns of the Four Leaf Towers. In
Four Leaf Towers, however, the various patterns of the skin severely compromise this reading, reducing it to
just another reading among many. As
a result, the frame of Miesian
modernism is reduced in significance
by Pelli, just as the skin was reduced
in significance by Mies. It is the skin
that is iconographically active for

Pelli, not the frame; if Mies's frames conveyed a utopian sensibility, the skin in Pelli's Four Leaf Towers conveys the opposite.

Frame as Fact
While the frame may have been a source of iconographic power for early European modernism as well as for the later International style in America, it was, as Colin Rowe has suggested, more of a convenience to the American proto-modernism of Chicago: "In Chicago it might be said that the frame was convincing as fact rather than as idea."[7]

Louis Sullivan was the greatest exponent of the frame as fact. Regarding the frame as a means to an end rather than as an end in itself, Sullivan did not express his iconography in technological symbolism or ideal order. It is his ornament that conveys his interests, just as it is Mies's ornamental, applied frame that expresses his preoccupations. Vincent Scully articulated the animated relationship between ornament and structure when he described Sullivan's Bayard Building of 1897–98 (figure 92):

The eye of the observer follows [the columns] upward to their split capitals. Above these, under the shadow of the cornice, stand female figures like crucified victories . . . under their outstretched arms the arches are pushed flat—as if close to fracture at their springing. The forces which pull them are those exerted by what seems to be the downward pull of the mullions. The "tension" of these members tugs at the intermediate arches until circular voids appear, and from these the eye runs down the mullions, round and tight like stretched cables, until it comes to rest finally upon the lowest spandrels. These spandrels stretch across two window bays and are massively textured as

92 Louis Sullivan, Bayard Building, New York, 1897–98

hung weights. Below them open clearly recessed window voids so that no confusion may arise between those elements [the piers] which are visually in compression and those [the screen of mullions and spandrels] which are visually in tension and which appear to have been pulled down as a screen or curtain between the supporting piers. Now the building not only clearly articulates the special structural and functional characteristics of its parts but also embodies a full drama of forces in which the observer can physically participate.[8]

While the use of colored panels of glass in Four Leaf Towers is not applied ornament in the sense that Sullivan's turn-of-the-century terra cotta and wrought iron were, it nevertheless achieves related expressive effects, for the same reason—the frame is active as fact, not as icon. This can be seen in the treatment of the pink panels.

These panels provide the strongest of the four surface readings (see figure 88) and create the only surface pattern easily identifiable from a distance. The stepped profile of the top of the curtain wall implies a division of each facade into three vertical sections (see figures 74, 75). The two heavy masses of pink panels in the outer sections beneath the fifteenth floor are connected by ribbons of pink panels to the terraces of the penthouses and look like flattened cables hung from them. If one imagines a Miesian box whose top is defined by the ceiling of the penthouses, then these "weights" attached to the corners of that prism have exerted a force that has pulled the roof line of the box down, shearing it away from the central octagonal shaft. As if connected by pulleys, this downward force is counterbalanced by

the upward motion of the central colored shaft of the building's upper two-thirds, which punches through the new position of the flat roof (the penthouse balconies) to form the shaft of the building's top.

The dynamics of these forces are recorded in the notch that occurs three floors down from the fifteenth floor in the side masses and three floors up from the fifteenth floor in the central shaft. The Four Leaf Towers stretch up to meet the sky and weight themselves heavily as they near the ground. This quality is absolutely foreign to a Miesian building.

The Ambiguity of the Skin
But while Sullivan's nineteenth-century humanism is unambiguously displayed in the empathy with which he invests his architecture, the ambiguity of perception in Pelli's curtain wall indicates only an illusion of movement toward a humanist position. The use of glass in Four Leaf Towers permits and encourages oscillations between four different and contradictory readings of the skin, which depend on the angle of vision and on how light is striking the building. All four readings are present at once from under a quarter of a mile, but certain lights will reveal one reading over another or make two different readings clear on different faces simultaneously. This enigmatic attitude surrenders control over the most basic meanings of the work in a way that is utterly contrary to the self-confidence of Sullivan's humanism. Sullivan's buildings have "a curious power of potential action; turn

your back and Carson-Pirrie-Scott
may cast off and float silently down
the street behind you. The Grinell
Bank may take one sudden hop and
gather you in. Turn around, most of
all, and the Guaranty may take its
giant step across the square."[9] Four
Leaf Towers show no inclination to
move. The towers witness, but they
do not act.[10] They commit themselves neither to the nineteenth-
century humanism of Sullivan nor
to the technological idealism of Mies;
rather, they engage both, distancing
themselves from each, allowing first
one and then the other to dominate.

SILENT WITNESS

Both in their massive carved form and
in their enigmatic and ephemeral
skin, therefore, the towers embody a
sensibility of silence. The towers are
in no way accomplices in the transi-
tory nature of life. Rather they are
witnesses to the fact of human existence. Herein lies the essential difference between the monumental and
the scenographic building. The latter
represents a condition that derives its
potency from the reality of day-to-day
life; the former from the immemorial
heartbeat of the human race.

The monumental building does not
require the movement of human beings to give it meaning and it constructs no mirror of the city's life.
Instead, it derives its strength from
the time scale of the city itself; and,
while resigned to the folly of its mak-
ers, is open to their brief moments of
serenity.

4 THE NATURE OF
THE NEW SUBLIME
Portland Public Service
Building, Portland, Oregon
Michael Graves,
Architect (1982)

PORTLAND

Violent Mount Saint Helens and
stately Mount Hood, twin poles of
Portland's landscape, command its
horizon on clear days (figure 93).
Mount Hood in the east, symmetrical
with its pointed summit, terminates
one axis of Portland's grid of squares.
Mount Saint Helens, blasted by erup-
tions, acutely angled to the horizon,
terminates the other in the north
(figure 94). Between these mountains
the Columbia River plunges into the
valley of the Willamette, which lies
between Oregon's Coast and Cascade
ranges.

The city of Portland occupies a gentle bend in the Willamette River before its confluence with the
Columbia, and it commands the base
of a long, triangular valley that
stretches south (figure 95). The downtown area takes up the Pacific side of
the river's flood plain, bounded to the
west by the steep, sheltering bluff of
the Tualatin Mountains, a ridge of
small hills deeply sliced by canyons
and topped with plateaus.

One can comprehend Portland as a
city lying at the intersection of two
axes, one joining the Tualatins with
Mount Hood, and the other joining
the Willamette River valley with
Mount Saint Helens.

The Tualatins are friendly, protec-
tive hills, dotted with desirable suburban houses whose terraces overlook
the city's downtown core. From Portland Heights, the core reveals its geometry (figure 96). The grid is
oriented along the line of the river,
and its spine is formed by Jefferson
Street, which connects the road
through the Tualatins with the Willamette. The lofty First National
Bank marks this artery near the river

where Fifth Avenue, a major shopping
street, crosses Jefferson. The bank
tower occupies the southwest corner
of a three-block park which, fronted
by important buildings on all sides,
forms the center of the downtown
area.

Michael Graves's Portland Public
Service Building occupies the central
block of the three blocks that take up
the west side of the park (figure 97).
To the left of Graves's building is
Whidden and Lewis's unusual, manneristic City Hall of 1895. To the
right is the same firm's later and
more conventional American Renaissance Multnomah County Courthouse of 1909–13. Two blocks back
from the park behind Graves's building is the 1931 Federal Courthouse by
James Wetmore in a spare classical
style betraying Art Deco influences.
These three buildings in particular,
with the surrounding corporate office
towers of the postwar period in general, form a palette of modern and
classical references on which Graves
has drawn in the design of the Public
Service Building (figure 98).

The Multnomah County Courthouse
The giant pilasters of the Portland
Public Service Building's park elevation continue the rhythm of the columnar screen of the Multnomah
County Courthouse (figure 99). This
colonnade of Ionic columns is
superimposed over an ancestor of
Graves's curtain wall—large sheets of
glass separated by spandrels and decorated with brackets marking the
floors. Above each column is a decorative blank rosette on the frieze before the dentil band. Graves has

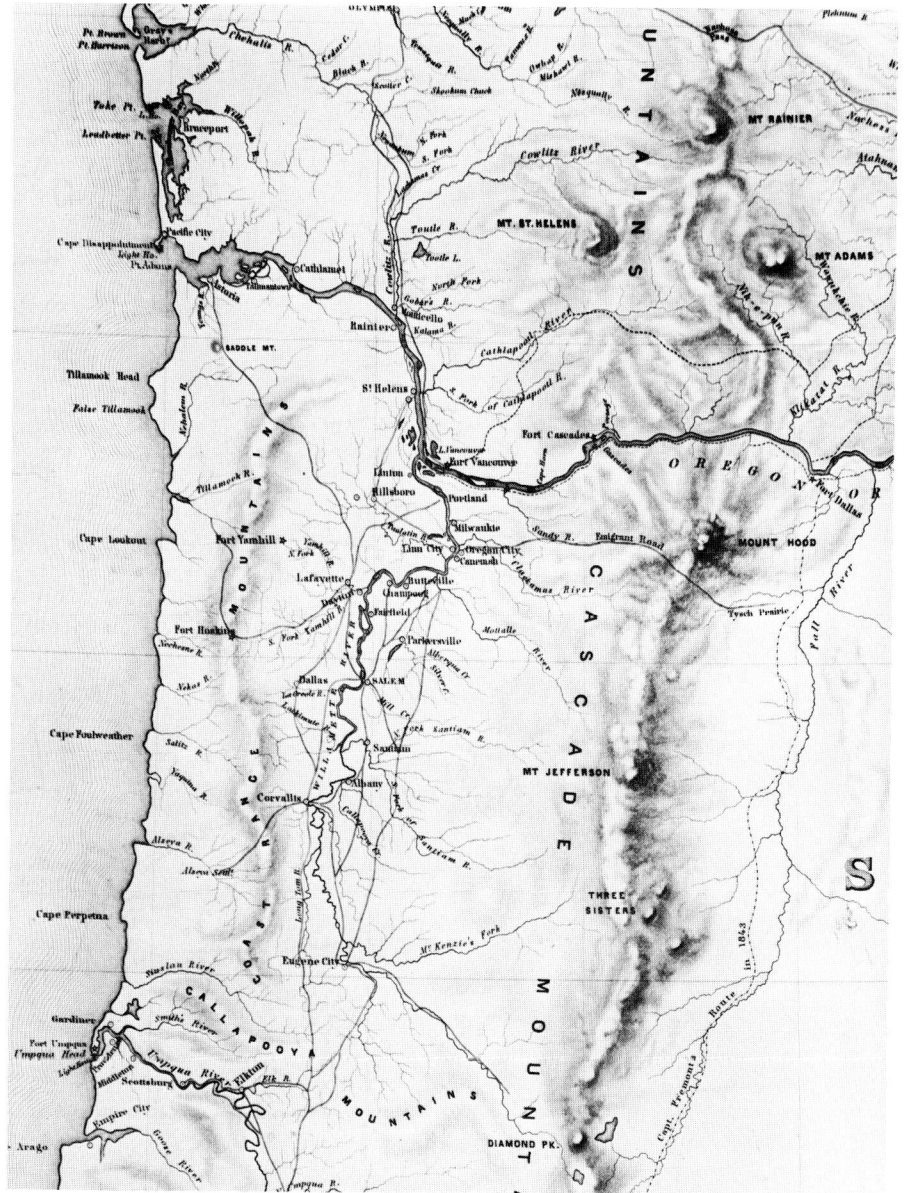

93 Oregon, 1873

94 View of downtown Portland from Portland Heights showing the relation of the grid to Mount Saint Helens

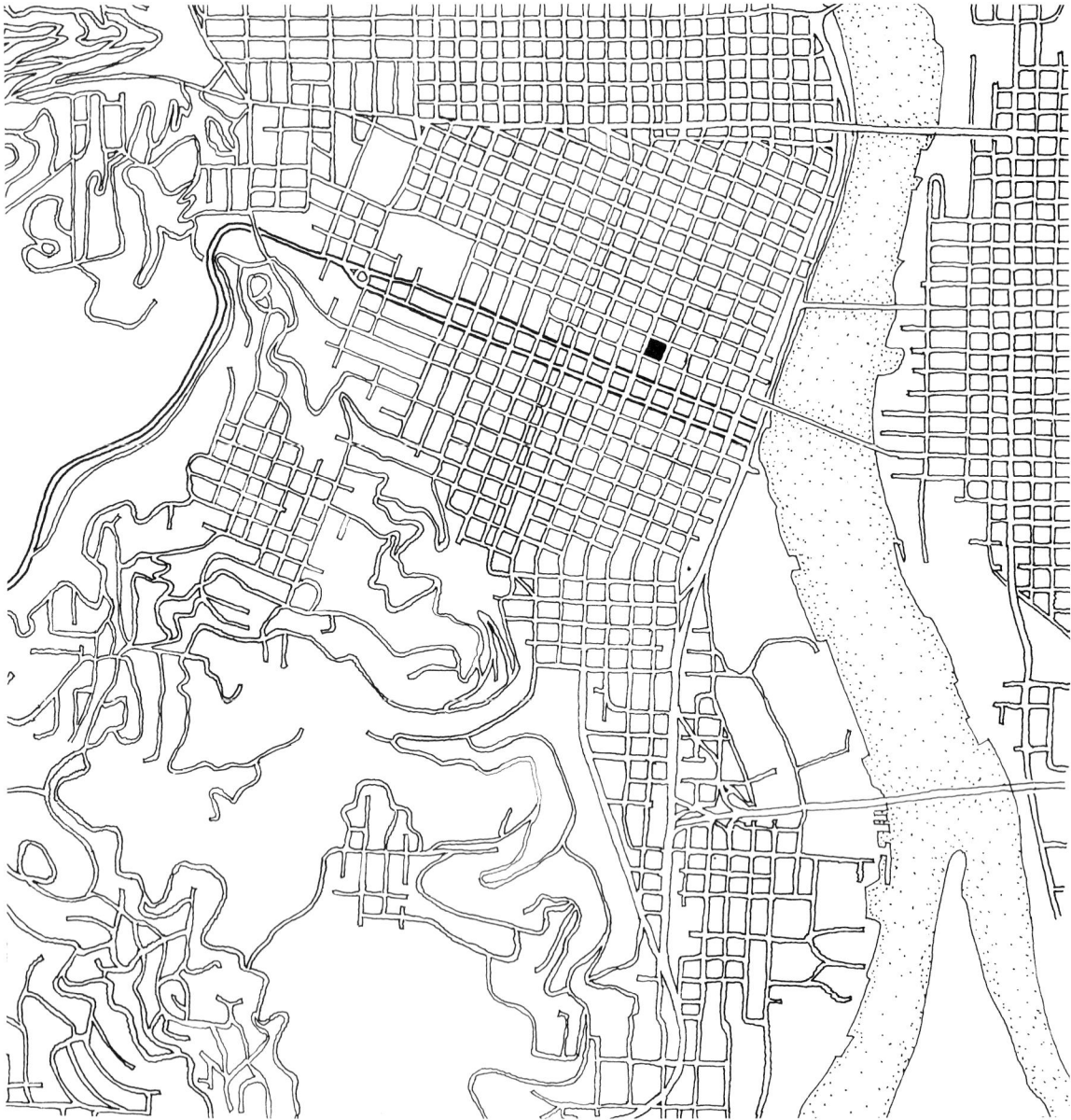

95 The road system of Port-
land and the location of the
Portland Public Service
Building

96 Perspective view of
downtown Portland from
Portland Heights showing
the relation to mountains

97 Axonometric view of
downtown Portland showing
the relation of Portland
Public Service Building to
the park and surrounding
buildings

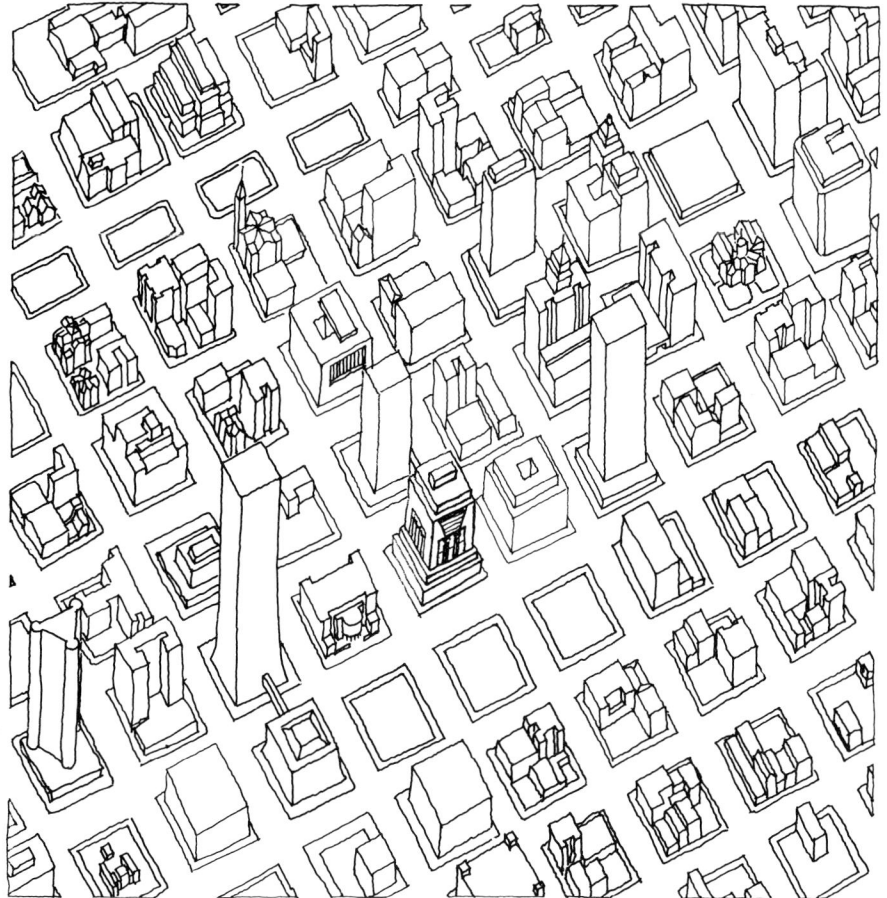

98 Portland Public Service
Building

99 Whidden and Lewis,
Multnomah County Court-
house, 1909–13, and the
Public Service Building
under construction. First
National Bank in the
background.

incorporated this motif on his Madison and Main Street elevations in the colossal roundels to which the flattened garlands are secured. At a similarly distorted scale, the striations of the keystone-shaped motifs continue the horizontality of Whidden and Lewis's cornice, with its tripled fascias on the architrave and band of modillions as well as dentils.

The projection of Graves's capitals is clearly related to the angle of Whidden and Lewis's cornice, just as the framing of Graves's colossal order within heavy masonry corners is derived from the articulation of the courthouse wall. Graves has made convincing use of Whidden and Lewis's solid corners, with their break in the cornice line and double pilasters against blank, four-story panels, as a transition from the sculptural colonnade of the courthouse to the planarity of the Public Service Building.

Finally, the base of Graves's building is directly related to its neighbor, for both are divided in two, are roughly the same height, and support a flat band on which the columns and pilasters rest.

The Federal Courthouse
A closer stylistic affinity, however, exists between Graves's pilasters and those of Wetmore's Federal Courthouse two blocks west of Graves's building (figure 100). The pilasters of Wetmore's building are five stories high, have six flutes each, and have very restrained bases and capitals. Here also the corners of the building are treated massively. Interestingly, Wetmore opened up the top two stories between each pair of pilasters into a continuous glass expanse, surmounting the void "columns" so

formed with flat, Ionic ornamentation in the shadow of a cornice. Graves has changed this rather beautiful feature of Wetmore's design: he enlarged the glass plane so that the whole central section of the facade is glazed, leaving the floors recorded in ghostly mullions, and replaced the ornamentation with a less delicate but equally flat keystone.

Graves's pilasters are two stories taller than Wetmore's and have less attenuated proportions, yet they are closely related in the flatness of their forms and the low relief of their flutes. Nevertheless, in Graves's building there is a graphic quality alien to Wetmore's. The Portland Public Service Building impresses one as emerging from the flat plane rather than disappearing into it—like an idea, partly awkward still, becoming reality rather than a tradition, fully developed, smoothed away almost to nothing.

While the Portland Public Service Building has many affinities with the Art Deco style, the sophisticated games of scale in which Graves's building indulges are less Deco than they are mannerist. It is a happy coincidence, therefore, that Whidden and Lewis's City Hall is right next door.

Portland City Hall
The City Hall (figure 101) is high Renaissance turning mannerist in detail, but French Revolutionary in massing. The simple arrangement of its masses is distinguished by a semicircular council chamber that projects over a triple-depth colonnade of half-rusticated columns, through which the building can be entered. The semicylindrical drum of this projecting mass has a disturbing relation to the

100 James Wetmore, Portland Federal Courthouse, 1931

101 Whidden and Lewis,
Portland City Hall, 1895

columns. The columns seem far too
small for the enormous weight above,
creating an uneasiness that is deliberately increased by the confinement of
the rustication to the lower half of
the columns, which leaves slender
shafts at the point of greatest pressure. The window openings of the
second floor are oversized for the
openings in the colonnade beneath,
while the flatness and delicacy of the
Ionic pilasters and the wall surfaces of
the top floor are in pronounced contradiction to the cavernous darkness
and forceful plasticity of the ground
floor. These manneristic juxtaposi-
tions of scale and texture are aggressively continued on the side facades
(figure 102), where, in the upper three
stories, there is an even wilder display
of mannerist effect. Areas of intense
decoration alternate with expanses of
plain wall in the manner of
Michaelangelo's Porta Pia. Strange
games of scale are everywhere, from
the tiny columns and huge windows
to the huge decorative wreaths and
tiny mortar joints.

These are exactly the same con-
trasts of scale evident in Graves's
building, but his manipulation of
scale serves a different end. While
Whidden and Lewis's games of scale
are urbane, Graves seeks the primitive power that derives from empathetic responses.

CREATION OF EMPATHETIC RESPONSES

Manipulation of Scale

The perceived dimension of the perfect cube that forms the central section of Graves's building is increased
by the small windows that perforate
it. These windows are small enough
to dissolve the familiar office-building

102 Whidden and Lewis,
Portland City Hall, 1895,
side elevation

proportions of window to floor, creating an impression of a surface texture of endless extension, a wallpaper of dots. This is an impression furthered by the mullionless and perceptually frameless windows. They appear simply as small voids and are set far enough back from the surface to give strong shadows, which suggest that the cube in which they are inscribed is a block of solid material. This is an effect heightened by the scored lines on the exterior surface, which give the impression of massive stone blocks piled on top of one another.

The base on which this cube presses down reinforces the sense of heaviness. The three tiers of the base compress progressively as the eye ascends, and the openings in the tiers become smaller, creating a sense of forced perspective that increases the apparent size of the cube. In addition the openings in the tiers of the base are not vertically centered but are either below center or pushed to the bottom of their respective tiers, as if by the weight of the building bearing down on them.

At the top of the building there is a similar manipulation of scale, but for opposite ends. The miniaturized pilasters of the temple on the roof, the miniature primitive huts sitting in the indentations near the roof on the Park and Fifth Avenue facades, and the tiny square apertures at the roof line with their diagonal cross motifs —all these exercise the eye on distant details. Such details increase the apparent bulk of the building and at the same time create the impression that the building is stretching toward the sky, thus reversing the compressive tendencies of the base.

103 Whidden and Lewis,
Portland City Hall, 1895,
plan

104 Portland Public Service
Building, plan of first floor

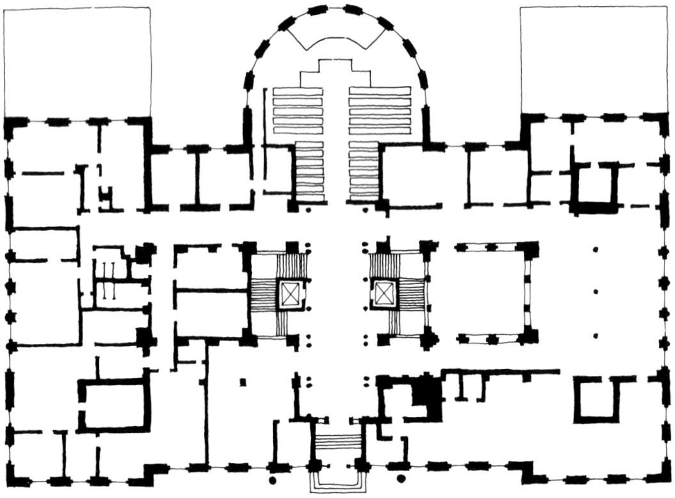

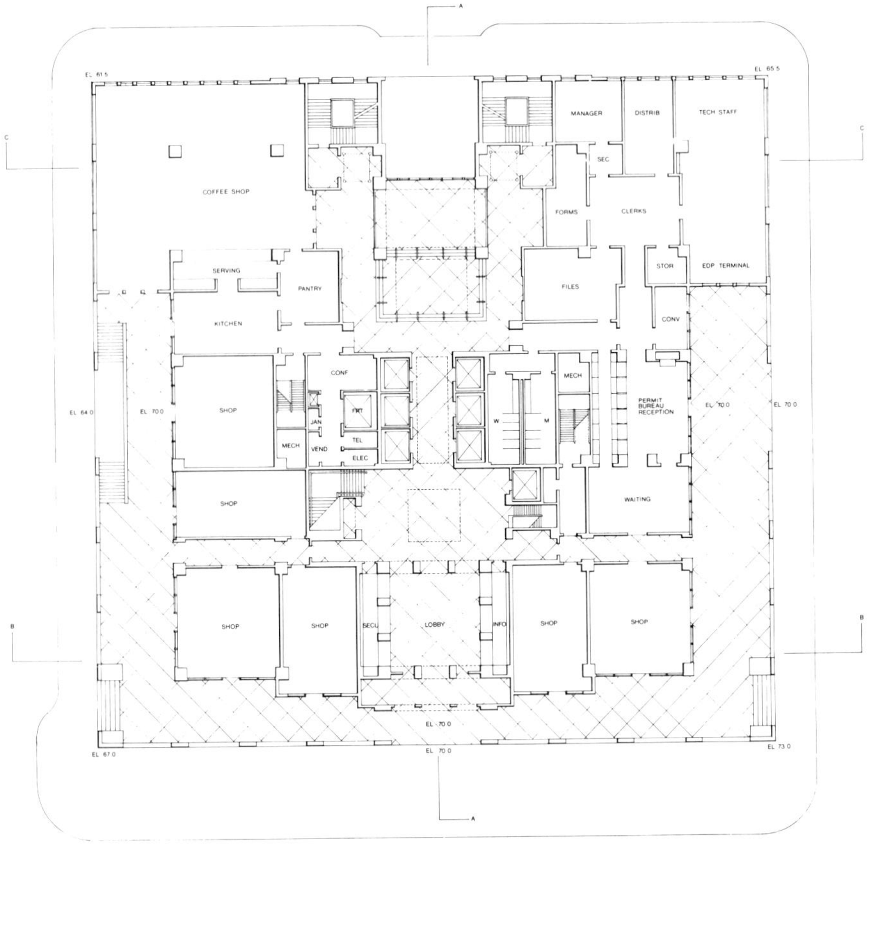

As a result of these manipulations of scale, our primary reading of the Portland Public Service Building is empathetic. It arouses our physical memory of the action of great weight on our own bodies because the apparent mass of the building is so exaggerated. The use to which these empathetic forces are put can be observed in a comparison of the plans of Whidden and Lewis's city hall and Graves's building.

Both buildings are symmetrical, with a major east-west axis. In both, the vertical circulation is placed in the center and the main entry is at one end (figures 103, 104). Both buildings locate a semicircular council chamber on the second floor (figure 105); but while Whidden and Lewis expose the chamber, Graves does not. In the City Hall, Whidden and Lewis exteriorize the unique form of the chamber, drawing attention to it by the mannerist relationship of the chamber to the columns below it. Their building communicates *at the scale of the city.*

In the Portland Public Service Building, Graves interiorizes the chamber so that it does not detract from the colossal form of the building, thus helping the overall mass appear more colossal than it really is. His building communicates *at the scale of the landscape.* The primary impression created by the building is the physically experienced presence of a mountainous mass, for it is Mount Hood and Mount Saint Helens, ultimate facts of the landscape, more than the buildings of the local context by which Graves's building is finally most deeply influenced.

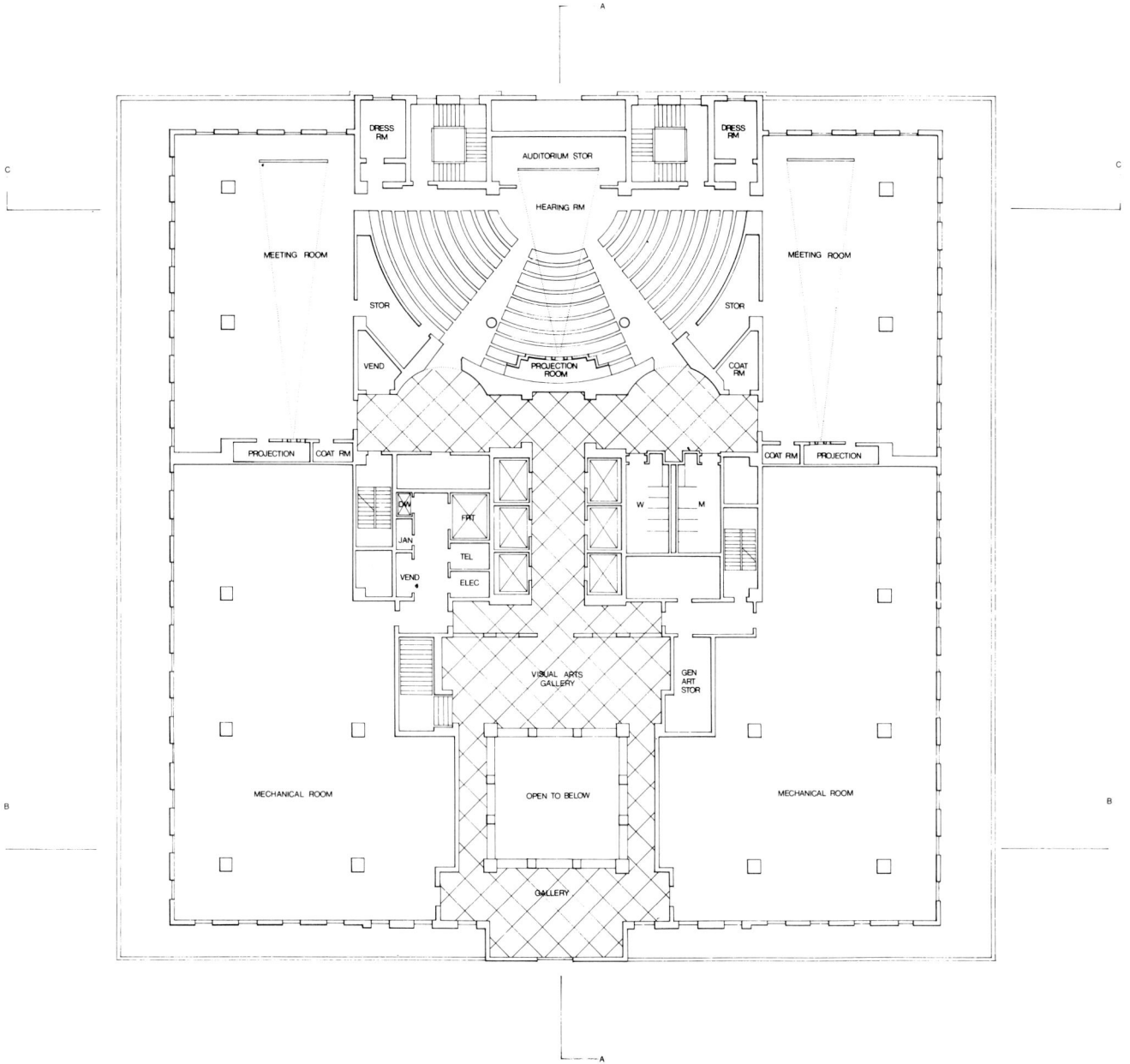

105 Portland Public Service
Building, plan of second
floor

Metaphor

The Portland Public Service Building is above all a metaphoric mountain empathetically experienced. It is also decorated with associative elements that support this mountain imagery. The building has a green base like foothills, continuing the color of the park, and the arcade that continues on three sides and opens toward Fifth Avenue is a columnar forest through which the building is entered. On all sides, rising above both this treeline and the trees of the park, the giant fluted pilasters resemble abstract waterfalls of glass, ribbons of streaming liquid cascading from outcrops of rock, like the great cataract of the Columbia itself. On the sides of the building these pilasters are connected by enormous concrete garlands of a metaphorical nature. On the front and back sides, facing Fifth Avenue and the park, they support giant keystones, like massive geological formations. The plateau on which a miniature temple stands, oriented toward Mount Saint Helens, is analogous to the residential buildings on the Tualatin Mountains but answers to the distant mountain peaks, to a primeval landscape rather than to a suburban one.

Monumental Anthropomorphism

The projections of the base, the pilasters, capitals, and keystones of the Fourth and Fifth Avenue facades create a monumental, though unfortunately rather flat, representation of the human body. Planted on the ground and stretching into the sky, the figure is like a giant rising above the park (figure 106). On the other two sides, the pilasters create monu-mental representations of a pergola in an idealized garden decked with mythic flowers.

Nothing could be more different from Utopian modernism, with its dreams of perfection, than the poignancy of this giant figure in its distant, mythic garden pergola and rooftop landscape. Utopia is no longer earnestly attempted on the ground; it is staged upon the roof, a reference point against which to match the imperfections of the actors and their play below. For the figure looming over the observer among the faceless buildings of Utopian modernism is an inhabitant of the city at colossal scale, a monumental actor in a scenographic architecture, an inhabitant who may aspire to the garden he has left, but who is an actor in this world and not one from another.

As in Pelli's towers, it is in the combination of the empathetic response to the building's mass and the intellectual response to its surface elements that the secret life of the building is to be found. But where Pelli distanced his towers from language, Graves eschews the sensibility of silence for the language of the sublime.

THE CONCEPT OF THE NEW SUBLIME

Graves's cultivation of the colossal has its roots in eighteenth-century aesthetics. The classical conception of beauty had been of a universal harmony and order cerebrally contemplated, not the sensation of awe produced by vast dimensions either of space or time. To Winckelmann and the neoclassicists, as to the ancients, beauty was the splendor of absolute

106 Portland Public Service
Building, perspective view
from across the park

truth. Appreciation of the colossal in the eighteenth century, however, implied that classic beauty might not be the only worthy form of aesthetic experience.

Edmund Burke

The figure of Edmund Burke lies behind this point of view. In *A Philosophical Enquiry into the Origin of Our Ideas of the Sublime and Beautiful* of 1757,[1] Burke defined two competing categories of aesthetic worth—the sublime and the beautiful—and thereby threw into question the absolute nature of classical beauty. This initial division was elaborated by the early-nineteenth-century theorists of the picturesque, who sought to define a third category of beauty; further fragmented during the eclecticism of taste in mid-century; and rounded out by late century awareness of industrial beauty. This is the heritage of diverse aesthetic modes to which we are today the heirs, able at last to see its promise for the twentieth century after half a century of false absolutes.

To Burke visible objects affected the passions through the instincts, by way of the senses, and not the mind through a cerebral perception of natural harmony. All passions were ultimately divisible into those which turn on pain and danger, belonging to instincts of self-preservation, and those "which . . . cause love, or some passion similar to it,"[2] belonging to "society," to self-propagation, or to any form of affection among living things or toward inanimate objects. Emotions in the first category were capable of producing the sublime; those in the second of producing the beautiful. Actual feelings of pain or fear, however, were "simply painful when their causes immediately affect us; they are delightful when we have an idea of pain and danger, without being actually in such circumstances; this delight . . . I call sublime."[3] Burke then characterized the particular qualities that excite the sublime. The components are greatness, artificial or actual infinity, succession and uniformity, obscurity, difficulty, magnificence, and "all general privations . . . vacuity, darkness, solitude and silence."[4]

The Cult of the Colossal

Before Burke's *Enquiry* gave them a philosophical basis, the qualities of greatness of dimension, obscurity, difficulty, and darkness had reached a peak in the *Prisons* of Piranesi. The drawings of Boullée brought dimension and artificial infinity, succession and uniformity, solitude and silence to a similar peak some years later.

Greatness of dimension was the easiest quality to produce in buildings, but, as Burke was careful to point out: "Designs that are vast only in their dimensions, are always the sign of common and low imagination. No work of art can be great but as it deceives, to be otherwise is the prerogative of nature only."[5] Thus, in the late-eighteenth-century cult of the colossal that developed from the general acceptance of the sublime as an aesthetic category, not mere size alone but an expression of enormous heaviness was desired. What advocates of the colossal pursued was an architecture like the ruined temples of Paestum illustrated by Piranesi, or, even better, an architecture directly

comparable with the "natural architecture" of cliffs and mountains,
which would embody the belief that
"the effects of art are never so well illustrated as by similar effects in
nature."[6]

It is this sensibility concerning the
sublimity of vast landscapes and colossal mass on whch Graves's Portland mountain draws. The perspective
view of the building gives us a clue to
these Romantic roots, for it uses the
conventions of the eighteenth-century
Romantic landscape. Our eye is
guided to the building along a path
whose benches are borrowed from designs of Thomas Hope, exemplary
Romantic, the greatest *grand touriste*
of all (figure 107).

Such colossal architecture is nowhere more sublime in its attitude to
nature than in the architecture of
Ledoux; and the massive blocks of
Ledoux's Propylaea of Paris, the toll
houses that ringed Paris before the
revolution, provide clear formal prototypes for Graves's Portland building.
The Barrière de l'Étoile (figure 108),
for example, conveys precisely the
same quality of weightiness: the twin
cubic blocks form peaks in the landscape that announce Paris to the approaching traveler, and the massively
rusticated columns press the buildings into the ground the way heavy
excise stamps press into sealing wax.

Graves's work at Portland reflects
the influence of other colossal projects of Romantic classicism, such as
Friedrich Gilly's monument to Frederick the Great (figure 109), with its
tripartite vertical organization, central
penetration, huge side columns, and
iconic temple roofscape. George
Dance's Newgate Prison (figure 110)

107 Thomas Hope, *House-
hold Furniture and Interior
Decoration*, 1807, plate V.
"Third room containing
Greek vases."

108 Claude-Nicolas Ledoux,
Barrière de l'Étoile, 1785
(demolished 1857), steel en-
graving by C. Heath after
painting by Batty

109 Friedrich Gilly, Monument to Frederick the Great, Berlin, 1797

110 George Dance, Newgate Prison, London, 1770

and Karl Ehrensvard's dockyard gateway project (figure 111) are other examples that demonstrate similarities
of form and sensibility. A surprising
amount of recent work can be directly
compared to this architecture:
Graves's Portland Building, Plocek
residence, or Humana building (figure
112) no less than European examples
such as James Stirling's Bayer Center
at Monheim, Ricardo Bofill's Arcade
du Lac, or Rossi's Modena Cemetery.
All are "sublime." Yet it is a very different kind of sublimity from that
familiar to the eighteenth century.

Fragmentation

The breaking of the classical rules of
unity and permanence produced in
the work of Ledoux and Boullée, as in
that of Dance or Gilly, what Emile
Kaufmann has called an "atomization" of individual elements. The
"concatenation, integration and gradation"[7] of the seventeenth century
gave way to the "breaking loose . . .
of the single features from the
whole."[8] With each part stressed,
with "equivalence more important
than gradation,"[9] the whole depended
upon a composition of individual elements; no longer were the parts sub-
ordinated to the whole in an easily
perceived hierarchy or interdependent
according to unquestionable rules.

Graves carries this atomization of
classical elements to new extremes,
fusing the cult of the colossal with
the fragmentation developed in the
landscapes of Cézanne and brought to
its apotheosis in Cubism. For the
Portland building forms no ideal, classical unity but is a balance struck between warring fragments. Thus, the
landscape of the roof is as separate
from the cube below it as the building's shaft is from the street. Lacking

111 Karl Ehrensvard, model
for a dockyard gateway,
Karlskrona, Sweden, c. 1785

112 Model of Humana building, Louisville, Kentucky,
1982. A monumental
actor in a scenographic
architecture.

the classical moldings that could unite them, the pilasters are gigantic presences jostling with the keystones. So, too, is the central window a form at war with every other as it explodes from the building's heart. The unity of the Renaissance tradition is altogether gone. While this was also in part true for Ledoux and Boullée, for them Nature was still a binding force.[10] For Graves, however, the landscape of the Portland building roof has taken on a nostalgic quality, has become a landscape separate from life, a protected myth. It is not the cosmic harmony of the Renaissance, the Nature of the Enlightenment, or the machines of Utopian modernism but the nature of the new sublime that holds the fragments of the Portland Service Building in uneasy unity.

Natural and Human Force
The terror behind Burke's sublimity was infused with reason, as it had the objective distance of a controlled experiment. This attitude can be discerned in Burke's scientific and minutely observed description of pain: "I say a man in pain has his teeth set, his eyebrows are violently contracted, his forehead is wrinkled, his hair stands on end; the voice is forced out in short shrieks and groans, and the whole fabric totters."[11] This description is like a page from an eighteenth-century medical treatise on insanity—controlled and dispassionate. It is like the scientific sensibility embodied in the sixty-four bizarre heads sculpted in the 1770s by Franz Xaver Messerschmidt as likenesses of his own features when con-

torted with pains inflicted by stabbing different areas of his body with needles (figure 113).

Twentieth-century terror is not as controlled (figure 114), and the fabric that threatens to rend is now universal.

It is through Emmanuel Kant that the eighteenth-century sublimity starts to be more like our own,[12] for although Kant's appeal is still to reason, it is to the individual intellect rather than to the more impersonal "reason" of the *philosophes*. To Kant "instead of the object, it is rather the cast of the mind in appreciating it that we have to estimate as sublime. This makes it evident that true sublimity must be sought in the mind of the judging subject, and not in the object of nature that occasions this attitude by the estimate formed of it."[13] Yet for Kant too an objective distance was still possible, and it is this distance that for him defines the sublime:

Bold, overhanging, and, as it were, threatening rocks, thunderclouds piled up the vault of heaven, borne along with flashes and peals, volcanoes in all their violence of destruction, hurricanes leaving desolation in their track, the boundless ocean rising with rebellious force, the high waterfall of some mighty river, and the like, make our power of resistance of trifling moment in comparison with their might. But, provided our position is secure, their aspect is all the more attractive for its fearfulness; and we readily call these objects sublime, because they raise the forces of the soul above the height of vulgar commonplace, and discover within us a power of resistance of quite another kind, which gives us courage to be able to measure ourselves against the seeming omnipotence of nature.[14]

113 Franz Xaver Messer-
schmidt, *Grimacing self-
portrait*, c. 1780

114 Still from Eisenstein's
film *Battleship Potemkin*,
1925

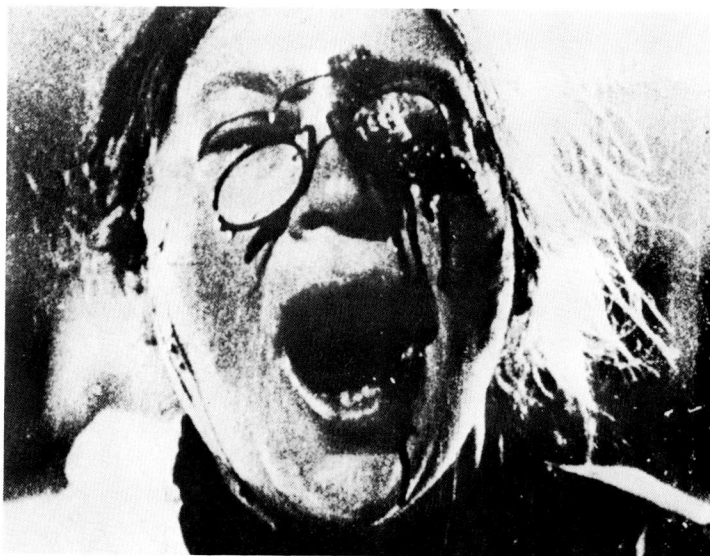

But whose position is anywhere "secure" today, what "courage" now sufficient? A sense of imminent and irrational disorder has replaced the trust in reasoned order of the Enlightenment; terror is no longer a quality that can with certainty be separated from any other; and Burke's "self-preservation" is now a universal condition, provoking not a *frisson* of sensual delight, but a deep disquiet that is cerebrally registered. This is why the sublime in Graves's building cannot be conveyed by empathy alone and why his building eschews the sensibility of silence. For Burke's concept of the sublime, relying on the perception of objects through the senses and on communication through these senses with the subconscious instincts and not with the conscious mind, operates by the same mechanism as empathy. In either, as Henri Focillon has written "art must renounce thought."[15] In the architecture of the new sublime, however, art renounces thought only at its peril, for it is not the awe of natural power perceived directly that now awakens our sense of self-preservation but the uncertain dread of human force abruptly imagined and ignored.

The New Sublime
For this reason the temple on the roof of the Portland Public Service Building is not dedicated to a god whose power is palpable in nature's form but to one whose will it is to control nature even in the face of her volcanic power. It is dedicated to individual man, to the colossal figure of the main facade.

Like the temples of the Acropolis in Athens (figure 115), animated, as Le Corbusier observed, "by a single

thought, drawing around them the desolate landscape and gathering it into the composition,"[16] Graves's rooftop temple gathers in the western landscape. The two are situated along similar axes as well; at Athens the axis runs from the horned mountains of Hymettos to the sea at Salamis,[17] while at Portland it runs from Mount Saint Helens down the fertile valley of the Willamette to the river's source (figure 116).

On its other axis, too, Graves's Public Service Building gathers in its distant landscape. The two major facades of the building, one facing the Cascades, the other the Tualatins, have fundamentally different meanings. In Graves's original scheme this difference was recognized by an important distinction in the motifs that decorated each facade at the roof line. The Fourth Avenue facade (figure 117), facing the park and confronting the distant Cascade range with a perpendicular view of Mount Hood (figure 118), was ornamented with a miniature primitive hut that corbeled out over the central "window" and stretched toward the mountains. The Fifth Avenue facade (figures 119, 120), facing the suburban houses on the Tualatin Mountains and the city fabric in between, received a standing anthropomorphic figure with a pitched roof head. Unfortunately, this figure was removed and replaced by a primitive hut identical to the one that was to have projected from the park facade. In the end, neither of the huts was corbeled out beyond the plane of the wall (figure 121). Nevertheless, because of their contexts, these two huts can still be read as referring to

115 Le Corbusier, *The
Acropolis. The site*

116 View from the terrace of
the Portland Public Service
Building showing Mount
Saint Helens in the distance

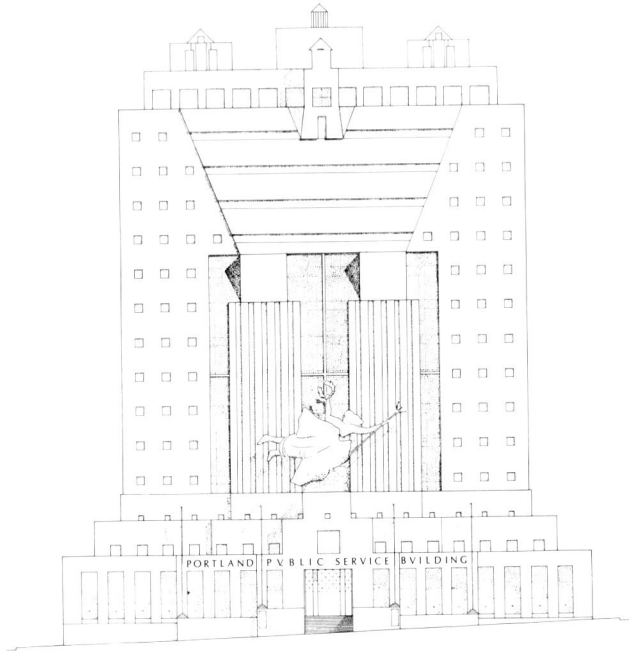

117 Portland Public Service
Building, preliminary
scheme, Fourth Avenue
facade

118 View from inside the
Portland Service Building
showing Mount Hood in the
distance

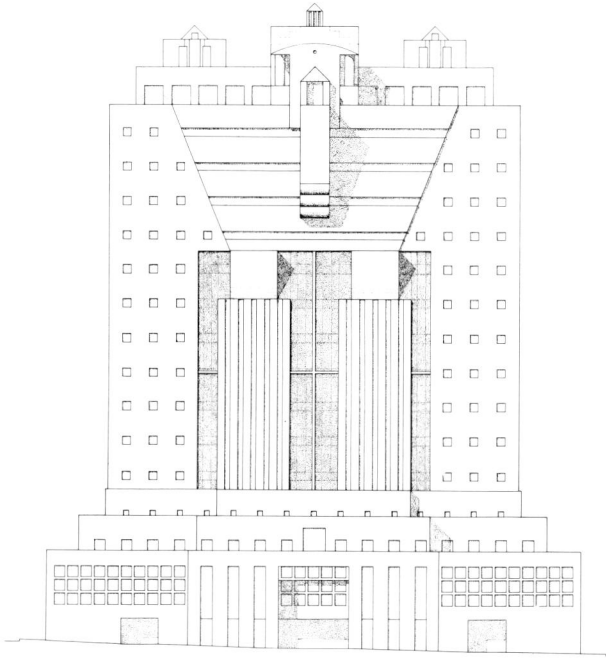

119 Portland Public Service
Building, preliminary
scheme, Fifth Avenue facade

120 View from inside the
Portland Public Service
Building showing the Tualatin Mountains and suburban
houses in the distance

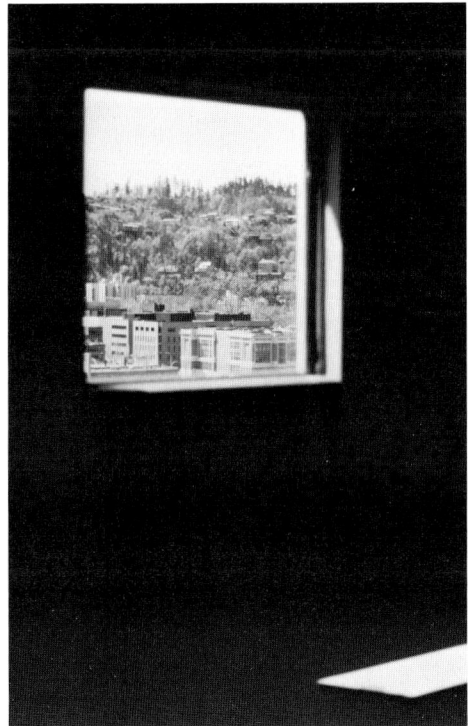

the different conditions of primeval existence in nature on the one hand and sophisticated city living on the other. One represents the first of man's habitations, the other man in what might be his last.

In the primitive huts of the main facades, Graves depicts a human journey from Classical Greece with its temples to the anonymous person in the modern city. Individual man, vulnerable and threatened, charts his course alone, at first facing his nakedness in nature and at the end facing his own creations. The sublime now represents the foreboding, not with which man considers the power of nature, but with which he looks upon himself as superhuman. The explosive force of the gigantic pilasters, with their rushing flutes rising out of darkness, and the spreading horizontal bands above, like energy emitted from the capitals, blasting the keystone from civilization's arch, irradiating alike the iconic human body and his mythic shelter, the beginning and the end of time—this is the twentieth-century version of the sublime.

121 Portland Public Service Building, perpendicular view

Keith Haring, *Untitled*, June
1982, vinyl ink on vinyl tar-
paulin, 10 × 10 feet. Photo
by Ivan Dalla Tana, Tony
Shafrazi Gallery, Ara Arsla-
nian Collection.

5 SCENOGRAPHY AND THE PICTURESQUE

Bozzi House
East Hampton,
Long Island, New York
Robert A. M. Stern,
Architects (1983)

EAST HAMPTON

Near the tip of the smooth, south-facing Atlantic shore of Long Island, on a good day two and a half hours by road from Manhattan, lies the ancient village of East Hampton (figure 122). One of a string of resort communities on the island, East Hampton has preserved its seventeenth-century heritage better than most and has been lucky enough to have escaped the disasters of fire and hurricane that have struck other communities in the same area over the years.

The Development of the Summer Colony

Before it became firmly established as a resort around 1890, East Hampton was a remote agricultural village. It was set back from the ocean and built around a broad, grass main street distinguished at either end by two windmills. The houses of the village were simple geometric shingled forms: sharp-edged, upright, independent, with lean-to, gambrel, or pitched roofs.

The windmills remain, as does the original broad character of Main Street. The architectural success of East Hampton's development as a resort community is in large measure due to the summer colony's building upon and enhancing the seventeenth-century forms of the village rather than separating itself from them.

This development began in the early 1870s with the extension of Main Street along Ocean Avenue, which, winding and narrow, connected the historical village with the shore (figure 123). Later the land facing the ocean between Hook Pond and Georgica Cove was developed along Lee Avenue and Lily Pond Lane. These three streets form the backbone of the original summer colony.

As Stern has shown, the first resort houses along Ocean Avenue were the Stick style cottages of wealthy businessmen and the Gothic cottages of clergymen, houses that could not be said to have made any particular gestures toward "the local landscape, development patterns or to the architectural traditions of East Hampton."[1] By the time East Hampton was "discovered" in 1877, however, when *Scribner's* magazine commissioned a group of writers and artists from New York to report on the villages of Long Island, there had been a significant shift in taste coincident with the rise of the Shingle style.

Architectural taste in the late 1870s and 1880s reflected a renewed interest in American traditions. The 1876 centennial and the financial panic of 1873, led, as Henry-Russell Hitchcock has noted, "to a general mood of repentence after the extravagances, architectural and otherwise, of the post-war boom."[2] In contrast to the houses of the decade before, the houses that East Hampton's summer visitors built in the 1880s drew inspiration directly from the original modest, shingled salt-boxes and barns.

The older, simpler, and somehow nobler buildings of America's thrifty colonial times provided convenient forms for embodying the "yearning for roots"[3] latent in the Shingle style and for expressing the sentimental desire for "an unpretentious kind of life."[4] Attention was focused on the old towns, where "life was regarded as having once been simpler and cleaner [than] it had become in the teeming cities of nineteenth-century

122 Long Island and the
mainland, 1878

123 East Hampton road system and location of Bozzi
house

America,"[5] places where "one could
build vacation houses and hope to
achieve, or play at achieving, the ancient values once more."[6]

The Revived Shingle Style
It was in the Shingle style that Stern
built his first house in 1965–67, along
the shore at Montauk for the Wiseman family, and it has remained one
of his strongest influences. Stern's
earliest East Hampton houses, for example the Mercer house of 1973 on
Ocean Avenue (figure 124), do not
possess the volumetric clarity of their
nineteenth-century predecessors.
However, if the formal clarity of an
1880s Shingle style masterpiece like
Arthur Little's Shingleside (figure 125)
is absent, the individual elements of
that particular house are much in evidence. As Vincent Scully has noted,
in the Mercer house Stern was ready
to take on Little's Shingleside "not
only with two storied volumes of interior space, but also with the layered
exterior and curving glass bay."[7]

In Stern's Bozzi house the overall
massing is clearer[8] (figure 126). It consists of a pitched roof hipped at either
end over the rectangular plan, which
corresponds to the simple geometry of
East Hampton's colonial prototypes,
to the town's original revival of these
forms as epitomized by the Moran
studio of 1884 (figure 127), and to the
more monumental of the Shingle
style masterpieces of the early 1880s.

This massing suggests the possibility of recovering that empathetic
quality of the nineteenth-century
Shingle style which Caroll Meeks has
characterized as the desire "to have
the building seen in the round and
from many points of view, from each
of which [it] . . . would compose differently"[9] (figure 128). But this is not

124 Stern and Hagman, Norman Mercer house, Ocean
Avenue, East Hampton,
1972

125 Arthur Little, Shingleside, Swampscott, Massachusetts, 1880–81

126 Bozzi house, from the
road

127 Thomas Moran house,
Main Street, East Hampton,
1884

128 Arthur Little, Grass-
head, Mrs. James L. Little
house, Swampscott, Massa-
chusetts, 1882. Little's house
demonstrates the pictur-
esque massing of secondary
volumes around a major
volume, which permits
the house to "compose
differently."

its purpose. Rather, it provides a sympathetic and consistent background
for the arrangement of associative elements. In the Mercer house these elements were tentative borrowings from
Little, uncertainly placed; in the
Bozzi house they are richer, strongly
evocative of American summers in
Atlantic resorts. Together they create
a sophisticated scenographic architecture. Stern has absorbed the forms of
the Shingle style and used them to
create a mood appropriate to a historical resort. The playful use of these
forms also comments, however, on
how fragmented modern life is compared to the solid Victorian family
structure of the late nineteenth
century.

DRAMATIS PERSONAE

The house occupies a site that was
formerly the side garden of a neighboring house in the heart of the original summer colony on Cottage
Avenue between Lee Avenue and
Georgica Road. It is screened from the
road by tall, tightly spaced trees, and
the front of the house maintains this
plane with a flat surface. In the back
the house breaks up into a dance of
geometrically shaped rooms, which
open diagonally to the southwest to
catch the prevailing breezes (figure
129). These rooms are contained
within a rectangular perimeter
marked by columns.

The elements composed on the
straightforward volume of the house
can be considered either as things
added to or subtracted from the mass.
On the south elevation is an added
chimney with subtracted voids on
either side. On the front elevation

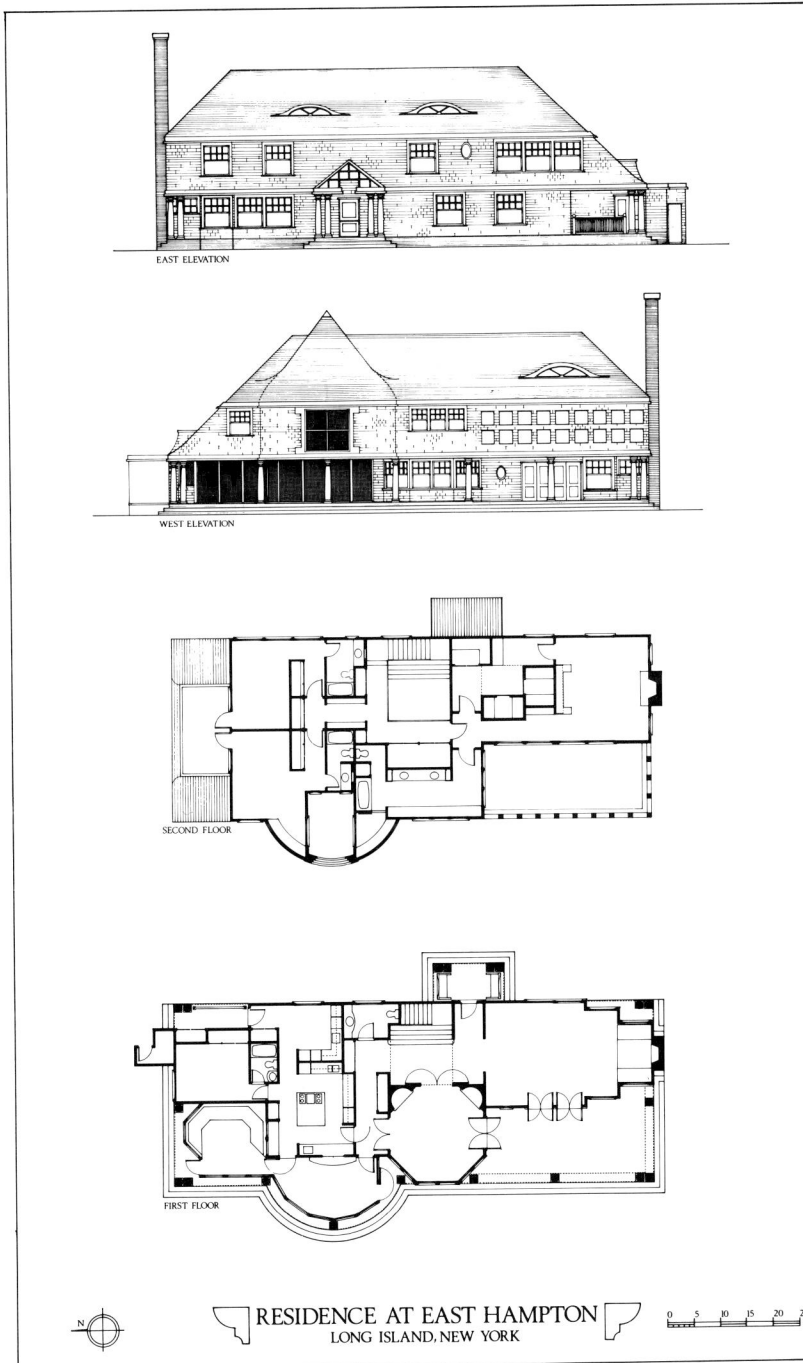

EAST ELEVATION

WEST ELEVATION

SECOND FLOOR

FIRST FLOOR

N

RESIDENCE AT EAST HAMPTON
LONG ISLAND, NEW YORK

0 5 10 15 20 25

129 Bozzi house, elevation
and plan

there are three additions, the porch and two eyelid dormers, and also two subtractions, the first floor voids at either end. The north elevation has the addition of the extra slope of roof with a subtraction within it, the balcony; and the garden elevation contains another addition and subtraction, the tower to the left and the piazza with its screen to the right.

The Chimney
Near the entry gate, the ground floor of the Bozzi house steps back to the tall brick chimney, which rises out of the three steps of the plinth on which the house stands. In the original Shingle style houses, the chimney was almost invariably an element whose verticality was related to the horizontality of the roof by interpenetration, as in John Calvin Stevens's House by the Sea of 1885, William Ralph Emerson's Glover house of 1879 (figure 130), or the East Hampton houses of its best original Shingle style architect, I. H. Green, Jr. Normally the chimney was a form expressive of interior volumes, a central point in the swelling spatial order. Even when the chimney was external, as in Wilson Eyre's Charles A. Newhall house of 1881, the roof embraced it so that the two were related to one another. In the Bozzi house the form of the chimney is attached as an associative element from outside. While not empathetically connected to the other elements, it is successful scenographically, acting as a signal to the approaching visitor and terminating the view from the front gate.

130 William Ralph Emerson,
Glover house, Milton, Massachusetts, 1879

The Porch

Raised on three brick steps and projecting like a proscenium from a
shingled curtain, the porch floats
freely along the lower cornice, avoiding the axis between the dormers
(figure 131). It is not derived from the
classic Shingle style, where entry is
typically from within the body of the
building, either from a piazza or from
a *porte-cochère*. The porch is a feature
borrowed from the classical reaction
that began in the later 1880s, in
which classical elements were combined with Shingle style principles. It
recalls the porches of McKim, Mead
and White at the Misses Appleton
house at Lenox; their Wavecrest at
Far Rockaway (figure 132); or, in the
context of East Hampton, a house
such as the Carson house on Lee Avenue. The Bozzi porch, however, disrupts the straightforwardness of these
porches with a horizontal cornice that
under its latticed pediment is broken
in an ironic manner, suggesting the
possibility of its imminent collapse
on an unsuspecting visitor mounting
the steps.

Apart from this difference, McKim,
Mead and White's porches at Far
Rockaway and Lenox are also intermediate events between external
spaces (the arcade or entry court), internal spaces (the central space of the
hall with its axial vestibule), and
semi-external spaces (the bay window
or the terrace). These porches are part
of a unified spatial sequence through
the entire house, to which the porch
acts as a key (figure 133). The porch
of the Bozzi house, by contrast, is not
located on the exterior by relation to
other spatial sequences that develop
from a sense of the wholeness of the
house but is connected tangentially,

131 Bozzi house, front porch

132 McKim, Mead and
White, Wavecrest, Mrs.
Cowdins house, Far Rocka-
way, Long Island, New York,
c. 1885

133 A. Bozzi house, East
Hampton, 1983

B. McKim, Mead and White,
Misses Appleton House,
Lenox, Massachusetts,
1883–84

C. McKim, Mead and White,
Wavecrest, Far Rockaway,
Long Island, New York,
c. 1885

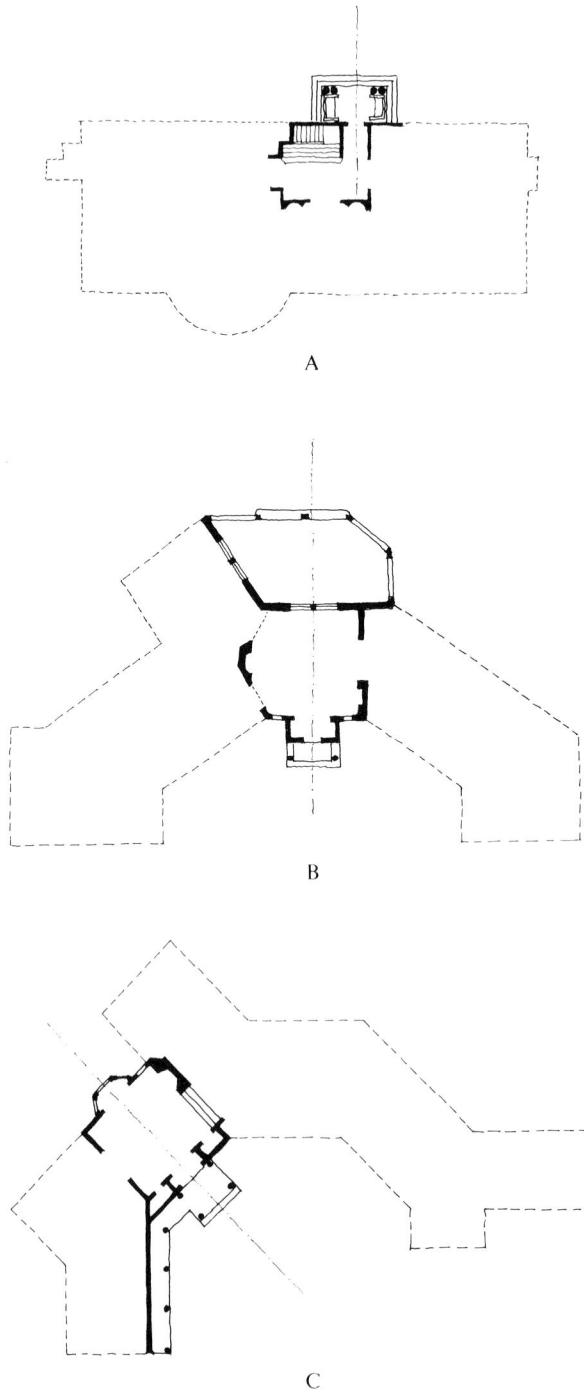

A

B

C

not axially, to an interior composed of discrete spaces instead of flowing, serial spaces in the Shingle style manner. It is an independent element enjoying its own playful joke.

Similarly, the sheltered space cut out of the mass of the house to the right of the porch and protected by porch rail and columns is not like the space revealed by the cutting away of planes, as in Wilson Eyre's Potter house in Chestnut Hill (figure 134), and integrated by the projecting gable and its symmetrical partner. Rather it too is a floating atmospheric incident, not related to the void on the left by an intermediate element such as the Potter house gables.

The Dormers
The eyelid dormers above the porch look down and sideways. Such dormers are frequent features in East Hampton; they resemble, for example, those of the neo-Elizabethan East Hampton Free Library of 1910–11, by Aymar Embury II. If they are compared to the eyelid dormers of other buildings of the nineteenth century, however, especially those by H.H. Richardson or East Hampton's Schuyler Quackenbush house by Cyrus Eidlitz, they will be found to be quite different.

Richardson's and Eidlitz's dormers are like surgical incisions made by slivers of glass cutting into the building's shingled skin. In Richardson's Crane Memorial Library (figures 135, 136), the three dormers articulate the swelling spaces of the two interior volumes, the library and the reading room, and look as if they could be folded closed and stitched. In Eidlitz's design each dormer is visually related to one of the projecting gambrels (figure 137). They enable the eye to

134 Wilson Eyre, Potter
house, Chestnut Hill, Pennsylvania, 1881–82

135 H. H. Richardson, Crane
Memorial Library, Quincy,
Massachusetts, 1880–83

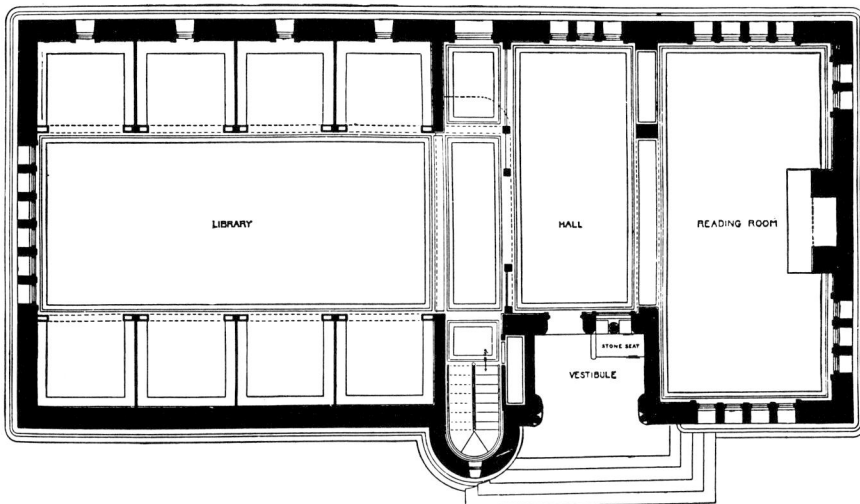

136 H. H. Richardson, Crane
Memorial Library, Quincy,
Massachusetts, 1880–83,
plan

137 Cyrus L. W. Eidlitz, Schuyler Quackenbush house, Lee Avenue, East Hampton, 1898–99. Note how the porch slides sideways, weakening the corner where the gable falls.

more easily register the empathetic movement of rising and sinking volumes. The rising volume signifies the fixed end of the front facade, while the falling volume leads the eye around the corner, already de-stabilized by the apparent sideways slide of the long porch. The house therefore takes advantage of its site, "composing differently" with the movement of the viewer. By contrast, the dormers of the Bozzi house are bigger and rounder; they are emblems individually placed on the roof, lacking the visual connections that would enable them to "compose differently" from many points of view yet acting most successfully as props in the unfolding action.

The Roof

To the north, past the turning circle, the mass of the Bozzi house is extended into what seems at first glance to be an eminently Shingle style sweep of roof. Yet the sweep of roof is less an integral feature of a roof striving to quell the restless incidents it embraces, as in Emerson's Glover house (see figure 130), than it is the incidental recollection of a sweeping roof. It is not a roof that preserves the uninterrupted quality that was essential to the Glover house, tipping and spilling from the topmost gable almost to the ground. The roof is interrupted first by the upper cornice, contradicting the lateral push of the shingle roof with the containing tendencies of the American Renaissance, and then by the balcony. Here the flood of shingles is prevented from descending further, caught, like water in a pool. The balcony itself, symmetrical in the north facade, is a delightful set-piece, decked already with the coffee and the *New York Times*, with morning light cutting over the slope of the roof.

The Screen

The gridded screen over the piazza originates in Emerson's Hemenway house at Manchester-by-the-Sea (figure 138). In that house the lean wooden post at the corner is an integral member of a larger structural order, and we perceive the shingles as a thin membrane applied over a wooden frame. The lean post reveals a concern for the economy of the Colonial prototypes; and the lightness of the skin, made lighter by the perforations, is a metaphor for camping out in nature, for escape from the grime and overcrowding of the nineteenth-century city. This corner post and screen perfectly embody the twin feeling for structure and nature present in the original Shingle style.

In the Bozzi house the screen is juxtaposed with columns that avoid a structural or visual relationship with the screen's solid elements. Whereas in the Hemenway house the acknowledgment of the corner posts produces a differentiation between the width of the corner and the width of the other verticals in the screen, bringing the perimeter of the facade to a clear halt and giving the house a sense of self-containment, in the Bozzi house these conditions are undifferentiated. The screen is a fragment disconnected from its supports (figure 139), and it overwhelms the smaller scaled and more delicately massed neighboring house (figure 140). From the point of view of creating a stage, however, the screen is extremely successful; and the exterior space behind it epitomizes this quality of the house, for

138 William Ralph Emerson, Hemenway house, Manchester-by-the-Sea, Massachusetts, c. 1883

139 Bozzi house, detail of screen

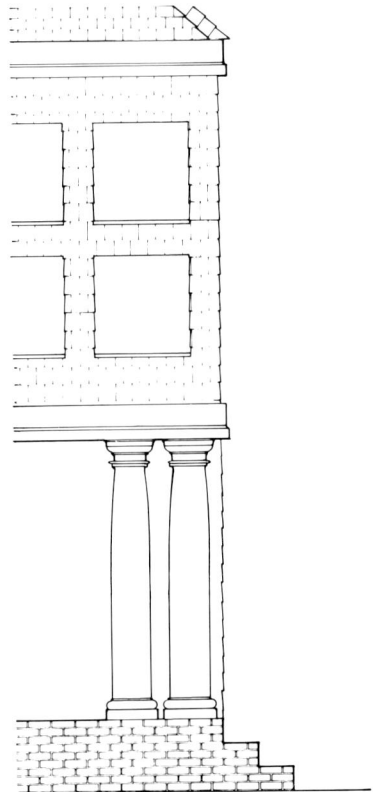

the screen not only seems like a curtain poised either to close or to open
on a fresh act, but also provides sensuous theatrical lighting effects in the
form of gridded light and shade (figure
141). The double-height space thus
dramatized, with its bedroom windows above to be serenaded and double French doors downstage, abounds
in charm. If this is the foremost stage
of the house, however, the tower to
its left is the leading player.

The Tower
Standing on three columns, the tower
is a half circle in plan (figure 142). It
is cut on the diameter along the line
of the wall that separates the interior
space of the tower from the rest of
the house. This space is a screened
porch on the ground floor but is channeled into a rectangular slot in the
center that is a little over thirty feet
high, only about eight feet wide, and
lit by an oval window twinkling at
the top.

The tower of the Bozzi house is
rendered largely static in the horizontal plane, for it is given an intensely
vertical axis by the location of a single column directly under the center
of the largest window in the house,
on axis with the point of the half
cone. This is contradictory to Shingle
style practice, in which horizontal
movement is used to connect elements, such as a tower form, with the
rest of the house.

In Richardson's Stoughton House of
1882–83 (figure 143), for example,
only a quarter of the tower is exposed
and the shingles seem to race over the
curved surface of the tower and into
the flat surface over the entrance.
There is no vertical axis to impede
their flow. Indeed, the larger windows

140 Bozzi house and its
neighbor

141 Bozzi house, screen

142 Bozzi house, tower

143 H. H. Richardson,
Stoughton house, Cam-
bridge, Massachusetts,
1882–83

are placed over the smaller ones, establishing a relationship that is inherently unstable visually and directing attention away from the tower to aid the expression of movement. In Emerson's house at Bar Harbor (figure 144), the tower's fenestration is even more dynamic in the horizontal plane: the spiraling of the tower's stair is expressed in the moldings that connect the windows, and the balconies spin like the base of a humming top. The free and flowing plan (figure 145) is reflected in the movement on the facade.[10]

If the static quality in the horizontal plane of the Bozzi tower is uncharacteristic of the nineteenth-century Shingle style, its movement in the vertical dimension is equally uncharacteristic. The central column "supports" a large opening above, while at the same time the visually heavy tower appears to "float" over a void, producing ironic fluctuations in the vertical dimension. This sophisticated, knowing movement is as remote from the nineteenth-century Shingle style as the cut in the back of the tower, which deliberately separates it from the rest of the house and makes it a self-contained image applied to the house.

THE PICTURESQUE

The emblematic incidents in the Bozzi house are therefore not connected by the original Shingle style technique of "composing differently." Stern does not seek the historical Shingle style's unity of "plastic and richly surfaced mass, various and coherent, indicative of plastic volumes within."[11] The organic wholeness of the Shingle style is in fact

144 William Ralph Emerson,
Thirlstane, Mrs. R. B. Scott
house, Bar Harbor, Maine,
c. 1885

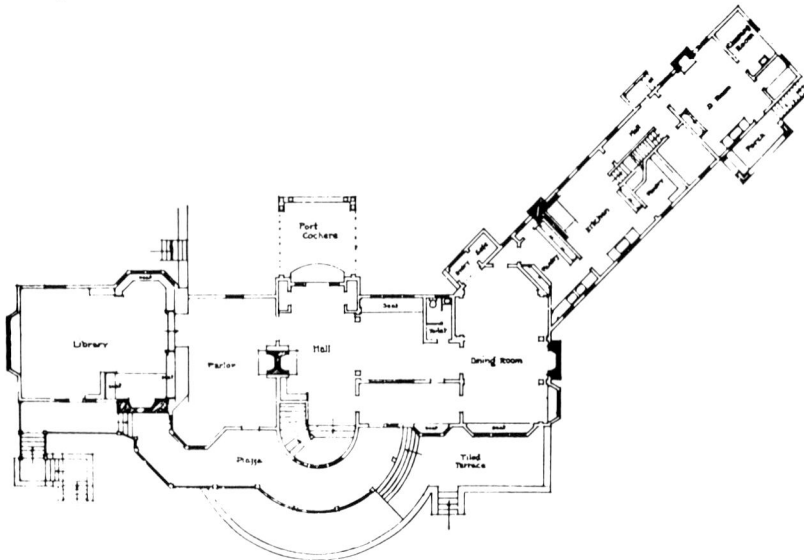

145 William Ralph Emerson,
Thirlstane, Mrs. R. B. Scott
house, Bar Harbor, Maine,
c. 1885, plan

consistently denied in the Bozzi
house. For the picturesque incidents
of the house are, rather, individual
players in a scenographic architecture.

Romantic Rationalism

Stern's denial of the organic wholeness of the original Shingle style is a
denial of the principles of Romantic
rationalism from which the coherency
of the nineteenth-century Shingle
style evolved. These principles were
formed in America by the conver-
gence, in the work of Andrew Jackson
Downing, of the English theories of
the picturesque with the later moral-
ism of the Victorian era.[12] To Downing, as to Ruskin, "all beauty is an
outward expression of inward good."[13]
This "outward expression" tended toward the revelation of the "inward
good" of the structural wood frame,
first with the simple board and batten
of Downing's "Villa in the Bracketed
Mode," then with the articulated
framing members (whether actual or
not) of the 1860s and early 1870s.
Next the "inward good" was trans-
ferred from the frame of the Stick
style to the volumes of the Shingle
style, which borrowed from the lightness of skin implicit in the often tent-
like qualities of English Regency
work[14] and the spatial developments
of the English Queen Anne style. Finally, as the Shingle style progressed
into the mid-1880s, the transformation was from the order of a flowing
spatial unity to the power of monumental expression, such as one sees
in the work of John Calvin Stevens
and Clarence Luce and as epitomized
in McKim, Mead and White's Low
house (figure 146).[15]

146 McKim, Mead and
White, W. G. Lowe house,
Bristol, Rhode Island, 1887

Stern's scenographic Shingle style does not possess the abstract order of Stevens or Luce and may reject what Gervase Wheeler, developing Downing's ideas, described as the "reality"[16] of organic wholeness and what Downing himself called its "truth,"[17] but it has an order of a different sort. It substitutes a collage of images (figure 147) for the archetype and turns to the more pictorial Shingle style of Lamb and Rich (figure 148). It finds inspiration in East Hampton's earliest Shingle style house, the delightful Moran studio, with its unexpected and wonderful interior stage, complete with balcony, or in the eclecticism of the more exuberant Colonial Revival houses of the late nineteenth century, such as the house of Pierre Lorrilard, Jr. at Tuxedo Park (figure 149), designed by the unpredictable Bruce Price. Stern's work is not in the tradition of the monumental Shingle style, summed up by the shatteringly primitive gesture of the Low house. The picturesqueness of Stern's approach is not that of inherent spatial characteristics empathetically expressed in the movement of external masses, such as one sees in many of the greatest orthodox Shingle style works, where the volumes all "compose differently" from different points of view. It is from an alternate late-eighteenth-century view of the picturesque as primarily a matter of associations that Stern's architecture can be said to ultimately derive.

Archibald Alison and the Theory of Association

Edmund Burke's distinctions between the sublime and the beautiful—and the development of his line of reasoning by Uvedale Price in his *On the Picturesque* of 1794[18] to include a

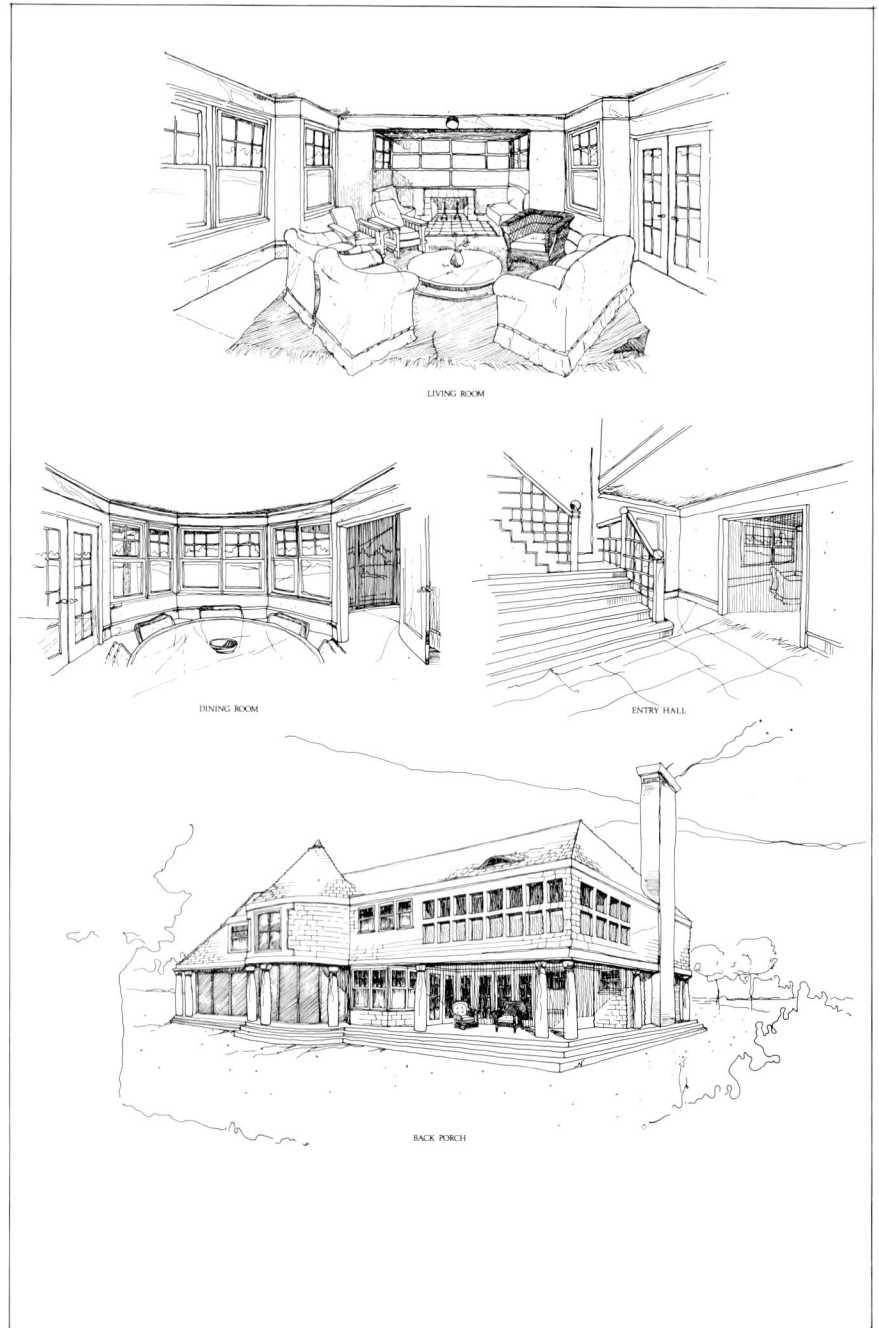

147 Bozzi house, interior sketches by Terry Brown

148 Lamb and Rich, Sunset Hall, S. P. Hinckley house, Lawrence, Long Island, New York. Sketch of the interior by Rich, 1883.

149 Bruce Price, Pierre Lorillard, Jr. house, Tuxedo Park, New York

third standard of beauty characterized by movement, texture, and light and shade—rely on the belief that the inherent visual characteristics of matter cause aesthetic emotions. In his 1790 study *Essays on the Nature and Principles of Taste*[19] written in reaction to Burke, Archibald Alison posits that the *associations* aroused by forms produce aesthetic emotions.

Alison's theory is based on the premise that the activation of a train of thought about an object causes the "Emotion of Taste," that is, the sensation of aesthetic pleasure:

When any object, either of sublimity or beauty, is presented to the mind, I believe every man is conscious of a train of thought being immediately awakened in his imagination, analogous to the character or expression of the original object. The simple perception of the object, we frequently find, is insufficient to excite these emotions, unless it is accompanied with the operation of mind, unless . . . our fancy [is] buried in the pursuit of all those trains of thought, which are allied to this character or expression.[20]

To Alison, therefore, "the object itself appears only to serve as a hint, to awaken the imagination, and to lead it through every analogous idea that has place in the memory."[21]

Trains of thought about all things are of course present at all times. Alison's theory circumvents this problem by imposing two conditions on those trains of thought that produce the emotion of taste. First, the ideas that compose the train must be "Ideas of Emotion"; in other words, they must be ideas meaningful enough to disengage an individual from trivial concerns. Second, the ideas in the train must be "distinguished by some general principle of connection, which subsists through the whole extent of the train."[22] Alison's concept of the aesthetic experience, which is made clear by his choice of numerous examples from poetry, is of a kind of reverie, a dreamlike state in which a stream of thoughts connected to one another by analogy succeed each other in a smooth flow.

This theory of association became the foundation of an attack on Uvedale Price by Richard Payne Knight. To Knight, in his *Analytical Enquiry into the Principles of Taste* of 1805,[23] Price's "great fundamental error, which prevails throughout the otherwise able and elegant Essays on the Picturesque, is seeking for distinction in external objects, which only exist in the modes and habits of viewing and considering them."[24]

SCENOGRAPHIC ARCHITECTURE

The elements of the Bozzi house are not connected by visual means, such as those set out by Price and continued into the nineteenth century and the Shingle style, but by association in the manner of Alison and Knight. The forms transport us to Atlantic resorts, to vacations, to American summers by the sea. The tower inhabits its garden and gazes out toward us and toward the pool and trees. We retire to the sea breezes and sharp, checked shadows of the terrace and then to enclosure and the warmth of the fire within. The house is an album of images that reconstruct this experience for a society wishing to "play at achieving the ancient values" once again.

There was an element of such the-
ater in the original Shingle style cottages, but in the Bozzi house we
experience a detachment from the
sense of organic wholeness produced
in them by the unified movement of
picturesque forms. Instead, the associative elements of the house create
a stage on which day-to-day life is
carried out and are also architectural
actors in a play within a play. The individual inhabitant of this scenographic architecture becomes at once
actor and subject, and "truth" is no
longer a universal, moralistic expression in space and structure but com-
passion for the multiplicity of
everyday life acted out in architectural form.

6

THE CONTINUITY
OF THE
CLASSICAL
Manchester Superior
Court Building
Manchester, Connecticut
Allan Greenberg,
Architect (1980)

MANCHESTER

Manchester, Connecticut, is a typical small New England town. Its history is one of storybook Yankee ingenuity and a kind of nineteenth-century industrial feudalism.

The town was dominated during the century of its expansion, from its incorporation out of East Hartford in 1823 to the economic crash of 1929, by two things: silk and the Cheney family. Some early mechanical silk-spinning inventions together with restrictive tariffs on imported silk imposed during and maintained after the Civil War established Manchester's wealth. This wealth was largely in the hands of the Cheney family, who owned most things of importance in town but also stuck by a traditional policy of god-fearing philanthropy. So extensive was the "Cheney principality," as it has been called,[1] that by the town's centennial in the peak years of the silk industry, Cheney Brothers employed one quarter of the total population. The Cheneys also owned roughly a quarter of all property, which was disposed in a neat geometrical configuration.

The town has a typical crossroads plan (figure 150). There is a Main Street running north to south, from the immigrant concentrations to the commercial core, intersected by a Center Street which runs east to west and was built on an old Indian trail that led down to the Connecticut River on the other side of East Hartford. Of the four quadrants so formed, the Cheneys owned most of the southwest chunk. Accordingly, it is not surprising that the civic heart of Manchester, Center Park, occupies a rectangular piece of land, given by the Cheney family, south of Center and west of Main where these roads meet. It is to this park that all buildings of importance in the center of Manchester address themselves.

Civic Style
Of these buildings four stand out: the white clapboard Congregational Church of 1904 in the Colonial Revival style, the Town Hall of 1926 by Frank Farley (figure 151), the Mary Cheney Library of 1937 by the same architect, a Cheney relative (figure 152), and the Post Office of 1932. These last three are all in the urbane masonry classicism of the American Renaissance and are neither outstanding nor less than skillful. The library stands in the park; the town hall and the Congregational Church front the park; the post office adjusts itself diagonally from across the intersection to face the park. Until recently a memorial fountain to the Daughters of the American Revolution designed in the same period by Charles Platt (another Cheney relative) stood in the middle of the intesection opposite the post office. A fountain with wrestling bears by Platt still stands in the park. The American Renaissance was the style in which Manchester expressed its civic pride at the moment of its greatest success, after a hundred years of prosperity, a style made somehow rather poignant in retrospect by its modest grandeur in the face of imminent decline.

Center Street falls off to the west along the slope of the hill and is lined with the tight-edged wooden prisms of typical vernacular Greek Revival houses, interrupted here and there by a gas station or fast food restaurant.

150 Manchester road system with major public buildings at the center of town and the Manchester Superior Court Building on the left

151 Frank Farley, Town
Hall, 1926

152 Frank Farley, Mary
Cheney Library, 1937

The proportion of new to old increases as the hill levels off where Center Street parts in a fork around a long, triangular sliver of park. Blocking this rising tide of sprawl, the Superior Court Building spans the two parts of Center Street and forms a dam at the base of the park (figure 153).

Manchester Superior Court
The new building is a renovation of what was a decaying supermarket (figure 154). Greenberg transformed a sickly and debased descendant of the International style into a robust classical building cast in the mold of the American Renaissance, which establishes an intelligible equilibrium with the civic buildings at the top of the hill.

The secret life of the Superior Court Building is expressed through the variations on its classical sources. There are three levels at which these variations occur: through the action of empathetic forces, through the associations with classical precedent, and through the quest for those ideal values the classical embodies.

EMPATHETIC FORCES

The Interior
Manchester Superior Court is a single-story brick box with a structural system consisting of twenty steel columns connected by lightweight steel trusses. The front elevation of the original supermarket was glazed, like any suburban example of the type, and had white bricks fronting Center Street at its division. The renovation made two major changes. In the interior a series of enclosed spaces was created by joining columns with walls

153 Manchester Superior
Court Building in its context

154 The supermarket before
renovation

in various ways and then subdividing many of the spaces so formed. On the exterior the glass wall was replaced by a classical facade.

The public spaces form a layered sequence from front to back that consists of a vestibule, an antechamber and lobby, and three courtrooms (figure 155). The remaining spaces form a habitable *poché* between the public spaces and the exterior walls. These public spaces are organized along two axes. A major axis penetrates the front elevation in the center and passes through the vestibule, antechamber, lobby, and central courtroom, terminating in a judge's seat. A cross axis passes down the length of the lobby and out through the two side vestibules.

As one enters the courthouse, the internal organization is completely unambiguous, yet subtleties gradually reveal themselves. The lobby is barrel vaulted above a deep entablature and is painted blue to represent the sky. The Tuscan columns that inhabit the lobby under this "sky" seem to be in a state of perpetual anticipation, mirroring the anticipation of all who wait there (figure 156); and the courtroom doors in their Pompeian colors gaze into the lobby, inscrutable countenances seeming to draw the columns toward them (figure 157). Three of the four columns contain structural members. The columns are matched with two pilasters each, one facing them across the vaulted space, the other ornamenting the courtroom wall behind. Each set of three is linked by a dark gray stripe in the terrazzo floor pattern so that the columns appear capable of sliding from pilaster to

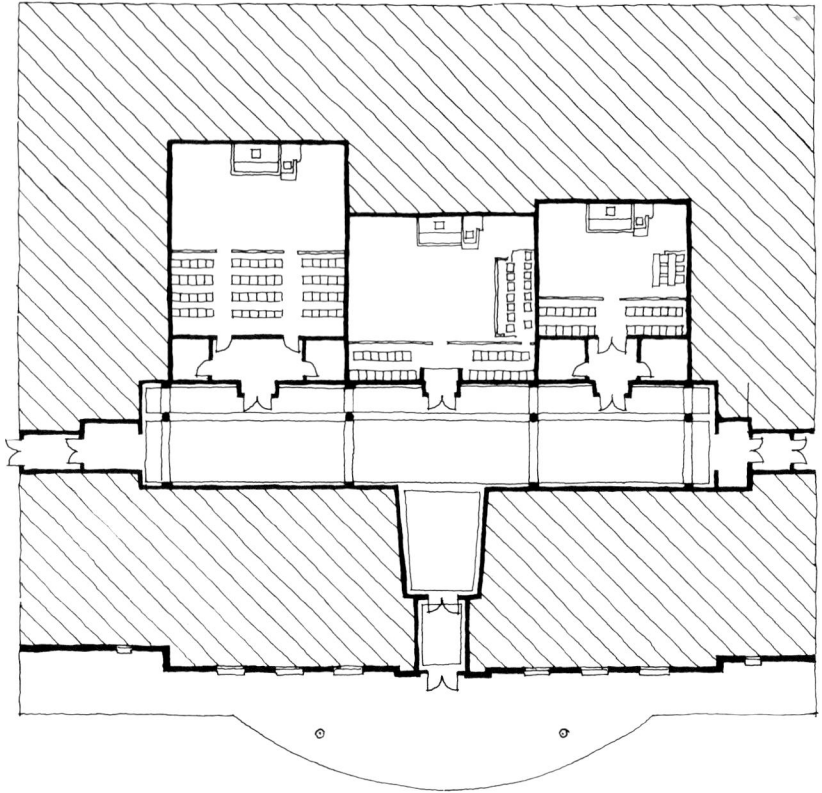

155 Manchester Superior Court, plan showing major public spaces

156 Manchester Superior
Court, interior view

157 Manchester Superior
Court, interior view with
courtroom door

pilaster along the stripe, as if in a
groove, and of causing the barrel-
vaulted ceiling to yawn wider, or
snap shut.

Greenberg has used the Tuscan Order from Palladio (figure 158). This
Order has the advantage of being
seemly without being pretentious and
is suitable for what is a significant
but not grandiose public building.
Also, as Palladio notes, "if simple col-
onnades are made of this Order, the
spaces or intercolumniations may be
very wide because the architraves are
made of wood."[2] This allows Greenberg to conform with the existing
structural grid and therefore to reflect
in the tripartite division of the lobby
the layout of the three major public
rooms.

The wide intercolumniations of the
lobby have resulted in slight variations to the Tuscan designed to increase the sense of sturdiness in the
columns. Greenberg has slightly increased the width of the abacus, used
a twelfth rather than a sixteenth diameter for determining the astragal
molding, and made a minor adjustment in the relationship between
cincture and torus in the base by
slightly increasing the height of the
former.

It is in the entablature, however,
that the most significant changes occur (figure 159). The architrave is normally equal to the frieze in a Tuscan
entablature, each being half the diameter of the column base. Here the architrave is compressed to about a
third of the diameter, making the
frieze taller so that it can easily accept its large lettering. An extra fascia
and fillet added to the bed mold com-
plement the increased scale of the
frieze, and the normal cyma reversa

Cymatium
Corona
Bed Mold
Frieze
Architrave
Abacus
Echinus
Necking
Astragal
Cincture
Cyma Recta
Plinth

158 The Tuscan Order ac-
cording to Palladio. Note
that Palladio gives two column bases for this Order,
one with a cyma recta as
shown and one with a large
torus or half round. Greenberg had modified the latter
version.

159 Detail of the entablature in the interior of the Manchester Superior Court Building

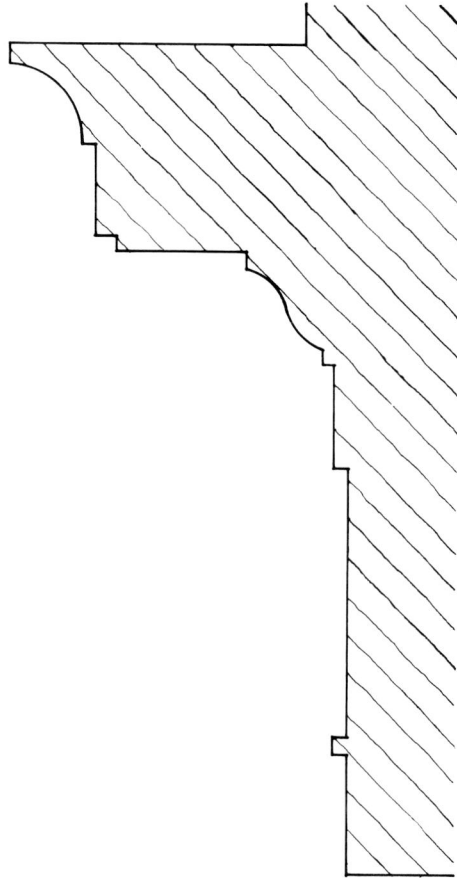

was replaced with a cyma recta to announce and reflect the vault above. These modifications permit the entablature to span the wide intercolumniations necessitated by the existing grid without appearing strained.

These extended features, however, are abruptly contraindicated by the corona, which is greatly compressed. The corona also projects much further than one normally finds in a Tuscan entablature, approaching that of a Doric corona but without dentiles or mutules to support it. The corona appears to slide on its bed mold, and the subtly placed fillet beneath it gives a further impression of movement, as the corona advances from the fillet into a vaulted space. Finally, Greenberg replaces the normal ovolo of the cymatium with a cavetto, adding thrust to the projecting section of cornice and recalling the larger curve of the vault above, for which one has been prepared by the cyma recta of the corona's bed mold.

If the columns suggest movement along the gray stripe in the floor pattern, so too the corona suggests horizontal movement over the bed mold and frieze. The pilasters that ornament the courtroom wall exert a stronger visual pull on the columns than those on the opposite wall because they are nearer and connected by shallow, dropped beams. By this action, they seem to open the space of the vault further. The coronas, on the other hand, appear more likely to continue sliding toward one another than to recede. This movement appears to close the vault. The contradictory forces at work seem to strain the vault, which, subjected to the force of light and landscape at either end, is also pulled on its long axis (figure 160). The vault is elongated and

160 Manchester Superior
Court, interior view

tense; one senses the sky opening and closing as the columns slide along the dark bands in the floor and the coronas crash together overhead, as the law is applied and sentence passed, and as guilty and innocent pass into the darkness of their incarceration or are delivered onto the land.

The Exterior

Similar forces are at work in the facade (figure 161). The facade retains the step-in plan of the original supermarket. The glass and aluminum skin was converted into a red brick and cream-colored stone facade, which is the same palette of materials used in the American Renaissance buildings around Center Park. The asymmetrically placed, glazed entrance of the original building was replaced with a centered astylar pavilion set in front of the rest of the facade by eight to ten inches. That no Order is used on the exterior is certainly no hinderance in a classical building. As the Abbé Laugier observed in his *Essai* in 1753:

The five Orders are not suitable for every kind of building because they involve expense which not everybody is able to afford . . . . Attractive and even beautiful buildings can be built without the help of entablature and columns . . . .

The beauty of [such buildings] . . . depends mainly on three things: accuracy of proportions, elegance of forms, and choice and distribution of ornaments.[3]

For a simple decoration it is sufficient to mark the corners of a building from top to bottom by quoins and the stories by a plain band projecting slightly, to give doors and windows plain casings, and to have the whole building crowned by an uncomplicated and gracefully designed cornice. Since in decorations of this kind

161 Manchester Superior
Court

the plain wall must necessarily appear, there are no great objections to making the heads of doors and windows in the shape of a segmented or even semicircular arch.[4]

Laugier's words describe remarkably well the approach taken at Manchester Superior Court. The quoins generate bands that meet the springing of stretchers over the window arches, give the facade a base, and also determine the vertical spacing of the rustication around the entrance. The "uncomplicated cornice" is a frieze with the barest architrave below, the cornice above in brick, carrying the name of the building, and an attic story and cap on top. In the central pavilion this entablature meets a fully detailed raking cornice in stone, but the frieze merges with the tympanum, despite the projection of the central pavilion (figure 162). This is rather unfortunate as the otherwise vertical thrust of the entrance pavilion is necessarily compromised by the horizontality of the frieze.

An admirable piling up of rustication is achieved around the entrance, however, emphasizing the building's centrality and controlling its length. The bands appear to shoot out horizontally from the entrance pavilion, and so strong is this horizontal force that the quoined ends of the facade appear to be pushing further apart as if to cover completely the remaining sections of white brick wall. This movement is denied, however, by the small windows in the white walls, which pick up the central four panes of the arched windows and compress the facade, seeming to push it toward the central pavilion.

As the facade is stretched out between tension and compression in this way, it has become very thin, like a taut sheet of fabric. There is very little modeling in the facade, although enough to give it body. The rustication does not project at all and so casts no shadow; when seen at an angle, the arched openings lack the three-dimensional quality conferred by the plastic notching of raised rustication and therefore have a punched out rather than a molded quality. The single bricks laid end to end, which separate the rusticated bands, add to the stretched-out quality, as does the frieze with its linear lettering.

The raking cornices of the pediment, which are not fully connected by a horizontal cornice, seem to be collapsing, pulled out by the escaping surface of the tympanum, which also appears to be spreading horizontally (figure 163). The tip of the pediment, just peeping out over the cap of the attic story, has a very tenuous connection with the sky, which tends to add to the impression of collapse, as if the weight of the sky had already forced the pediment down and was pushing it even further. The compressed relation of the raking cornices to the extremely thin, horizontal brick cornice of the frieze that joins the split fillet reinforces this impression, as do the enlarged proportion of the cymatium and the compression expressed in the layers of rustication beneath.

ASSOCIATIONS AND PRECEDENTS

Overall, the courthouse is immediately associated with Frank Farley's American Renaissance town hall and

162 Manchester Superior Court, detail of facade portico

163 Manchester Superior Court, detail of facade portico

Cheney Library in the center of Manchester. All three buildings are simple brick enclosures with a projecting portico (suggested rather than actual in the courthouse). Obviously, because the library is a single-story building where the town hall is not, the courthouse has a closer affinity with a library. Both buildings have a central projecting element with three arches on either side, although the court building is flat roofed and the library is not. The library is also the only major civic building near Central Park without a cupola or spire.

It is clear, however, that in massing and detail the courthouse and the Cheney Library are quite different. The courthouse politely acknowledges its civic counterparts and does not upstage them; but its more potent associations lie elsewhere, for its struggles with context, both spatial and temporal, are of an altogether different order. It is to the seventeenth- and eighteenth-century roots of American architecture, to the Colonial, Revolutionary, and Federal periods that Greenberg turned for models that addressed the problem of architectural identity in a period of dislocation.

The facade of Manchester Superior Court exhibits two contrasting strains of American architecture. On one hand, the body of the facade betrays the influence of the Colonial—the Georgian architecture descended from Inigo Jones, Christopher Wren, James Gibbs, and ultimately from Palladio, as simplified and filtered through English and American pattern books to suit the sensibilities and materials of the New World. The windows and decorative aspects of the facade are influenced by the Federal style, the post-Revolutionary America version of the Adam style. On the other hand, in the outline of the superimposed central pavilion, with its temple front proportions and correct, pedimented cornice, one catches the influence of Jefferson, of the Revolutionary neoclassicism of the Virginia State Capitol, of the symbolic architecture of the Enlightenment.

Georgian Influence

The simple, vernacular Georgian architecture of the oldest courthouse still in use in America, the King William County Courthouse in King William, Virginia, of c. 1725 (figure 164), provides a Colonial model for Greenberg's arched facade; but the modest details, the simple cornice, and the subtle springing of the arches are replaced by more decorative touches in the Federal mode. The Federal delight in setting arched windows in arched openings, present also in the recessed windows of the Mary Cheney Library and stemming from such projects by Robert Adam as the House of the Society of Arts, Manufacturing and Commerce (figure 165) or the house of Sir Watkins Williams Wynn, is recalled at Manchester by the separation of the central nine panes of each window from the thinner outer band of ten panes. In the playful rustication with its flat, linear articulation, one also senses the delicacy of Federal proportions.

Jefferson's Influence

On this simply ordered elevation is superimposed the temple front, a form that has conveyed the continuity of the ideals of American government for two hundred years and that is rooted in the architecture of Thomas Jefferson.

Jefferson's Virginia State Capitol building (figure 166) was the first building in either America or Europe to use an antique temple for a contemporary purpose. Its primary message is clear: Roman architecture embodies the noblest aspirations and ideals of Republicanism and is therefore morally correct for America. Additional messages emerge, however, as one traces the differences between Jefferson's buildings and his Roman model, the Maison Carrée at Nîmes (figure 167).

The first design, illustrated by Jefferson and Louis Clerisseau's model of the capitol (figure 168), is quite different from its progenitor. It has a different arrangement of columns, the half columns are omitted, windows are inserted, Ionic is substituted for Corinthian, and there is an enlargement of scale. In the Maison Carrée, the columns continue around the building and are intersected by a wall to form half columns starting at the third intercolumniation back from the facade. Jefferson made his building more frontal by removing the half columns and by compressing the portico so that it became only two intercolumniations deep. The Ionic capital Jefferson substituted for the Corinthian further emphasizes this frontality, as the volutes are flat in the plane of the facade, where the Corinthian capitals of the Maison Carrée are in the round. Even the pilasters of the final building, though they dilute the effect portrayed in the model, preserve the frontality that replaced the peripteral temple form of the Maison Carrée, since they cannot be confused with the columns of the portico. Finally, the windows that Jefferson

164 King William County
Court House, Virginia,
c. 1725

165 Robert Adam, House of
the Society of Arts, Manufacturing and Commerce,
the Adelphi, London,
1772–74

166 Thomas Jefferson, Virginia State Capitol, completed c. 1790. The steps shown on Jefferson's drawing still had not been built when this view was taken in 1880.

167 Maison Carrée, Nîmes, France, first century A.D., view from the northeast

168 Thomas Jefferson and Charles Louis Clerisseau, model for the Virginia State Capitol, 1785

located on the exterior wall make it plain that this is an architecture for man, not for the gods, for it is from this capitol, with its new and increased scale, that the laws of man emanate and extend over the land.

Jefferson's final and complete evocation of this new force was achieved in the University of Virginia library (figure 169), where the Roman Pantheon is converted from a temple—dedicated to all the gods, blind, save for the oculus, pivot of a terrifying vertical shaft of charged space—to a great, many-windowed, domed drum, like a brain that pours the fruits of reason out over the hills and valleys in great horizontal waves to the distant Pacific.

Continuity

It is to this fundamental point in American architecture that Greenberg returns, but through the lens of twentieth-century experience. Greatly different as our age may be from Jefferson's, however, the laws that were created then are fundamentally those by which America is governed still; and although the now familiar western sea may no longer hold the promise of heroic challenge, the myths of possibility and promise are no less deeply ingrained today than they were then. In short, there are profound similarities between the eighteenth century and our own that define a continuity of American culture (figure 170). Greenberg asserts this continuity in the quotations from Locke and Jefferson he has placed on the entablature on the courthouse interior.

Locke is represented by: "The end of law is not to abolish or to restrain, but to preserve and enlarge freedom, for in all the states of created beings capable of law, where there is no law there is no freedom."[5] It is the anarchy of seeming freedoms created by the historical avant-garde that is restrictive, Greenberg implies. The laws of classicism, however, are not restrictive but liberating because they give the architect clear models and rules to refer to, develop, and carry out.

From Jefferson, Greenberg chose: "Laws are made for men of ordinary understanding, and should therefore be construed by the ordinary rules of common sense. Their meaning is not to be sought for in metaphysical subtleties."[6] The forms of classical architecture, Greenberg suggests, have a civic potency lacking in the novel forms of Utopian modernism because they can unambiguously convey the shared values that constitute a cultural continuity.

THE CLASSICAL IDEAL

The analogy between architecture and law may derive from the Enlightenment and may establish a continuity with that time, but at a deeper level the classical implies a sense of continuity based on absolute values that are unchanging over far longer periods of time. The classical implies that whatever profound differences may exist between the present and the past—differences which to the Utopian modernists seemed so irreconcilable—there are greater similarities. The perception of such enduring truths is the basis of all classical re-

169 Thomas Jefferson, University of Virginia campus, Boye print, 1828

170 Thomas Jefferson, Rotunda at the University of Virginia inscribed in a circle

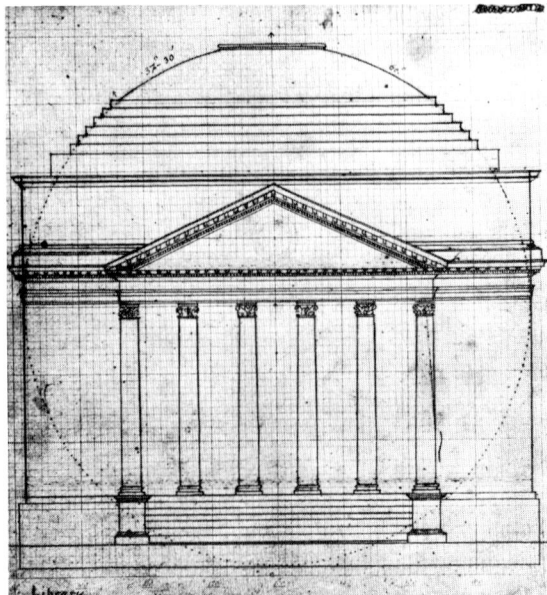

vivals. In his quest for the classical
ideal, Greenberg turned to the greatest twentieth-century classicists: he
has found inspiration in the English
architect Sir Edwin Lutyens and in
Lutyens's contemporary in America,
Charles Follen McKim.

Lutyens

Lutyens's influence is pervasive in the
courthouse, but Greenberg's sensibility is quite different. This difference
can be observed in a comparison of
Greenberg's courthouse with Lutyens's Midland Bank of 1922, located
in Piccadilly, London (figure 171).
Midland Bank is a simple geometric
block, as is Manchester Superior
Court. Both buildings are of the same
red brick with stone trim. But where
Midland Bank is an assertive cube of
space, the Manchester building is flattened and pulled horizontally, as if
the ground under Lutyens's bank had
become elastic and begun to stretch.
Its arched openings are tripled, its attic story crushed, and the horizontal
bands that hoop Lutyens's building
are broken and reset in a single plane,
no longer closed but extending laterally. The keystone retains its idiosyn-
cratically curved soffit and the
vertical chamfer of the sides. Even the
typeface used in Lutyens's building is
retained, but is stretched out instead
of compact and vertical.

While Greenberg may refer to Lutyens's forms in both the interior,
where the restatement of a ceiling
opening in a floor pattern is a typical
Lutyens motif (figure 172), as well as
the exterior, these forms are used for
virtually opposite purposes. For where
Lutyens's work is full of paradox,
serving a society cast in the mono-
lithic mold of empire and imperial

171 Sir Edwin Lutyens,
Midland Bank, Piccadilly,
London, 1922

172 Sir Edwin Lutyens,
Midland Bank, Poultry,
London, 1922, safe-deposit
corridor

ideals, Greenberg's is clear and unambiguous, ministering to a pluralistic society that is itself inherently paradoxical.

The "love of paradox"[7] so characteristic of Lutyens's work is well illustrated in the Midland Bank by his manipulation of the small, nearly square windows in the attic story. The rhythm established on the elevation perpendicular to the street leads one to expect three more windows where their places are indicated by floral decorations on the front elevation. The windows, however, have dropped out of the attic story and have come to rest over the keystones of the arches. In their new location they have a contradictory relationship with the enormous scale of the swelling central window of the front elevation. A double paradox therefore arises, as the large window ascends and the small ones fall.

Greenberg avoids Lutyens's paradoxical relationships by simplifying his forms. As if to underscore the lack of ambiguity, the banding gives the building a bottom-heavy quality that makes it firmly grip the ground, where the extended attic story of Lutyens's bank tends to lift it above the congested street on which it stands. The use of movement at Manchester is so much less ironic than in Lutyens's bank that it cannot but convey a different sensibility, even though it derives from the same empathetic movement of implied forces. It is not the representation of paradox but the search for clarity in the face of it that is Greenberg's concern; yet from Lutyens Greenberg has drawn one important lesson, the lesson of the "qualified monumentality [that] enabled Lutyens to simultaneously imply greatness, yet accept the mundane."[8] This qualification of the monumental is crucial to Greenberg's attempt to adapt classical language to express the beauty of ideal order for the modern world.

McKim, Mead and White

The expression of this ideal order is present in the architecture of McKim in a way that it is not in the work of Lutyens, and it is to McKim that Greenberg has turned for a recent model of classical order.

Leland Roth has demonstrated the manner in which McKim, Mead and White, the most prolific architects of the American Renaissance, used precedent imitatively, that is, without copying, just as Greenberg uses it and as the quote from Locke suggests it should be used.[9] Their New York State Building at the World's Columbian Exposition (figure 173), for example is modeled after the Villa Medici in Rome, designed by Annibale Lippi in 1544 (figure 174). But as Roth notes:

In the garden facade of the Villa Medici the central element is recessed behind the side wings, and the roof heights, string courses, and all other horizontal lines of the villa are discontinuous from the wings to the center block. In the New York State Building, on the other hand, all horizontal lines are continuous, running completely around the building. The roof lines and cornice are made particularly prominent. Although some of the relief sculpture of the villa is absent to allow for more windows, an entirely new band of sculpture is introduced as a frieze below the cornice, containing within it small square windows. This richly modeled frieze further emphasizes the horizontal lines of the cornice.[10]

173 McKim, Mead and White, New York State building at the World's Columbian Exposition, 1893

174 Annibale Lippi, Villa Medici, Rome, 1544

Greenberg's adaptations from Lutyens are directly in line with this method, and the horizontality, regularity, simplicity, uniformity, hardness, tautness, and strengthened relationship to the ground visible in McKim, Mead and White's adaptation of the Villa Medici are also crucial to Manchester Superior Court, as in so many American artifacts.

These qualities are even more evident in McKim's greatest building, the Boston Public Library (figure 175). The models for the Boston Public Library were Henri Labrouste's Bibliothèque Sainte-Geneviève of 1843–50 (figure 176) and Alberti's S. Francesco in Rimini, begun in 1446 (figure 177). McKim retained Labrouste's concept of an arcaded second floor set on a heavy base with small windows. But where Labrouste expressed the thinness of the iron columns of the interior in the tall, fragile pilasters of his arcade, seeming to set a frame with infill panels on his base, McKim adopted Alberti's understanding of the pier as the only way to sustain the impression of a wall structure. To avoid the implied repetitiveness of Labrouste's extendible light frame, McKim reduced the number of arches in the arcade from nineteen to thirteen, thereby expressing a Roman massivity. McKim also gave the Boston Public Library three entrance arches instead of Labrouste's one, which increased the expression of the building as a solid mass by seeming to draw the sides toward the middle. The expression of horizontality is still there, however, and can be seen in the richer and more emphasized moldings of McKim's work. McKim strengthened the connection

to the ground and simplified the complexity of Labrouste's half-glass, half-stone infill panels by increasing the amount of glazing.

Manchester Superior Court clearly owes an intellectual debt to the Boston Public Library, but the newer building is modest rather than grand, qualified rather than imperialistic, and this modesty is derived from Alberti rather than McKim. Greenberg uses horizontal banding only where it is used by Alberti—the base, the springing of the arches, and the entablature—and both S. Francesco and Manchester Superior Court derive considerable expressive force from unadorned blank surfaces, while these are largely avoided by McKim. At Manchester, Labrouste's first floor is replaced by the slight plinth of S. Francesco. The number of arches is further reduced from thirteen to seven, back to the number in the south elevation of Alberti's church; but Labrouste's single opening is retained, recalling Alberti's front elevation. This elevation was the very first to graft a Roman triumphal arch onto a wall, and Alberti used as his model the Arch of Constantine (figure 178). Through Lutyens, McKim, Labrouste, Jefferson, Palladio, and Alberti, therefore, Greenberg reaches back to the architecture of Rome itself, and that distant triumphal rhythm is remembered in Greenberg's building, while the echo of Rome sounds in its details.

Perfectibility
Greenberg's courthouse establishes a continuity not solely with the ideals of eighteenth-century America, but

175 McKim, Mead and White, Boston Public Library, Boston, Massachusetts, 1887–98

176 Henri Labrouste, Bibliothèque Sainte-Geneviève, Paris, 1843–50

177 Leone Battista Alberti,
S. Francesco, Rimini, 1446

178 The Arch of Constan-
tine, Rome, 315 A.D., north
facade

also with the ideals of classical antiquity. The idealized representation of
man's perfectibility, patterned on the
majesty of nature and embodied in
the Orders, is the absolute value on
which Manchester Superior Court is
based.

It is not to irony, therefore, not to
the contradiction between the classical ideal and the impossibility of at-
taining it that Greenberg is drawn.
Rather he is drawn to the continuity
of this ideal and sees it as something
by which the seemingly chaotic state
of things is to be measured. Greenberg does not limn the world as it is,
as it ought to be, or as it might be,
but refers instead to a world in which
it is still possible to aspire to a more
perfect state despite the destruc-
tiveness of modern life. Unlike those
modernists to whom the utopian
apocalypse was not only possible but
imminent, Greenberg expresses a classicism that is not utopian but that attempts to open our eyes to what is
still noble in human nature, still
touched by the divine, and that excludes our weakness not because it
is not there, or because it can be
ignored, but precisely because it will
always be there.

Allan Greenberg, project
for a Holocaust memorial,
Battery Park, New York,
1984. Courtesy of Allan
Greenberg.

THE IRONIES OF
THE DIFFICULT
WHOLE
Gordon Wu Hall
Princeton, New Jersey
Venturi, Rauch
and Scott Brown,
Architects (1983)

THE PRINCETON CAMPUS

Princeton University rests on historic ground that slopes gently from Nassau Street south to Lake Carnegie (figure 179). Spreading laterally against the slope and confronting the town is Nassau Hall, which was built in 1756 and shelled during the Battle of Princeton (figure 180). A tall colonial spire rivets the building to its site at the apex of the campus. From the projecting southern wing of Nassau Hall, which thrusts down the hill like the barrel of a gun, runs the axis of the university. It passes first between isolated buildings from the nineteenth century, then tumbles through the varied courtyards of the twentieth, and finally passes through open fields to the lake.

Stylistic Diversity
From Cannon Green, through Tiger Mall, between the Greek Revival twins of Whig and Clio, then diagonally across open space, the axis runs its course to the mighty block of Brown Hall. Like a rock set in a river, Brown Hall, John Faxon's Richardsonian palazzo of 1891, diverts the axis from a single stately flow to rapids on either side, to the passage from court to court of collegiate Gothic.

Cuyler and 1903 Halls, of 1912 and 1929 respectively, form a pure collegiate Gothic group behind Brown Hall that takes its style from Day and Klauder's Holder group of 1910 and Cram and Ferguson's Graduate College, finished in 1913. The enclosed quad between Cuyler and 1903 Halls passes into a larger, longer, and more irregular court between Walker and Patton. While Walker is of the same collegiate Gothic vintage as 1903 Hall, Patton, finished in 1906, belongs to the earlier and less pure tradition of Princeton's East Pynne and Blaire Halls, to the Hampton Court Tudor of Henry VIII, castellated and quoined, with turrets for gables and towers in place of spires.

Extending southward down the slope from the swelling, octagonal tower of Patton are the diluted but still sensitively scaled collegiate Gothic buildings of 1915 Hall, the dormitories built in 1949 that make up one half of the newly formed Butler College. The other half of Butler is Venturi, Rauch and Scott Brown's Gordon Wu Hall, the dining, social, and library facility of the college. A narrow space between the new building and the returning wing of 1915 Hall (figure 181) forms an entry to the Gothic quads from the south, which complements in a larger scale the arched passages formed where Cuyler and 1903 and Cuyler and Patton meet.

Immediately to the east of the new building lies the sadly soulless Wilson College group of 1961, a parody of Mies van der Rohe's IIT campus posing awkwardly in Gothic rags. To this group belong both Gauss and Wilcox Halls; Wilcox connects directly to Gordon Wu Hall at the north, and Gauss is to the east and slightly separated from it. To the south lies Hugh Stubbins's unashamed Laurie-Love complex of 1964, the last buildings before open fields and the lake. The Stubbins buildings, however, are separated from the other campus buildings by the major cross axis of the campus, which is terminated in the west by the Gothic spire of the Graduate College and in the east by the modern Jadwin science tower (figure 182).

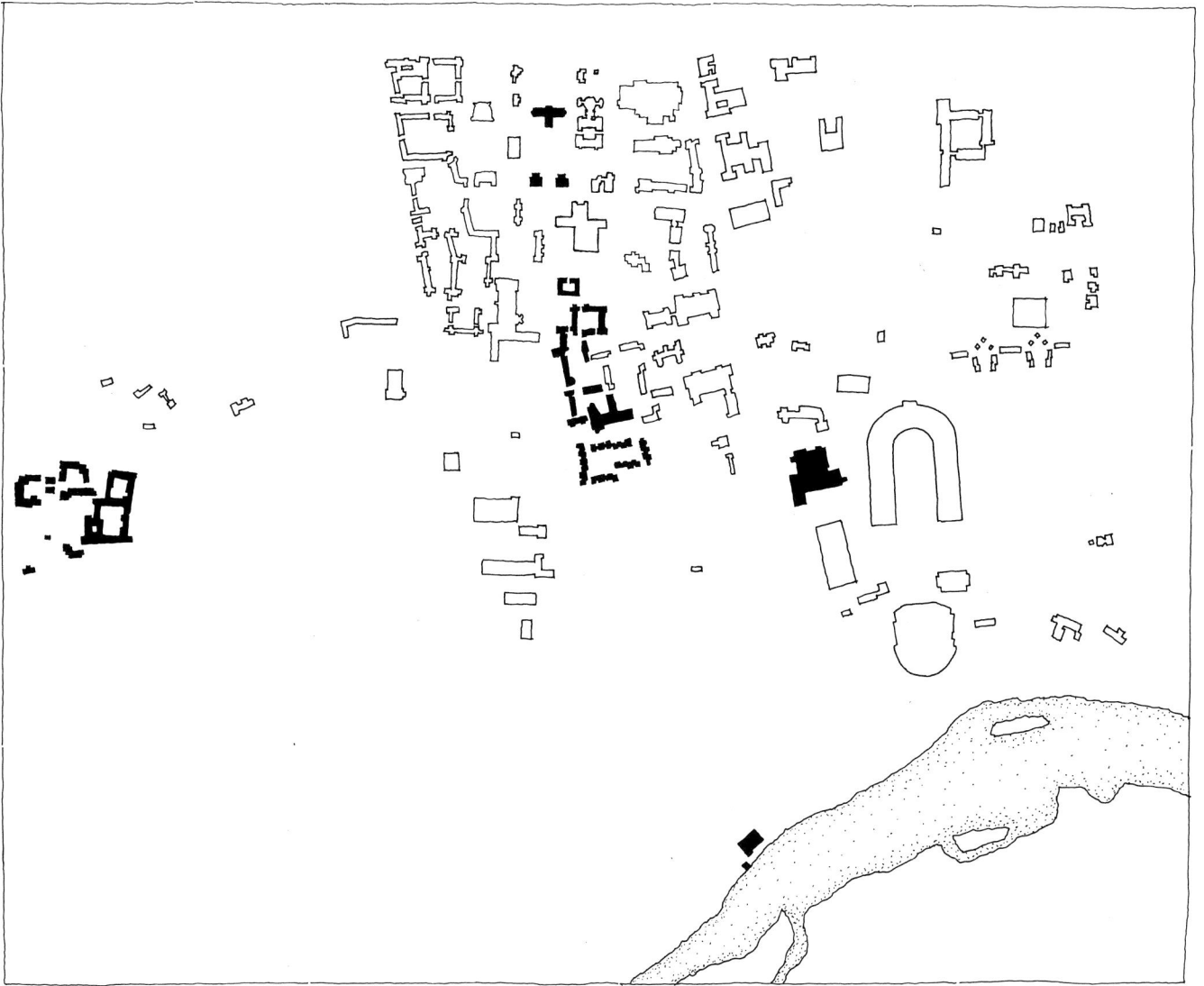

179 Figure-ground study of the Princeton campus showing the central axis and the cross axis defined by buildings drawn solid

180 Tiger Mall, Cannon Green, and Nassau Hall

181 Princeton campus with 1915 Hall on the left, Gordon Wu Hall on the right, the tower of Patton in the distance

182 The cross axis with Jadwin in the distance, Gordon Wu Hall and 1915 Hall on the left, and Laurie-Love on the right

Gordon Wu Hall therefore occupies a site exactly at the crossing of two major axes of the campus. The site is at the end of a procession of buildings in six completely different styles and is also part of a smaller series of enclosed courtyard spaces that flow into one another.

Butler College

In the campus as a whole, the institutional buildings, such as the library, chapel, infirmary, professional schools, and stadium fall generally to the east of the central axis; the residential halls fall mostly to the west. This separation reflects the historic development of the university, for in 1836 West College, the first dormitory building, was built to the west of Nassau Hall and in 1873 Chancellor Green, the first library building, was built to the east. The layout of Butler College can therefore be seen as analogous to the layout of the institutions of the campus because the dining, social, and library facilities of Gordon Wu Hall fall to the west of the axis and the dormitory buildings of 1915 Hall fall to the east.

More importantly, however, the spine of Butler College, running between the old buildings and the new, retraces the chronological development of the campus down the slope of the hill. It is divided into three sections: a flight of steps at the top, a stepped ramp in the middle, and a gentle slope down to the cross axis at the bottom (figure 183). While the flight of steps that passes between two large stone balls recalls Tiger Mall, the stepped ramp between two walls recalls the intimacy of the Gothic courts, connected by their easy gradient and punctuated by short flights of steps. The slope, with its elongated flower boxes and views on either side—east into the dining hall through a glass curtain wall and west out to the tennis courts—is similar to the fall of the open fields to the south. The spinal passage is terminated at the crossing of the campus's axes by a column topped with a flat marble tiger. The column stands in a patterned ellipse like a miniature lake of decoration, which distorts the curb (figure 184). The flat tiger is seen axially between the two stone balls at the top of the spine, completing and tying together the microcosmic image of the campus from Tiger Mall to Lake Carnegie.

Gordon Wu Hall

The spine emphasizes the most striking feature of Gordon Wu Hall, its linearity and the resulting flatness. The elevation is so flat that it seems as if the facade had been stretched tight by the pull of the axis (figure 185). Nothing projects beyond this plane save the eaves of a short length of pitched roof and its drain pipe. This sense of flatness is increased from a distance, when the angle at which the facade is seen is acute. At closer quarters, as the angle of vision approaches ninety degrees, the flatness is mitigated by a series of closely packed layers, compressed indentations parallel with the axis, which create a rhythm, advancing and receding, that gives a sensation of depth to the facade.

The tightly stretched facade is capped at either end by large semicircular bay windows, one at the southern extremity of the dining hall, the other at the northern tip of the grand

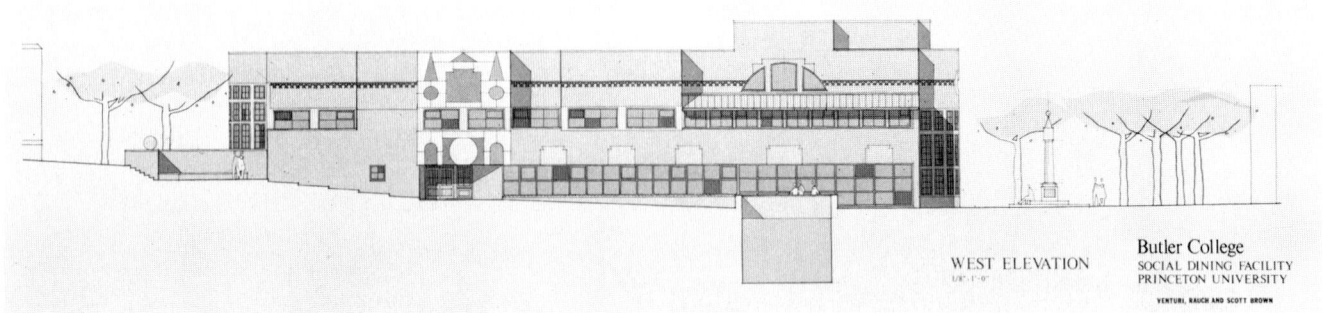

183 Long section through
the central axis of Butler
College, showing the long
elevation of Gordon Wu Hall

184 Gordon Wu Hall, with
the flat marble tiger in its
lake of decoration

185 Gordon Wu Hall

staircase. Although the latter is perfectly symmetrical, the former is not;
it rotates toward the tiger column and
away from Wilcox Hall, as if turning
the other cheek to the Utopian modernist buildings of Laurie-Love which
it faces.

Since these two bays are on the
university axis and will be seen immediately by anyone going up and
down the hill, they are made stylistically sympathetic with the majority
of buildings that surround them.
Their style is almost literally collegiate Gothic; that is, they hark back to
the sixteenth century in England, to
the modest domestic architecture of
the Tudor and Elizabethan periods
(figure 186), and echo such buildings
on campus as the McCosh Infirmary
(figure 187). The long facade of Gordon Wu Hall, on the other hand,
which will be seen at right angles by
students of Butler College passing
from 1915 Hall to the new building,
is stylistically independent of the
campus. It adds yet another style to
the procession along the central axis
and therefore imparts to the new college a uniqueness and an identity.
This style, which is the style of the
heraldic marbles over the entrance
gate to Gordon Wu Hall, derives from
the grand Elizabethan and Jacobean
"prodigy houses" of the late sixteenth
century in England, but it is treated
abstractly rather than literally.

Stylistically, then, what is invoked
in Gordon Wu Hall is the architecture
of late medieval England, the architecture of the years immediately
preceding Inigo Jones's proper classicism, the years when the old Gothic
traditions were being gradually over-
laid with the new fashion for classical

186 Kirby Hall, Northhamp-
tonshire, 1570–75, detail
showing bay windows

187 Isabella McCosh Infirmary, Princeton campus

details, emanating from Italian mannerism and arriving in England by way of France and the Low Countries.

STYLISTIC IMPURITY

The precedent at Princeton for the English medieval style was set in 1910 by Day and Klauder, whose complex of four dining halls, clustered around Holder Hall, provided the first collective eating facilities on the campus. Before these buildings were finished in 1918, students had eaten either in their rooms or at the numerous private dining clubs on Prospect Avenue. Gordon Wu Hall continues the tradition of collective eating started in Holder and the halls, but provides for the trend toward smaller groups.

The style of Holder, however, is academic, a scholarly recreation of the point at which the perpendicular Gothic was broken off during the reign of Henry VIII, after the dissolution of the monasteries. This, no doubt, is why Ralph Adams Cram, that fervent Goth of the perpendicular persuasion, praised the Holder group as "one of the most distinguished architectural creations in America" and claimed, somewhat optimistically, that "there is nothing better in Oxford or Cambridge, at Winchester or Eton."[1]

If the work by Day and Klauder, as that of Cram and Ferguson in their own Graduate College of 1913 is, in Cram's words, a "living architecture"[2] of pure perpendicular consistency, Venturi, Rauch and Scott Brown's Princeton building is by contrast a most impure architecture, binding together yeasty forces in an entirely different kind of living architecture.

This is as true in plan as it is in elevation, as true in regard to type as it is to style (figures 188, 189, 190). Gordon Wu Hall is based on the English medieval hall, with its bay window or oriel, elaborate entry porch, wooden screen separating entry and hall, grand staircase, and with the baronial fireplace displaced upstairs. Just as the architects of the Elizabethan hall maintained the construction techniques typical of the Gothic but added classical mannerist motifs to them, so Venturi, Rauch and Scott Brown make no apology for the construction techniques of modern architecture. The modern building tradition of adjoining Wilcox Hall is maintained. The enormous span of the long facade, for example, which one sees on the oblique above the ground floor, is not compromised by structurally unnecessary columns or arcades. The flat keystones recall the superseded structural system, however, but they are cut through with the expansion joints that are necessary in modern skin construction (figure 191). These keystones give the wall a rhythm that would otherwise be missing. They make the wall articulate in a way that the puerile, abstract patterns of Wilcox Hall's *brise soleil* do not. Similarly, the interior space of Gordon Wu Hall is open like modernist space; we are not presented with the enclosed rooms of a classical plan but rather with an open space reminiscent of Aalto, yet one that is loaded with complex allusions and references.

The desire for impurity prompts Venturi, Rauch and Scott Brown to return in the symbolic marble entry

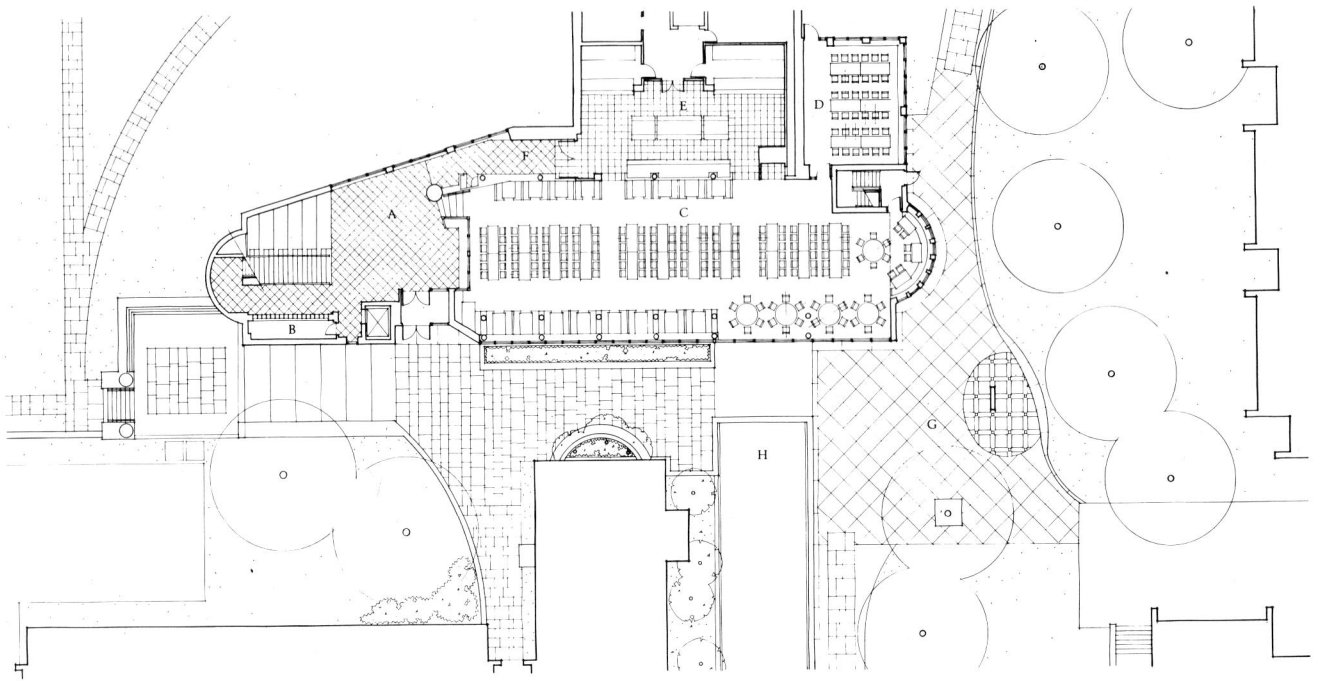

188 Gordon Wu Hall, plan of
first floor

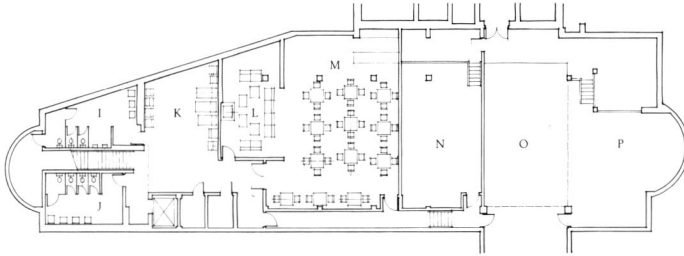

A Lobby
B Mail Room
C Dining Room
D Private Dining Room
E Serving Area
F Ramp
G Butler Memorial Plaza
H Service Ramp
I Men's Room
J Women's Room
K Game Room
L TV Room
M Coffee House
N Mechanical Room
O Loading Area
P Storage
Q Lounge
R Master's Office
S Secretary
T Office
U Workroom
V Conference
W Library

189 Gordon Wu Hall, plan of
basement

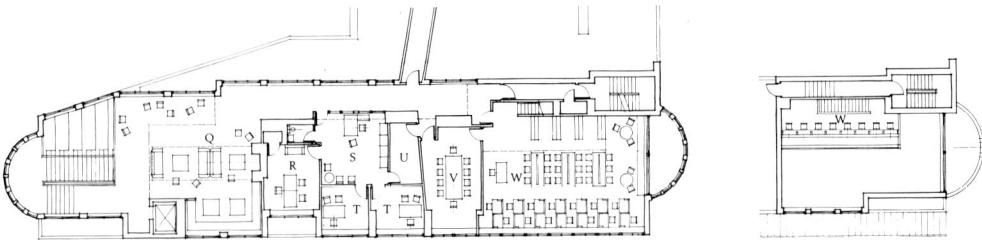

190 Gordon Wu Hall, plan of
second floor and mezzanine

191 Gordon Wu Hall, detail
of keystones on long
elevation

gate (figure 192) not to the pure
Gothic of the fourteenth and fifteenth
centuries, nor to the seventeenth-century purity of Inigo Jones's classicism,
but to the impure, eclectic architecture of the late sixteenth century, to
the Elizabethan and Jacobean prodigy
houses and those manneristic
"Jacobethan" halls at Oxford and
Cambridge universities.

It is not hard to identify the
Jacobethan motifs in the abstracted
heraldic marbles of the porch, which
faces onto the college courtyard as in
the medieval colleges at Oxford, such
as Wadham. A good comparison is the
marvelous courtyard porch at Burghley House of 1585 (figure 193). Its
basic rhythm is preserved in the Gordon Wu Hall gate. So too are the typically Elizabethan ornamental obelisks
surmounting strapwork circles and
the characteristic niches. The oversized motif between the two lions is
retained in the rectangular granite
panel of the center, and the central
pyramidal roof is amusingly recalled
by the miniaturized pediment surmounting the whole, a shape frequently found topping Jacobean
gables.

Just as Burghley mixes Gothic and
classical in an impure mannerist composition, so Gordon Wu Hall makes
an eclectic composition from modern,
Gothic, and classical elements. At
Burghley one finds a medieval bay
window wedged between pairs of correctly detailed Corinthian columns
harboring classical niches, whose
bases are ornamented with the mannerist strapwork of northern Europe.
In the gate of the Princeton building,
the medieval bay of Burghley has
been replaced by a pair of aluminum
windows, elegantly positioned in a

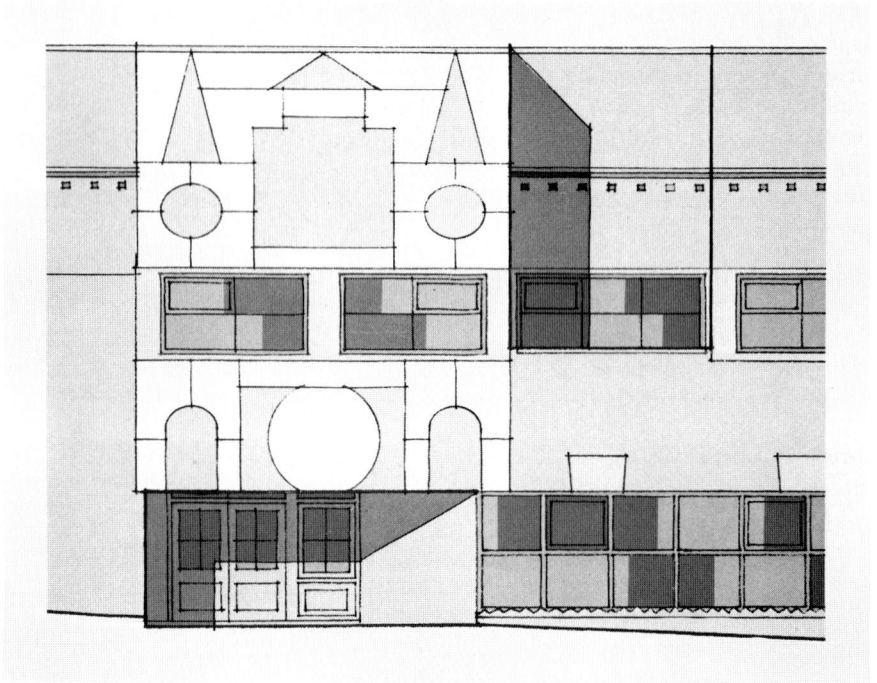

192 Gordon Wu Hall, entry
gate

193 Burghley house, North-
amptonshire, 1585, court-
yard gate

band of limestone that sets them off
against the flattened geometrical
shapes of their neo-Elizabethan neigh-
bors and disrupts the ABA rhythm of
the Burghley gate with the suggestion
of a continuous Corbusian ribbon
window. The flatness of these surrounding marble shapes is not without historical precedent, however.
Elizabethan fireplaces frequently had
elaborate geometrical overmantles
that are strikingly similar in appearance to Venturi, Rauch and Scott
Brown's gate; compare, for example,
those in the state dining room at
Bramshill house in Hampshire of
1603 (figure 194) and in the salon at
Charlton house in Kent of a slightly
later date. The geometries at Princeton, however, are rendered even flat-
ter and more abstract than these
Jacobean overmantles (figure 195).

No Jacobethan building, moreover,
would have lost the opportunity for
adding picturesqueness to its skyline
by making obelisks or pediments project above the roofline; indeed, all features capable of projecting vertically,
such as chimneys, gables, or balus-
trades, were exploited to the full.
Venturi, Rauch and Scott Brown deliberately avoid such opportunities
(figure 196). The chimney, for example, is suppressed, though it might
have projected, on axis perhaps, with
the entry gate; no pedimented gables
are introduced; and most of all, the
obelisks and pediment of the gate
touch the roof line with such astonishing reticence that they seem poised
for immediate blast-off, so powerful is
their upward movement, so tense
their tenuous pinpoint contact with
the sky. The forms beneath the obelisks and pediment seem to bear the
force of their suppression, as the ovals
are distorted from the circles of strap-

194 Chimney piece and
overmantle in the drawing
room at Bramshill house,
Hampshire, 1603. Drawn
and engraved by Henry
Shaw, 1839. "Altogether
executed in a . . . solid and
less ornamental style of art.
The design is classical after
the manner of Vignola . . .
the distribution of the
members is pure and regular
. . . the basement seems
almost too low for the order
above it."

195 Gordon Wu Hall,
overmantle

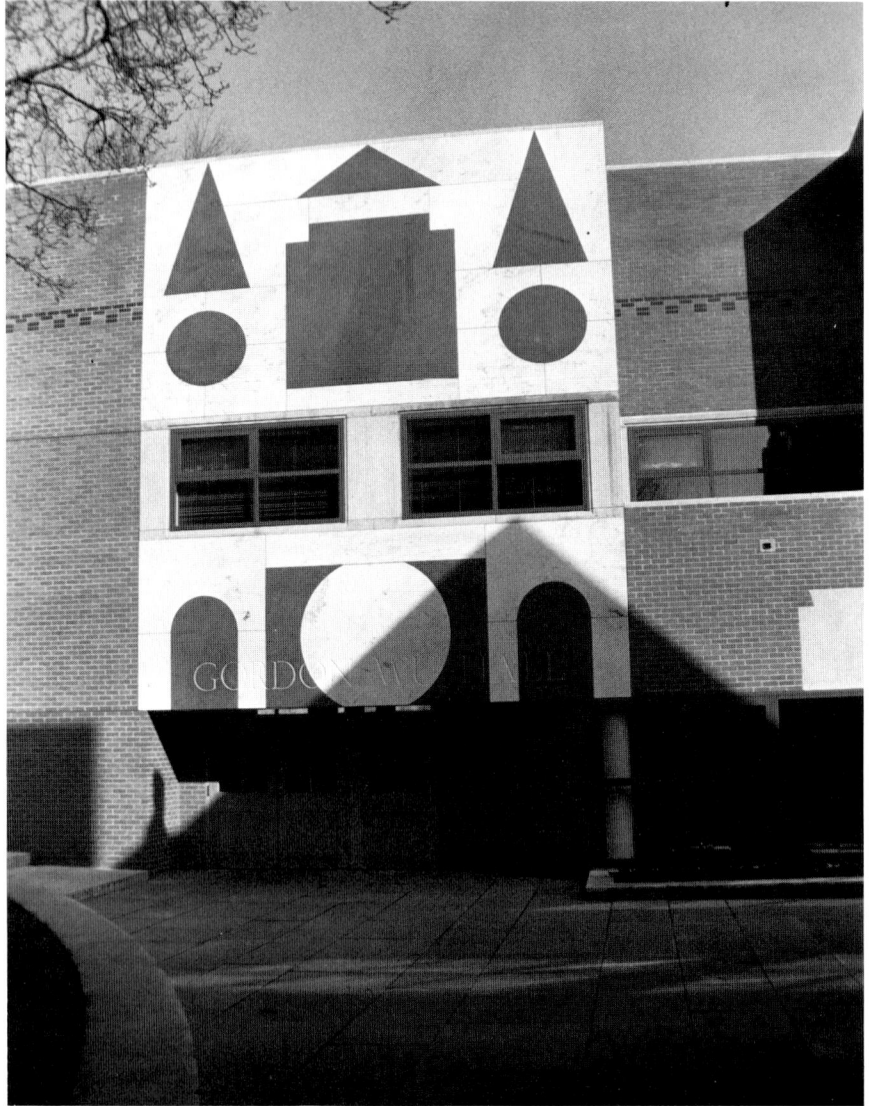

196 Gordon Wu Hall, marble
gate

work under the obelisks at Burghley
and the rectangle is distorted from the
square. The tension is also felt in the
sliced-off base of the decorative gate.
The niches seem very awkward without bases, as awkward as the odd proportions of the lowest horizontal
division in the background marble.
But this also lends the gate a tremen-
dous downward force, so that the two
compressed parts of the gate seem
ready to burst open with a blast of
sound, to shoot into the sky and slice
into the earth. Such indeed is the
character of Elizabethan porches and
gates. They are almost without excep-
tion extravagently vertical, while at
the same time ponderous, usually because of the piling up of Order upon
Order. In Gordon Wu Hall these mannerist, Jacobethan qualities are faith-
fully conveyed, but by abstraction,
which adds a level of distance, of
sophistication, of irony, to the oddly
naive architecture of the prodigy
houses as well as to the technological
idealism of Le Corbusier's ribbon
windows.

INFLUENCES

There are two predominant influences
on the way in which the elements
of Venturi, Rauch and Scott Brown's
impure architecture are combined in
Gordon Wu Hall: the architecture of
Le Corbusier and the architecture
of Sir Edwin Lutyens.

Le Corbusier

The Corbusian influence in Gordon
Wu Hall is evident in the proportion
of the facade at the point where it re-
sists the returning wing of 1915 Hall.
Here a standard pair of modern windows, made into a ribbon window by

their limestone backgrounds (backgrounds that derive from the construction of masonry windows, such
as those of Cuyler or other Gothic
quads), is surmounted by an apparently top-heavy mass of wall with a
large, continuous glazed opening beneath. This eccentric proportioning of
window to wall is much like that of
Le Corbusier's Villa Stein at Garches
(figure 197). Indeed, the central rectangular motif of the marble entry gate
takes on a ghostly after-image of the
central motival void of Le Corbusier's
composition.

As at Garches, the Princeton building has a perforated ground floor, an
extremely linear fenestration above,
and a high blank "attic" wall above
that. The ground floor, however, is
more transparent than it is at
Garches, and its function is to take
the place of those cuts in the facade
of the Villa Stein, the *coulisses* with
which Le Corbusier revealed the
depth of his building.

To the left of the rear elevation of
the Villa Stein (figure 198), for example, as also in the Pavilion de L'Es-
prit Nouveau, Le Corbusier allows a
view almost through to the back of
the front facade of the building. But at
the same time, overlapping this deep
space is a continuous, shallow slot of
space just behind the main frontal
plane. In the rear elevation of the
Villa Stein this is marked by the ter-
mination of the side walls of the roof
terrace and the back of the roof pavilion. On the front facade it is marked
by the interior of the central void in
the attic story. This shallow slot of
space just behind the main facade is
reiterated throughout the building.

The Princeton building, too, over-
laps deep space with shallow. One

197 Le Corbusier, Villa Stein
at Garches, 1929, front
elevation

198 Le Corbusier, Villa Stein
at Garches, 1929, rear
elevation

can see through the *coulisse* space of the ground floor glazing to a screen marking the plane of the back wall of the second floor. This is contradicted by the front doors, which mark a plane that extends across the front of the building and that is revealed several times as the plane of the second floor returns and advances. This plane is marked at either end externally by the returning bay windows and internally by the ends of the piers in the dining hall and the storage spaces near the stair (figure 199).

The use of such overlapping and interpenetrating deep and shallow space to produce "a simultaneous perception of different spatial locations"[3] has been termed *phenomenal transparency* by Colin Rowe and Robert Slutzky.[4] Rather than being a quality of substance, like the literal transparency of glass or Frank Gehry's literally deconstructed walls, phenomenal transparency is an inherent quality of organization. It is an abstract organizational structure based on layers of flat space, the full extent of which cannot be seen but can be understood conceptually. This organization of space in layers is as important in Gordon Wu Hall as it was in Venturi's early masterpiece, the Vanna Venturi house of 1962 (figure 200). As in the Villa Stein and the Vanna Venturi house, only more so, the result of phenomenal transparency in the Princeton building is that "central focus is consistently broken up, concentration at any one point is disintegrated, and the dismembered fragments of the center become a peripheral dispersion of incident, a serial installation of interest around the extremities of the plan."[5]

What differentiates Gordon Wu Hall from the Villa Stein as well as

199 Gordon Wu Hall, the
shallow slot of space

200 Venturi and Rauch,
Vanna Venturi house, Chestnut Hill, Pennsylvania, 1962,
front elevation

from the Vanna Venturi house is the degree of fragmentation caused by the extreme, mannerist development of the peripheral dispersion. In the Vanna Venturi house, Venturi did not stray from the formal unity of the Villa Stein. The large central window of Le Corbusier's ground floor became Venturi's entrance; the plane within the attic void, his fireplace mass, articulated the narrow slot of space; the ribbon windows were fragmented and forced lower in the composition, hugging the ground; the horizontal roof line, broken at the central void, was wrested into the archetypal gable of the late Shingle style. The "drifting Palladian memory"[6] of Frank Lloyd Wright's own Oak Park house was restated with new conviction.

As if the pieces had been put in a centrifuge, the Princeton building disperses the archetypal unity of these earlier buildings and elaborates the results produced at the Villa Stein by "the most catholic of eclectics,"[7] as Rowe has described Le Corbusier. The building is more qualified, less categorical. The "difficult whole" espoused by Venturi in *Complexity and Contradiction in Architecture* has been made more difficult, reviving the mannerist concept of *difficultà*, the conquest of formal and stylistic problems of deliberate difficulty in as apparently effortless a manner as possible.

Yet, while it may be that the compositional method of Gordon Wu Hall is derived from the phenomenal transparency of Utopian modernism, there is a great difference in the ends to which it is put. At Garches there was a strong spirit of rationalism, witnessed by Le Corbusier's *tracés régulateurs* and their mathematical

imprint on the facade. This spirit is to some extent still present in the Vanna Venturi house—the fragment of a circle is a *tracé régulateur* also—but it is now a different, more humanistic, more Vitruvian kind. In the Princeton building the post-Utopian sensibility is further developed; it is now the exact antithesis of Marinetti's explosive man-machine, "the man at the steering wheel, whose ideal axis passes through the center of the earth, whirling around on its orbit."[8] Gordon Wu Hall casts a more ironic and skeptical eye on late-twentieth-century man than the eye of the Renaissance humanist did on the *uomo universale* or than the Utopian modernist did on the "man at the steering wheel."

Lutyens
Where in the Vanna Venturi house there was the suggestion of Vitruvian man, though centered in a void, in Gordon Wu Hall Vitruvian man has come down from his cosmic arc of his own free will and has not been ripped from it, as in Eisenman's work. Man seems lonely in a way unknown to Alberti or to Marinetti. The centralized image of the traditional humanist man has been dispersed and this dispersal has led to a rejection of any obvious kind of hierarchy as a unifying principle. In its place is the most ambiguous of all the formal ordering principles of *Complexity and Contradiction in Architecture:* namely, the idea of "equal combinations."[9] But here the difficult whole of equal combinations is not achieved through the medium of classical elements, as in Michelangelo's Porta Pia, or through geometric abstraction, as in Sullivan's Grinnell Bank, but through

anthropomorphic imagery. This is
Venturi's greatest debt to Lutyens.

In the Jacobethan style buildings
Lutyens built at the turn of the century, such as Deanery Garden of 1901
or Marshcourt of 1901–4 (figure 201),
we can see his habit of allowing elements of an anthropomorphic character to push from the inside spaces out
onto a relatively neutral field. The projections of the long facade of Gordon
Wu Hall have exactly this quality of
being pushed out from inside, and they
are just as full of anthropomorphism.

In the long elevation of the new
building there are at least three main
faces looking out on the spinal column of the college—the architectural
portraits, as it were, of those who
pass beneath (figure 202). The most
dramatic of these faces is that of the
abstracted Jacobethan entrance porch.
A comparison with Lutyens's addition
at Abbotswood of 1901 (figure 203)
shows how close the attitude to
human features is in both cases.
Throughout Gordon Wu Hall, in fact,
windows become eyes and other
openings become mouths and noses.
This is a quality absolutely foreign to
a Corbusian building.

What is true of architectural elements is also true of the attitude toward the abundant architectural
sculpture of the Jacobethan period.
On passing through the gate of Gordon Wu Hall, one finds oneself
slightly above the dining tables, looking out over them to the bay windows
at the far end of the room, of which
only the bottom half can be seen.
The traditional screen of the Elizabethan hall is replaced with a carefully
situated seat. Early Renaissance
screens like the one at Audley End
(figure 204) are always ornately carved

201 Sir Edwin Lutyens,
Marshcourt, Kings Som-
bourne, near Stockbridge,
Hampshire, 1901–4

202 The faces on the long
facade of Gordon Wu Hall

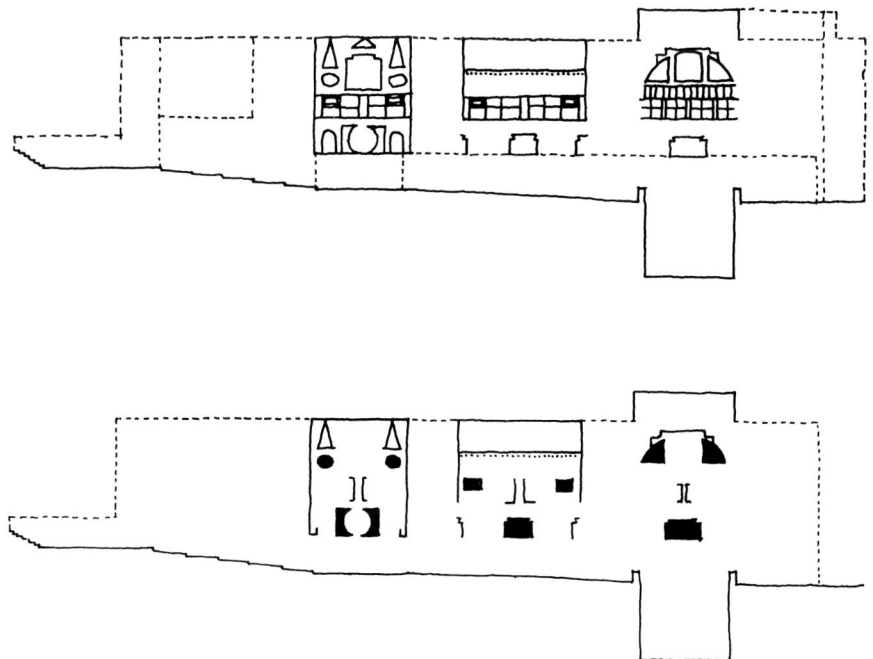

203 Sir Edwin Lutyens,
Abbotswood, Lower Swell,
Gloucestershire, 1901

204 Audley End, carved
screen in the Great Hall

and in most cases feature humanoid columns, such as those derived from northern European pattern books. The screens also continue but distort the Gothic tradition of telling stories on cathedral facades. By replacing the screen with a seat, by then putting the seat in its self-consciously axial location, and by raising it above the floor of the dining room so that those who sit on it are prominently displayed, the architects have neatly replaced the sculpture of the original model with the students of the college. Perhaps this attitude toward Elizabethan sculptural decoration also accounts for the odd proportioning of the niches in the entry gate; the sculpture has, so to speak, fallen out, moved through time, and become the actual inhabitants of the building.

This theme is brought to a climax in the generosity of the main stair, which is by far the grandest space in the building. The medieval stair is referred to in the Princeton building, but as its nineteenth-century American reincarnation, the living halls of Emerson, Eyre, and others of the mature Shingle style. These living halls developed from the influence of Richard Norman Shaw's evocation of the medieval hall in his so-called Queen Anne style (which was, in truth, neo-Elizabethanism). The result was a large, open hall for general use, more relaxed and fluid in character than the English Queen Anne, which featured a broad staircase that usually increased in width at the bottom. Often, light descended into the space from a stair landing. This is the immediate model for the Princeton staircase (figure 205), which resembles, for example, the one in Emerson's C. J. Morrill House at Mount Desert, Maine (figure 206), with its double-

205 Gordon Wu Hall, staircase

206 William Ralph Emerson, Redwood, C. J. Morrill house, Mount Desert, Maine, 1879, staircase

height space over part of the stair, generous stair landing, benches, and luminous bay window. Venturi has combined the Shingle style staircase with echoes of its ancestor, the sculpturally enriched Jacobethan stair. When the ample seating accommodations on the stair itself, at the half landing, and at the head of the stair facing the lounge are full of students, the scene recalls the conventional figure sculpture of Jacobethan newel posts and the required procession of family portraits up the walls of the stair, as in the famous example at Hatfield House or in the less well known staircase at Godinton in Kent (figure 207).

Gordon Wu Hall is a building permeated with anthropomorphism, therefore, not only in its forms, but in the absence of those forms most difficult to reproduce today, namely conventional architectural sculpture. Yet the building is far from symbolizing an anthropocentric condition because of the consistent dispersal of any hierarchic order into "equal combinations."

VESTIGIAL PERFECTIBILITY

The staircase may recall the Shingle style, but the dining hall is based on the original medieval examples. It is a navelike space with an apse at the far end and a regular rhythm of vaults marking the ceiling. The glazed wall area facing west increases as the hill falls off to the south, and this larger glazed area marks a transept that acknowledges the vehicular ramp down to the service dock. That, of course, is only the local reason for the cross axis. The larger purpose of the transept is to mark the cross axis of the

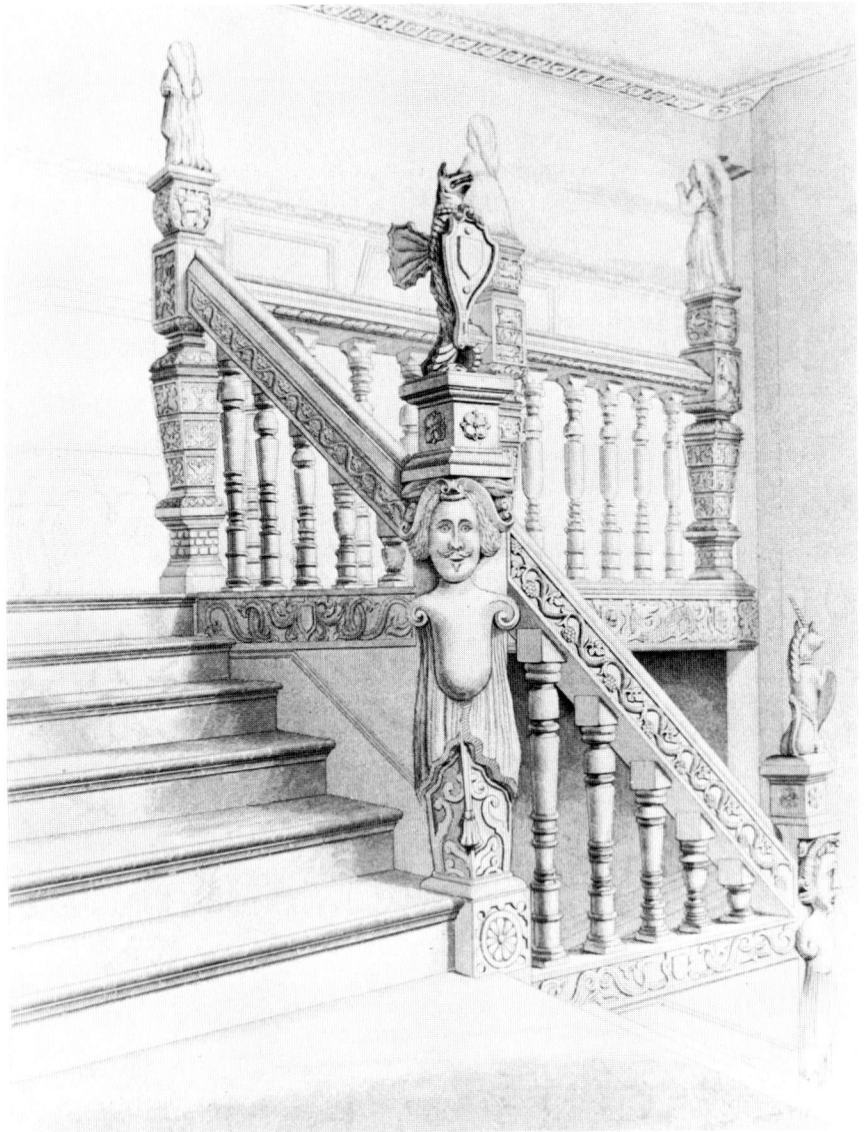

207 Staircase at Godinton, Kent, 1627. Seat of N. R. Toke. Drawn and engraved by Henry Shaw, 1839.

university. Thus the bay-windowed apse forms a terminus to the path from the Jadwin science tower, and the facade of the dining hall greets those crossing from the Graduate College by way of the tennis courts (see figure 182). This crossing of axes is registered in the dining hall by its central, cross-vaulted ceiling bay, the only bay not treated as a barrel vault, and by its cruciform lighting fixture (figure 208).

In addition to the dominant peripheral composition of the building, therefore, there is also a vestigial centrality. The marking of this centrality on the outside of Gordon Wu Hall says much about its secret life.

The crossing is marked on the long facade with a strong axis composed of five stacked elements: the ramp, a flat keystone, a length of pitched roof, an arched window, and a section of wall raised above the roof line. The three-part arched window, which is a clerestory light to the library, is the most dramatic of these elements. The triple-divided arch is a Roman motif, well known from the Baths of Caracalla. It was given currency again in postmedieval times by Palladio, who used it frequently, but perhaps nowhere more potently than in the Villa Malcontenta (figure 209). The Roman baths were magnificent centralized spaces, and in the Malcontenta Palladio consciously referred to them by creating a space no less centralized. In Gordon Wu Hall, however, the triple-divided arch is a sign of the loss of humanist centrality rather than another incarnation of it.

As in the Malcontenta, the arch of Gordon Wu Hall interrupts a horizontal cornice, which Venturi, Rauch and Scott Brown extend around the building as a binding element. While such decorative bands are a device Venturi has used on several occasions, as in the Guild House or in the Knoll Showroom in New York, to give coherence to a complex form, the band has a more specific meaning at Princeton. The cornices of Gordon Wu Hall and the Villa Malcontenta have similar compositions: the cymatium, the corona, and the modillions of Palladio's work are abstracted into a flat strip at the top, a broken strip underneath, and a row of dots (figure 210). This cornice defines a ratio between attic and piano nobile almost identical to that of Palladio's building. Moreover, the upper pediment of Palladio's building is restated above the semicircular window in Gordon Wu Hall by the raised section of wall.

The grave aspect of the Villa Malcontenta results from its top-heaviness, which is produced by the high attic and the upper pediment. Both press down on the rest of the building, and the pressure is increased by the inversion of the rustication, where the attic is rusticated while the base is smooth. This pressure is registered by the "roman baths" motif which seems to sink between the broken pieces of horizontal cornice. The effect in Gordon Wu Hall is similarly grave and yet it is witty also. The tall attic presses down on the building, the high lump of wall above the "roman baths" window presses down on the attic, the keystone falls from its arch, and the window "sets" beneath the horizon of the cornice, rolls off

208 Gordon Wu Hall, view looking up at light fixture in the center of the crossvault

209 Andrea Palladio, Villa Malcontenta, Mira, c. 1550–60, rear elevation

210 Detail of the decorative
brick band on Gordon Wu
Hall

211 The sun setting in the
arched window of Gordon
Wu Hall

the pitched roof, as it were, into the void created by the ramp.

This is no coincidental allusion. The window faces due west and at dinnertime the light of the setting sun streams through the curtain wall of the transept. Outside the sun does indeed set in the arch of the window, a great red ball slowly rolling down the ramp into the nether regions (figure 211).

If the sun sets on the humanism of the Renaissance and its symbolic centrality at the transept, as it does also on the perfectibility presupposed by Utopian modernism, then the day of a lyric modernism of impurity dawns in the fresh white circle of the entrance gate, and its ascent is proclaimed by the upward thrusts of the obelisks and pediment.

TYPES OF ORDINARINESS

This brings us to the core of Venturi's work: the transition from the idealism of early modern architecture to the belief that what is important is "the world as it is, not as it ought to be."[10]

Le Corbusier's 1923 comparison in *Towards a New Architecture* of a Delage automobile with the Parthenon (figure 212) focused attention on "the problem of *perfection*."[11] Once a standard was established for modern architecture as for the parts of a Greek temple or those of a car, Le Corbusier argued, refinement and competition would inevitably, by a kind of mechanical selection, produce "a speedy transformation. . . . A new aesthetic would be formulated with astonishing precision."[12] In *Learning from Las Vegas* Venturi, Scott Brown, and Izenour made a similar comparison between the Arch of Constantine and a Tanya billboard on Route 91 (figure 213). What is important now is the communication through signs of the sensibility of the world as it is. It is not perfection of form according to intrinsic "standards" (a perfection symbolizing the Utopia to be brought about through architecture—"Architecture or Revolution" in Le Corbusier's imperious phrase) that is embodied in Gordon Wu Hall. Rather, what is embodied in the building is the desire to articulate impure forms that will symbolize the existing conditions of life.

This concept of "ordinariness," of life as it is, has many levels of expression in Venturi's work. Early projects by Venturi and Rauch which sought this "ordinariness," such as the Football Hall of Fame, are obviously not merely ordinary but rather "represent ordinariness symbolically."[13] The approach was honed in later buildings and projects, such as those for BEST products and Dansk, where the American vernacular stands reflected, the glitter of Las Vegas's lights and the wagon wheels of Levittown. It is not by chance that in *Learning from Las Vegas* the lights of the Strip are likened to the mosaics of the Sicilian chapel of the Byzantine Martorama in Sicily, no longer glittering with the passage of the sun but dazzling the eye with the artificial movement of the neon light. Worlds turn, and man's gods change. With icy calmness Venturi points his finger at the world when in the gallery of the Football Hall of Fame (figure 214) he fills the vault of heaven with the stars of sport, as the Adam of Michelangelo's

THE PARTHENON, 447-434 B.C.

the run of the whole thing and in all the details. Thus we get the study of minute points pushed to its limits. Progress. A standard is necessary for order in human effort.

DELAGE, "GRAND-SPORT," 1921

212 Le Corbusier, comparison of a Delage automobile and the Parthenon, 1923

213 Venturi, Scott Brown, and Izenour, comparison of Tanya billboard and the Arch of Constantine, 1972

214 Venturi and Rauch,
Football Hall of Fame, 1967,
interior arcade

Sistine Ceiling floats, disconnected from his God, among the heroes of a new Valhalla.

But if such direct symbolism of the ordinary is appropriate to the entertainment of crowds at the Football Hall of Fame, is it also appropriate to house the dining, social, and library functions of a group of Princeton undergraduates? Obviously not. So what is it that the ordinariness of the Strip really represents after all its lessons have been learned? An acceptance of "the world as it is, not as it ought to be."

The world as it is clearly contains the Las Vegas gambler, the football fan, and the Ivy League student, and who is to say that one is superior to the other? The Princeton building does not represent ordinariness in a blatant way, for now decorum rules against the image of the Strip. Nor does it represent "ordinary" periods of architectural history, such as the Colonial, the Shingle style or the Greek Revival that are accessible to the American eye, for now history is servant to another master. It is the intrinsic "ordinariness" of people, the essential belief of American democracy in equivalence that underlies the architecture of Gordon Wu Hall. Through "equal combinations" of impure, anthropomorphic forms, Venturi restores to America the message of its constitution, just as in his houses on Nantucket he traced America's loneliness in its vast landscape through "ordinary" periods of history or in the Football Hall of Fame used the "ordinary" forms of the American commercial vernacular to record the isolation of its heroes in the flashy nearness of the Strip.

Gordon Wu Hall also holds up a mirror to reality, which is why it was conceived as a microcosm of the campus, drawing it in along its axes. The building is sophisticated, witty, erudite, and self-consciously disdainful of the Las Vegas aesthetic, though not of its lessons: in short, a mirror of the preppy undergraduate—stylish, clever, complicated, anxious about his or her deportment. No doubt the building is in part a humorously ironic look into Venturi's own Princeton undergraduate experiences. Strip, campus, or any aspect of the world as it is, the sensibility is the same. As Vincent Scully remarked long ago of the infamous television aerial atop the Guild House, that lightning rod of so much narrow-minded criticism: "Whatever dignity may be in that, Venturi embodies, but he does not lie to us once concerning what the facts are."[14]

THE DIFFICULT WHOLE

The representation of the world as it is at Princeton is achieved by a candescent show of erudition and scholarship. The full scope of that historical sense Venturi defined in the preface to *Complexity and Contradiction in Architecture* with a quote from T. S. Eliot has been unleashed:

The historical sense involves perception, not only of the pastness of the past, but also of its presence; the historical sense compels a man to write not merely with his own generation in his bones, but with a feeling that the whole literature of Europe . . . has a simultaneous existence and composes a simultaneous order.[15]

If Las Vegas is in the marrow of Venturi's bones, so too does he feel the whole history of architecture and thus expresses in Gordon Wu Hall Eliot's "simultaneous order."

As one of the most impure periods of architecture, the Jacobethan period provides an appropriate framework for the display of stylistic virtuosity in the Princeton building. The virtuosity of Venturi, Rauch and Scott Brown's building, crashing together Le Corbusier and Palladio, Lutyens and Gothic, mannerism and the Shingle style, Aalto and Rome, is a triumph of *difficultà*. Michelangelo's ghost on the vault of the Football Hall of Fame is a telling one, therefore, for his conquest of the human figure in the Sistine ceiling reveals that same sense of difficulty added to difficulty present in the Princeton building. Michelangelo's bodies twist this way and that, just as the complex references of the Princeton building interlock and mesh together, in each case maintaining that mannerist quality of *sprezzatura*, of well-bred negligence born of complete self-possession.[16]

Venturi, Rauch and Scott Brown's building uses *difficultà* to construct a mirror of reality, and this mirror presents both the polished surface and the inner tensions of the students it reflects. The silent portraits of the long facade, the empty niches of the marble gate, the hall's expanse of seat and stair: all await their *sprezzatura* sculpture. Hatfield House and Godinton will come to life again. The hall compresses like the squeezing of a giant bellows. Reality intrudes upon the careful artifice, and the bay windows stretch up their double height as if emitting a shrill whistle, the escaping steam from a tense and overwrought world.

But these are only one group of
players. If Adam is reborn on the
vault of the Football Hall of Fame, it
is Eve who is reborn as Tanya on
Route 91. The progeny of these
figures, Las Vegas gambler no less
than Ivy League student, are Ameri-
cans themselves. These are the people
who make up the "crowds of anonymous individuals without explicit
connection with one another"[17] that
people Venturi's America. From them
a canvas of contemporary life emerges,
and for them Venturi's architecture is
a wry offering of gentleness in the de-
humanized environment of the modern world.

The difficult whole

EPILOGUE
The City: A Machine for
Thinking In

"Do you suppose that some day a
marble tablet will be placed on the
house, inscribed with these words?

In This House, on July 24th 1895
The Secret of Dreams was Revealed
to Dr. Sigm. Freud

At the present time there seems little
prospect of it."[1]

THE PROBLEM OF CONTENT

In examining the secret life of buildings, I have inevitably been con-
fronted with the problem of content.
This issue is of the utmost importance for the development of modern
architecture because it addresses the
system of interrelations that cause
meaning. The subject has a distinguished modernist pedigree, having
been of fundamental concern to
Freud, Saussure, Levi-Strauss, and
Barthes, among others. An analysis of
content in architecture must build on
this tradition while avoiding overly
literal translations from other disci-
plines. I shall attempt to do this by
outlining three levels of content in architectural form: the literal, the representational, and the mythological.

Literal Content
In their analysis of the architecture of
Utopian modernism in *The International Style: Architecture Since 1922*,
Hitchcock and Johnson condensed
and exaggerated certain significant
and widespread tendencies of the
time. Their three principles—architecture as volume, regularity, and
avoidance of applied decoration—
were strictly formal ones by which an
outward expression of the one right
zeitgeist supposedly could be ensured.
Contemporary work of manifest value

in the Art Deco style or in the classical manner was either actively condemned or ignored outright. Since
there could be only one correct expression of the "terms of the day,"[2] as
they put it, there was no point in con-
ducting an examination such as the
one I have undertaken. This is not to
say that the concept of secret life
would have been alien to them or
their contemporaries, but simply that
in the ideology of the Utopian period
its investigation would have yielded
total consistency. Any other conclusion would have denied the force of
a homogeneous zeitgeist dispersed
throughout civilization. This ideology
led to an obsessive critical and professional interest in what we may call
literal content, to an amnesiac and
contextless concern for the purely
material aspect of buildings.

That we may now look back on the
great buildings of the Utopian period,
apply different methods of criticism
from those of the Utopian critics, and
see their secret lives as rich and in-
consistent is no contradiction. It is
simply the reflection of our own posthistoricist preoccupations. Great
buildings always transcend the ideology that brings them into being and
lend themselves to reinterpretation.
Each new generation can see itself
within them, for the secret life of architecture is affected not only by the
historicity of the building but also by
the historicity of the interpreter.[3]
This is precisely why cities are living
artifacts.

What should concern us, however,
is the lesson we can learn from the
impoverishment of the relationship
between literal content and secret life
during the Utopian period. The tendency in many works of Utopian

modernism was to mistake literal content for the secret life present in the greatest examples of the period. The resultant overemphasis on formal issues became extraordinarily destructive, especially toward the end of the Utopian period, producing an emptiness and banality unparalleled in the history of architecture. This tendency continues today and is responsible for sabotaging many current attempts to establish a wiser modernism. It is responsible for the spurious stylistic eclecticism that frequently bedevils contemporary work and has all too often led to a desiccated typological rationalism.

Stylistic eclecticism in itself simply provides a wider range of literal content. It eschews the idea of a zeitgeist that determines what may and what may not be acceptable manifestations of a period. This has great value as a tool; however, as dogma it simply compounds the problem inherent in Utopian modernism—mistaking literal content for secret life—by providing even more alternative guises.

As I stated earlier, the concept of type is as fundamental a tool of the lyric modernist as style. It is far saner than function for those processes of classification by which the past can be made useful as a mentor because forms endure over time while functions change. Yet as a doctrine for the making of architecture, the rationalism founded on typology is as limiting as one erected on stylistic eclecticism. It is flawed because it does not address the diversity of secret life in buildings derived from the same type. It may, in fact, be said to have substituted a tyranny of form for a tyranny of function. Functionalism

deprived architects of liberty in cultural representation by imposing on them a "spirit of the age." Rationalism exerts the same restraint through an "autonomy" of form supposedly found in the type and resulting from the endurance of form through great changes in function.[4] Rather than reducing form to the shape of an epochal essence, it instead demands the reduction of form to a typological essence. Such forms must be stripped of anything that would compromise the purity of the type and encumber it with the cultural experiences of the architect. Where previously the superhuman force was in the will of history, now it is in the world of objects. In short, functionalism, eclecticism, and rationalism are all useful as tools but destructive as dogmas since none in itself enables us to deal effectively with the secret life of buildings. Yet if we are to comprehend the transformation that modern architecture has undergone, we cannot afford to separate form from those meanings which comprise its secret life.

Representational Content
The Utopian obsession with literal content put architects in an enigmatic relation to imagery in buildings. Phenomena of the machine age inspired and excited them. Cubism, technology, or industrial processes seemed to embody the very meaning of the new world.[5] However, such phenomena were presented as offspring of a zeitgeist that would also give birth to an architecture deemed truly expressive of modern times. These phenomena were perceived more as so many aspects of a force destined to conquer the modern city than as what they

were in practice—sources of imagery
with which modern architects labored
to block out the past.

This negative conception of imagery was perfectly supported by the
Utopian modernist's view of memory,
expression, and morality. Both empathy and association, from which
imagery is derived, depend on memory. Since the past, however recent,
was for the Utopianist always inferior
to the present, both were also clearly
subordinate to the faculty of intuition, that sextant for historicist minds
adrift in the "eternal present."[6] Any
conscious use of imagery was therefore seen as at best, if resulting from
recent history, an illusion of the gen-
uinely modern forms possible only
through the union of intuition and
the spirit of the age, and as at worst,
if resulting from traditions of greater
antiquity, an assault on the unfolding
of history itself.[7] The use of imagery,
in other words, was condemned as a
counterfeit system of reality, to be
opposed by the full range of moral
arguments.

As the historicist underpinnings of
the Utopian period have collapsed, so
the web of justifications for begrudg-
ingly tolerating a narrow range of imagery in buildings has been torn apart.
The imagistic level of content—what
we may call representational content—is for us the means of visibly
articulating the fact of cultural diversity. All the works we have considered employ both natural and
architectural forms of representational
content, whether in the waves,
clouds, and fins of the Gehry house,
the mountains of the Portland building, and the faces of Gordon Wu Hall
or in the Piranesian deformations of

House El Even Odd, the romantic
classicism of Four Leaf Towers, or the
Shingle Style and American colonial
roots of the Bozzi house and Manchester Superior Court.

Despite the increased scope of both
natural and architectural imagery, one
image stands out as having successfully displaced the machine from its
preeminent position. This is the image of the human figure. The influence of the figure in its natural form
is extensive, from its overt anthropomorphic aspects, as we have seen
them in the Portland Public Service
Building, to its more abstract aspects,
such as the symmetry of the Four
Leaf Towers. The influence of the
figure in its architectural form is
equally far-reaching, through its embodiment in the classical vocabulary—from classical revivalism on the
one hand to the deliberate inversion
of classical precedent on the other.

The pervasive influence of the human figure in the representational
content of modern architecture has,
however, a significance deeper than
its value as a flexible currency of aesthetic expression. For while the figure
itself is by no means a universal image in modern architecture now, any
more than the machine was previously, it is symbolic of the general
shift from an identification of architecture with anonymous historical
forces to its identification with the
mystery and variety of individual personality. Thus, it is individual memory of the past as mentor that permits
representational content, displacing
unalloyed intuition from its hallowed
but hollow role as a weathervane of
the zeitgeist. Empathy and association
inventively applied now inform an ar-

chitecture expressing a breadth of cultural meaning that can arouse Scott's
"true ethical analogy" and echo in
our moral sense.

While Scott himself claims that the
purely physical experience of architectural form is primary and association
is destructive, he stresses that what
he calls "literary ideas" are nevertheless "its *ultimate* value." He states:

Since man is a self-conscious being,
capable of memory and association,
all experiences of whatever kind will
be merged, after they have been experienced, in the world of recollection—
will become part of the shifting web
of ideas which is the material of literary emotion. And this will be true of
architectural experience. . . . There is,
therefore, so to say, a literary background to the purely sensuous impression made upon us by plastic form,
and this will be the more permanent
element in our experience. . . . In the
last resort, as in the first, we appreci-
ate a work of art not by the single instrument of a specialized taste, but
with our whole personality.[8]

It is this experience that the deepest
level of content in the buildings I
have examined provides.

Mythological Content
Neither the exaggerated importance of
literal content nor the deliberately
weakened role of representational
content would have been possible in
Utopian modernism but for the ideology of historicism. The belief in the
unraveling of history according to social laws analogous to those of the
physical sciences produced among architectural theorists the unfortunate
belief that each age must produce
work unique to itself *in all ways*. The
embodiment in architectural form of

what we now perceive as deeply en-
trenched cultural beliefs that are
experienced "with our whole personality" I shall term mythological
content.

The misguided attempt of the Utopian period to develop a theory of homogeneous mythological content
disguised as scientific "truth" is the
single most destructive legacy of the
period. Its central myth—a techno-
functional determinism based on historicist ideology strong enough to
bring about the myth of the end of
myth—was aggressively anti-urban in
its demand for homogeneity of literal
content in the face of evident urban
diversity. Rejection of this myth does
not mean that lyric modernism is
necessarily antitechnological (rather,
it has enlarged the narrow scope of
Utopian representation) nor that it is
antivisionary (rather, the less mired in
historicism, the more winged mythological speculation may become).
Lyric modernism is fundamentally
urbanistic, based as it is on the belief
that an architectural mythology cannot but originate in diverse inhabita-
tion of the urban realm.[9]

As my analysis has shown, the collapse of a modernist ideology founded
on historicism has permitted a diversity of cultural expression in modern
architecture. The representational
content of form acts as a key to this
deep level of significance. Thus, the
marine imagery of Gehry's house enables us to understand a particular
condition of centrality, just as the
Jacobethan gate of Wu Hall leads us
to an understanding of a particular
condition of ordinariness. Ultimately,
these conditions address the varied effects of developed industrial culture
on man in the late twentieth century.

They articulate a diversity of mythological content no longer falsely controlled by a supposedly superhuman force, but rightly the result of individual human consciousness.

To understand the passage from the Utopian to the lyric period of modernism, and to effectively investigate work of this period, we must consider architecture as the expression of the many effects of industrial culture on man rather than as built historicist ideology; we must be concerned with the representational content of buildings rather than with the abstraction of essence from form; and we must free ourselves from the obsession with literal content for its own sake. In this way the comprehension of our present situation also opens the door to a comprehension of the full output of the modernist years.

An obsession with the historicist view of history meant that very few historians of modern architecture writing during the Utopian period considered the total architectural production of the years on which they focused.[10] Their examinations do not compare Lutyens with Le Corbusier, for example, or Asplund with Mies, or Cass Gilbert with Walter Gropius, despite the fact that these architects produced work of exceptional quality at precisely the same time. It therefore falls to us to consider the mythological content of this work and to construct a sane historical framework for modern architecture capable of providing a sound basis for its further development. In other words, we must acknowledge a unity of an altogether different order: not the false order of an imposed homogeneity, *but*

the living unity in diversity that is the fact of modern life.

That it should be American buildings and not European ones that best demonstrate the transformation of the Utopian period is no coincidence, because the period we have entered is profoundly affected by the tension and resolution in the fundamentally American condition of diversity within unity. History is no longer a burden to be cast aside by the triumphant man-machine; rather, immigrant architectural histories now find themselves in the melting pot of a developed industrial culture. We seek our great gestures now in the reconciliation of opposites, in the difficult art of joining, rather than in the undisputed fact of separation. This is why I speak of an American mythology for modern architecture.

The subject of these myths is the figure in the shadows who has been present throughout this book. My analyses have illuminated many different aspects of this figure, from the shattered, alienated individual of House El Even Odd to the beleaguered but resolute occupant of Manchester Superior Court. If we are to grasp the mythological unity of these buildings and to justify my contention that they are indicative of a new period of modern architecture, we must understand this figure. To do so I shall consider not the architecture of the city but the soul of a city—the secret city of lyric modernism, formed from the mythological content of my analyses. This city is no longer a utopian house for mechanized living but a machine for thinking in, the house of the figure in the shadows.

THE FIGURE IN THE SHADOWS

"Mr. Bloom stood far back, his hat in his hand, counting the bared heads. Twelve. I'm thirteen. No. The chap in the macintosh is thirteen. Death's number. . . . In Lower Mount Street a pedestrian in a brown macintosh, eating dry bread, passed swiftly and unscathed across the viceroy's path. . . . Golly, whatten tunket's yon guy in the macintosh? Dusty Rhodes. Peep at his wearables. . . . Don't you believe a word he says. That man is Leopold M'Intosh, the notorious fireraiser. His real name is Higgins. . . . What selfinvolved enigma did Bloom (as he undressed and gathered his garments) voluntarily apprehending, not comprehend? Who was M'Intosh?" The Man in the Brown Macintosh who passes through the dream of the book is no other than the author himself. Bloom glimpses his maker.

Vladimir Nabokov on *Ulysses*[11]

The method of criticism I have employed in this book is based on a reordering of the principal themes of modern architecture: memory, expression, and morality. I have used this method to penetrate the deepest level of content in the buildings under consideration. It is now necessary to consider the meaning of that mythlogical content. To do so I shall examine three characteristic conceptual concerns of lyric modernism: centrality, monumentality, and perfectibility.

Centrality

In considering the difference between Gehry's house and House El Even Odd, we confront the difference between a powerful centering effect produced by the act of perception in a world of the senses and a profoundly cerebral sense of the loss of center in a world of objects. These houses represent opposing tendencies toward, on the one hand, the centrality of an inner world of which the individual may or may not be master, and, on the other, a concern for the existence or absence of some larger order that can provide an external form of centering. Neither of these tendencies exist alone in any of the buildings I have analyzed, and indeed the coexistence of these inner and outer forces is what defines the nature of centrality in our present modernism.

In Gehry's house, as I have shown, man is an individual adrift in an ocean of being. The centrality of this inner world is conveyed both by literal content—the cross in plan with its unique focus—as well as by representational content—the marine imagery that perpetuates the immediacy of constant shock, keeping those memories that might invoke a traditional centering system at bay. Despite itself, however, the house also retains traces of the once-powerful external centralizing forces of earlier periods. We can see this residue in the kitchen's prismatic glass crystal, once the purifying symbol, as for Scheerbart and Taut, of a paradise of man's creation; or we may see it in the corner window of the house, now, through Malevich, doubly distant from the icons of the Russian church.

In House El Even Odd, by contrast, man is deserted in a hostile world of his own creations from which it would at first appear that there is no escape. This obsession with the loss of an external centering system is conveyed by literal content—the form of the el cube—and by representational content—the bitten apple of an Eden lost forever. The loss of center is defined, in fact, by a persistence of traditional centering systems through the technique of inversion, through the denial of the centrality of the cube as it has been used by Palladio, Ledoux, Le Corbusier, or Johnson. And yet, as in Gehry's house, but in reverse, there is a weak force in tandem with this strong force. It is the upward, escaping motion of the three axonometric models, the heartbeat of the house, which indicates a plan of battle and gives a glimmer of the inner centrality that is the strong force in the Gehry house.

Manchester Superior Court carries forward the classical centering system of the humanist tradition without the slightest trace of House El Even Odd's inversions. And yet the attenuated lobby of the courthouse, with its opposing forces that squeeze and dilate the barrel-vaulted sky itself, bears witness to the presence of that internal force I have described. The classical at Manchester is not, as Geoffrey Scott described the Renaissance tradition, "too alive to admit of analysis, too popular to require defense."[12] This analysis and defense, this forthright assertion of the enduring nobility of human nature, is carried out beneath a troubled sky whose contrast to the quattrocento dome shows the irrevocable impact on the classical of the isolation of this inner force from all external order. In the Bozzi house, on the other hand, it is the nineteenth-century humanism of the Shingle style, with its great volumes of sheltering space and its thematic principles of nature and of structure, that is in retreat. The individualized centering of each space and the discrete associative emblems of the exterior create of the remains of these

centering forces a stage on which the players act out this very inner force. So too at Houston the external centering force of Mies's technological universe, of Sullivan's empathetic one, or of Ledoux's mountainous embodiment of the Enlightenment is drained of its capacity, leaving us on a stage of silent witnesses to this loss.

But it is at Princeton and at Portland that we confront the centrality of lyric modernism at its point of balance, though this is no indication of greater merit, as imbalance has the intrinsic advantage of an implied force. In both buildings man as individual contemplates his distance from past centers, whether in the vestigial and poignant crossing beneath the window in which the sun descends or in the rooftop temple whose spirit is the vulnerable and threatened creator of the new sublime. Despite these differences of mythological content, however, despite the drama of the one and the irony of the other, the principle of a centering force derived in part from the isolation of an inner world and measured in part against and thus beholden to the certainties of outer forces remains the same.

In all the examples, in fact, we find a distancing from previous systems, whether from the humanism of the Renaissance as we can perceive it in the central plan churches of Bramante or in the fugal compositions of Palladio, from the Reason of the Enlightenment as it proclaims itself in Boullée's cenotaph to Newton, or from the machine world of the Utopians as we see it newborn in Sant Elia or at its denouement in Paul Rudolph. This distancing has pro-

duced a lingering sense of threat,
more evident in some examples
than in others, but nonetheless present in all.

Monumentality

Monumentality, like centrality, is
composed of two opposing forces.
And, as before, two buildings in particular most clearly show these separate forces.

Four Leaf Towers are carved,
rooted, and empathetically affecting
forms. They do not derive their meaning from the movement of the city's
inhabitants but from the structure of
the city those inhabitants have built,
from its primary artifacts and from its
space. The towers are monumental
for this very reason: in their mythological content they bear witness to
the fact of human existence over vast
periods of time.

The Bozzi house, on the other hand,
is significant precisely because it
looks to the side of the Shingle style
that is scenographic in nature and
that is based on the associational theories of the picturesque least concerned with timeless and intrinsic
qualities of matter. In its secret life
it is not a witness to life but a mirror
of life, and the drama its elements
enact is of the day-to-day events
that together make possible the
monumental.

As before, however, these impulses
can never quite exist alone. In Four
Leaf Towers the perceptual ambiguity
of the skin acts as an antisceno-
graphic foil to the monumentality of
the towers' form, since it describes an
accommodating condition that is then
robbed of scenographic potency by the
sensibility of silence. In the Bozzi
house, conversely, the chimney, the

porch, and especially the tower strive
toward an empathetic and monumental stand but are thwarted by their
emblematic treatment, which con-
tinuously returns them to a stage
they cannot transcend.

A similar opposition can be observed between Manchester Superior
Court and the Gehry house, although
both buildings move somewhat toward balance. At Manchester, the
classical is used to connect the building's mythological content with a
vast time scale, stretching back
through Lutyens, McKim, Jefferson,
Palladio, and Alberti all the way to
ancient Rome. And yet the building is
not just a witness, but an accomplice;
its didactic inscriptions are a script
for the partially scenographic qualities
of the courthouse facade. In the Santa
Monica house, by contrast, we are
kept always in the present and to
such an extent that the building cannot be said to mirror day-to-day life as
much as it strives to capture the actual experience of living from moment to moment. In this closeness to
the fact of life, in its superheated
scenography, its secret life escapes
like steam through a retort to con-
dense, paradoxically, as droplets of
that primeval sea to which the experience of the monumental returns us.

The issue of monumentality in
lyric modernism, in short, requires
the resolution of two forces; it is a
question of the extent to which the
ancient heartbeat of the human race
is threatened by the circumstances
which its day-to-day demands have
forged. This has a special meaning for
the modern architect not possible earlier in the century, a meaning made
explicit where the monumental and

the scenographic interlock in Portland's Public Service Building.

In Graves's building the *tabula rasa* of the International style curtain wall is emblazoned with the monumental actors of a scenographic architecture, figures who specifically recall the distant inhabitants of the primitive hut and yet are also modern urban beings. This monumental anthropomorphism, increasingly plastic in Graves's post-Portland work, has created an architecture of a new sublime, in which trepidation replaces delight and the tragic splendor of atomic man replaces the majesty of nature. Graves's resolution of the forces of the monumental, however, is by no means the only one; and in Gordon Wu Hall and House El Even Odd, other, subtler, balances have been struck.

The anthropomorphism that permeates Venturi, Rauch and Scott Brown's building avoids empathetic insistency; its scenographic figures are drawn, literally and figuratively, and the ripeness of the sublime is drained by a penetrating irony. And yet the figures escape their stage, as those of the Bozzi house cannot. The entrance gate, that most scenographic of elements, is alternately and equally an actor wryly soliloquizing on the loss of center and a simple pedestrian gazing at the camera's lens. Ultimately the building is a wistful acknowledgment of the ordinariness of human beings, of Vitruvian man come down from his cosmic arc and lost among the confusion and turmoil of the world.

Eisenman's balance could hardly be more dissimilar. The cerebral aspect of the new sublime and the renunciation of the physical reach an extreme detachment from the Vitruvian theme in House El Even Odd. Trepidation is piled on trepidation until a feverish anxiety results at the collision of man and object, of helpless actor and Piranesian stage. This is a collision captured in the el cube, which at once connects us with the ancient myth of loss and confronts us with our present nuclear uncertainties.

We must thus conclude that monumentality is inseparable from its sister centrality, for it concerns the very nature of man as individual, without which we cannot fathom his capacity to establish order as the certainties of older orders slip. In the resolution of these forces, we bring the fact of life into alignment with the sense of threat.

Perfectibility

The problem of perfectibility is the problem of the classical. Once again, the issue is defined by two opposing forces, embodied, in this case, by Manchester Superior Court and Gordon Wu Hall.

The courthouse continues the classical tradition by means of imitation, that is, by the inventive but scrupulous adaptation of classical precedents for the expression of mythological content. In so doing, the building carries forward the standard of ideal beauty based on the perfection of nature which is vested in the Orders. The architecture of the classical tradition is the fruit of this belief in perfectibility. The buildings and cities of this tradition are the habitat of a race deemed noble, indelibly stamped with the mark of the divine. In Greenberg's courthouse this system is brought to bear on day-to-day life at its point of greatest imperfection, and there is a

poignancy not only in the power of
classicism to confront transgressions
of the everyday in this particular case,
but in general to open our eyes to
what may even now be admirable and
magnanimous in human nature.

Wu Hall establishes an altogether
different continuity with the classical
tradition, for its adaptations of classical precedent are as much innovative
as inventive, more adulterous than
scrupulous. The building is not based
upon the Orders and carries forward
no standard of ideal beauty. On the
contrary, as we have seen, it strives
at every opportunity to draw its
strength from what is ordinary rather
than from what is perfect; not,
clearly, from the ignoble, but from
the imperfect, the vulnerable, the human. A continuity exists not because
the origin of the classical in man's
presumed perfectibility is still considered relevant but because the perceived deformation of this original
basis by modern culture is held to be
of even greater value. Wu Hall represents the assimilation of change by a
distortion of classical language;
Greenberg's courthouse represents acceptance of a given standard with
which to measure change by further
refinements to that language. Wu Hall
is not a sabotaging but a reformulation and an enlargement of the classical, made possible by the belief that
at its root should now lie the ordinariness of man and not his perfectibility.

We may therefore say that this final
issue is defined by two forces: the
first tends toward an absolute view of
classicism based on perfectibility,
through which a critique of modern
culture can be made by scrupulous
adaptation of classical precedent and

the Orders. The second tends toward
a view of man as ever less capable of
perfectibility, expressed through ever
greater distortions of the absolute nature of classicism, ever greater distortions of the Orders, of the memory of
the Orders, and finally of memory
itself.

In the Bozzi house the classical is
used, but it is emblematically used.
The Tuscan Order is correctly detailed by means of imitation, but it is
then made a fragment in a picturesque composition. Neither the spatial unity nor the all-embracing roof
of the nineteenth-century Shingle
style is used to compensate for the
lost hierarchical wholeness of part to
part inherent in the classical; and that
measure of the absolute which is embodied in the Orders begins to dissi-
pate. Still, however, the actors on the
Bozzi's stage fill up its space,
confident not of their perfectibility
perhaps but certainly of their
significance.

At Portland this dissipation is
intensified by the sublime, for the
strident presence of the Romantic
tradition makes the denial of any absolute standard unambiguous. The
pilasters of the main facades are now
distorted in scale and no longer recognizable as a specific Order. The condition of the sublime thus represented
separates man from any hoped-for perfectibility either through machines or
nature, but at the same time, in the
rooftop Arcadia, the possibility of its
recovery is insinuated.

In Four Leaf Towers the Orders
themselves are no longer evident, and
it is a distortion of the memory of the
Orders that is present. The marriage
of Loos's Tribune column with Mies's

Friedrichstrasse project presents a distortion in scale and meaning of the massive, carved forms of Romantic classicism, and the perfectible is replaced not now with ordinariness but with silence, with the witnessing of the ordinary rather than its expression.

In the Gehry house memory itself is distorted, drained of power, and finally replaced by individual perception. Even the classical prerequisite of gravity is lost and one is disengaged from the ground plane, tilted up and over a world for whose inhabitants the words perfectible or ordinary can have no meaning.

Finally, in House El Even Odd the classical, capable of no further distortion, is precisely inverted, literally and metaphorically. The collapse of the axonometric models by gravity is inverted to create the double axonometric model of the main facade which proclaims the loss of center. Man, at his journey's end, stands paralyzed at the void's brink.

The issue of perfectibility cannot therefore be divorced from the difficulty of action. This is the true significance of classicism for modern architecture. Whether inverted, distorted, or extended, it remains the only language through which architecture can address the issue of human magnanimity and can approach the question of whether it is possible to avert the catastrophe of man's ordinariness turned to pettiness and destruction.

The figure in the shadows of the secret city now has nowhere left to hide. The architecture of lyric modernism tells innumerable stories to explain man's relation to the world. It is constructing a new mythology of poetic richness and urbanistic potency. In the end, however, these stories all have the same subject. Its features are described in full when it is caught simultaneously in the sharp light of the sense of threat, the fact of life, and the possibility of action. And we see that it is ourselves.

NOTES

PREFACE

1.
See Alberto Pérez-Gómez, *Architecture and the Crisis of Modern Science* (Cambridge, Mass.: The MIT Press, 1983). Pérez-Gómez discusses the effect of the rise of science on architecture from the seventeenth century to the beginning of the nineteenth century.

2.
See Peter Eisenman, "The End of the Classical: The End of the Beginning, the End of the End," *Perspecta: The Yale Architectural Journal* 21 (1984), pp. 154–73. Eisenman comments, "The late twentieth century, with its retrospective knowledge that modernism has become history, has inherited nothing less than the recognition of the end of the ability of . . . architecture to express its own time as timeless" (p. 163).

INTRODUCTION: A METHOD OF CRITICISM FOR MODERN ARCHITECTURE

1.
Quoted in Karl R. Popper, *The Poverty of Historicism* (New York: Harper and Row, 1964), p. 8.

2.
Henry-Russell Hitchcock, *Modern Architecture: Romanticism and Reintegration* (New York: Payson and Clark Ltd., 1929).

3.
Le Corbusier, *Towards a New Architecture* (London: The Architectural Press, 1946), p. 17.

4.
Henry-Russell Hitchcock and Philip Johnson, *The International Style* (New York: W. W. Norton and Co., 1966), p. 19.

5.
Ibid.

6.
Ibid., emphasis added.

7.
See Alan Colquhoun, "Typology and Design Method," *Arena* 83 (June 1967).

8.
Hitchcock and Johnson, *The International Style*, pp. 36–7; emphasis added. Their discussion of these "free choices" in chapter VI and the emphasis they place on "interest," "a due proportion of several parts," and "asymmetry" should be compared with Andrew Jackson Downing's *Cottage Residences* (New York, 1842), pp. 17–20. Downing's distinction between uniformity and symmetry is continued by Hitchcock and Johnson although the meaning of key words is reversed.

9.
Le Corbusier, *Towards a New Architecture*, p. 9.

10.
Ibid., p. 19.

11.
Geoffrey Scott, *The Architecture of Humanism, A Study in the History of Taste* (London: The Architectural Press, 1980), pp. 158–59.

12.
Edward Dorn, *Gunslinger* (Berkeley: Wingbow Press, 1975). Book II first published by Black Sparrow Press, Los Angeles, 1969.

13.
Antoine Chrysostome Quatremère de Quincy, *Dictionnaire Historique d'architecture comprenant dan son plan les notions historiques, descriptives, archéologiques, biographiques, théoriques, didactiques et pratiques de cet art*, 2 vols. (Paris, 1832). The passage quoted is from vol. 2, the section on "Type."

14.
David Watkin's book *Morality and Architecture* (Oxford University Press, 1977) is a useful study of the theme of morality as it grew out of the nineteenth century and affected the Utopian period. Although Watkin is indebted to Geoffrey Scott, it is curious that he does not discuss Scott's concept of the true ethical analogy at all.

15.
Scott, *The Architecture of Humanism*, p. 162.

16.
Ibid.

THE REPRESENTATION OF PERCEPTION: GEHRY HOUSE

1.
See Gehry interview in Barbaralee Diamondstein, ed., *American Architecture Now* (New York: Rizzoli, 1980), p. 43.

2.
Quoted by Janet Nairn, "Frank Gehry: The Search for a 'No Rules' Architecture," *Architectural Record* 159, no. 7 (June 1976), pp. 95–102.

3.
Diamondstein, *American Architecture Now*, p. 36.

4.
Interview with Gordon Matta-Clark, Antwerp, September 1977, in *Gordon-Matta Clark*, International Cultureel Centrum exhibition catalogue (Antwerp, 1977), p. 10.

5.
Aldo Rossi, *A Scientific Autobiography* (Cambridge, Mass.: The MIT Press, 1981), p. 24.

6.
Gehry first used this form in the O'Neil hay barn in San Juan Capistrano.

7.
Diamondstein, *American Architecture Now*, p. 41.

8.
Michael Fried, "Ronald Davis: Surface and Illusion," *Artforum* (April 1967), p. 39.

9.
Camilla Gray, *The Great Experiment: Russian Art 1863–1922* (London: Thames and Hudson, 1962), pp. 136–38.

10.
Jean-Claude Marcade, "K.S. Malevich: From *Black Quadrilateral* (1913) to *White on White* (1917); From the Eclipse of Objects to the Liberation of Space," translated from the French by Sherry Goodman, *The Avant-Garde in Russia 1910–1930: New Perspectives* (Cambridge, Mass.: The MIT Press, 1980), p. 21.

11.
Diamondstein, *American Architecture Now*, p. 36.

12.
Note the painting of the Suprematist cross on the left hand wall of the *0–10* installation.

13.
Marcade, "From *Black Quadrilateral* to *White on White*," p. 22.

14.
Malevich was fascinated throughout his life by aerial perspective. See his book *The Non-Objective World* (Chicago: Paul Theobald, 1959), pp. 24–5.

15.
Author translation from the French translation of an unpublished Malevich text on volumetric Suprematism written after 1923. See Jean-Hubert Martin, "L'Art Suprematiste de la Volumo-Construction" in *Malevitch, Oeuvres de Casimir Severinovitch Malevitch (1878–1935)* (Paris: Centre Georges Pompidou, 1978), p. 15.

16.
Ibid.

17.
Le Corbusier, *Towards a New Architecture* (London: The Architectural Press, 1946), p. 166.

18.
G.A. Houses 6 (Tokyo: ADA Edita, 1979), p. 64.

19.
Ibid., p. 62.

20.
The tumbling cube of Gehry's house is, perhaps, also an echo of Philip Johnson's Glass House, whose "main motif" was also one of Malevich's elemental Suprematist forms. See Johnson's article "House at New Canaan, Connecticut," *Architectural Review* 108 (September 1950), pp. 152–59, especially paragraph 10: "Malevich proved what interesting surrounding areas could be created by correctly placing a circle in a rectangle. Abstract painting of forty years ago remains even today the strongest single aesthetic influence on the grammar of architecture."

THE ANXIETY OF THE SECOND FALL: HOUSE EL EVEN ODD

1.
See special issue on Peter Eisenman, *Architecture and Urbanism* 112 (January 1980), p. 69.

2.
Ibid., p. 31.

3.
Ibid., p. 29.

4.
Ibid., p. 33.

5.
Peter Eisenman, "Post-Functionalism," *Oppositions* 6 (1975), editorial pages, n.p.

6.
Eisenman, *Architecture and Urbanism*, p. 223.

7.
Ibid., p. 47.

8.
Ibid., p. 53.

9.
Manfredo Tafuri, "Peter Eisenman: The Meditations of Icarus," unpublished manuscript.

10.
Aldo Rossi, *A Scientific Autobiography* (Cambridge Mass.: The MIT Press, 1981), p. 23.

11.
Peter Eisenman, *Idea as Model*, Institute for Architecture and Urban Studies, catalogue 3 (New York: Rizzoli, 1981), p. 82.

12.
Le Corbusier, *Towards a New Architecture* (London: The Architectural Press, 1946), p. 100.

13.
Eisenman, *Architecture and Urbanism*, p. 25.

14.
See Bernhard Schneider, "Perspective Refers to the Viewer, Axonometry refers to the object," *Daidalos* 1 (1981), p. 81.

15.
Peter Eisenman, Interview, *Archetype* 1, no. 4 (Winter 1980), p. 32.

16.
Eisenman's own explanation of House El Even Odd centers on the idea that the house takes its origin from the *axonometric model* of House X. Thus the axonometric el of House El Even Odd is seen as the start, the "even" or neutral condition of its process of development. The "plan" and the apparently unmodified normal el then become axonometric projections of the axonometric el, the "odd" positions of the house. (See Peter Eisenman, "The Representations of Doubt: at the Sign of the Sign," *Rassegno* 9 (March 1982), fifth column of original English text). This explanation, while understandable, is not sufficiently distanced from the sequence of Eisenman's houses as a whole. Rather than the word "even" or "odd" in House El Even Odd, it is surely the word "El" that is crucial. This ties the meaning of House El Even Odd to the initial conception of House X, back from there to the geometrical configuration of House VI, and finally to Houses I and II themselves, which were regular "unbitten" cubes, not as yet betraying the idea of decomposition. In addition, the miniature els inside House El Even Odd refer to the "El" condition, not to the "even" condition in progressively stronger form as they reduce in size; thus the final smallest figure in the house is an el without any axonometric transformation.

17.
An axonometric projection of the axonometric model, whose vertical angles are all at forty-five degrees, produces a figure that is completely flat because the second forty-five-degree projection produces vertical angles of zero degrees.

18.
Eisenman, "The Representations of Doubt," fifth column of original English text.

19.
Le Corbusier, *Towards a New Architecture*, p. 166.

20.
See Eugenio Battisti, *Filippo Brunelleschi, The Complete Work* (New York: Rizzoli, 1981), pp. 102–13.

21.
Originally published posthumously as *Le Due Regole della Prospettiva Pratica di M. Iacomo Barozzi da Vignola con i Comentarij del R. P. M. Egnatio Danti* (Rome, 1583). It appears to have been written earlier, perhaps in 1527, according to Timothy K. Kitao in "Prejudice in Perspective: A Study of Vignola's Perspective Treatise," *Art Bulletin* (September 1962), pp. 173–94.

22.
Kitao, "Prejudice in Perspective," p. 184, quoting Vignola.

23.
Andrea Pozzo, *Perspective Pictorum et Architectorum*, 1693.

24.
Ferdinando Galli da Bibiena, *L'Architettura Civile*, introduction by Diane M. Kelder (New York: Benjamin Blom, 1971).

25.
Quoted in Kitao, "Prejudice in Perspective," p. 191.

26.
Giovanni Battista Piranesi, *Invenzioni Capric di Carceri* (Rome, 1745). The prison scene is a relatively common subject in surviving designs for early eighteenth-century stage sets.

27.
See Vincent Scully, *Modern Architecture: The Architecture of Democracy* (New York: Braziller, 1961).

28.
For an expanded analysis of similar kinds of ambiguity in the *Carceri*, see Patricia May Sekler, "G.B. Piranesi's Carceri etchings and related drawings," *Art Quarterly* (Winter 1962), pp. 331–63.

29.
Colin Rowe, "The Mathematics of the Ideal Villa," *The Mathematics of the Ideal Villa and Other Essays* (Cambridge, Mass.: The MIT Press, 1976), p. 15. Originally published in *Architectural Review*, March 1947.

30.
Ibid., p. 14.

31.
See Manfredo Tafuri, "Giovanni Battista Piranesi: L'Utopie negative dans l'architecture," *L'Architecture d'aujourd'hui* 184 (1976), pp. 38–108.

32.
Eisenman, "Post-Functionalism," editorial pages. (The term post-functionalism was first used by Alfred Barr in the preface to Hitchcock and Johnson, *The International Style* (New York, 1932), pp. 14, 15.)

33.
Peter Eisenman, "Introduction," *Philip Johnson Writings* (New York: Oxford University Press, 1979), p. 23.

34.
Ibid.

35.
Eisenman, *Archetype*, p. 30.

THE SENSIBILITY OF SILENCE: FOUR LEAF TOWERS

1.
See Sigfried Giedion, *Space, Time and Architecture* (Cambridge, Mass.: Harvard University Press, 1941), especially part VI, p. 402.

2.
Stanley Tigerman, ed., *Late Entries to the Chicago Tribune Tower Competition* (New York: Rizzoli, 1980), vol. II, p. 55.

3.
Aldo Rossi, *The Architecture of the City* (Cambridge, Mass.: The MIT Press, 1982).

4.
Peter Eisenman quoting Rossi in Editor's Introduction to ibid., p. 7.

5.
Aldo Rossi, *A Scientific Autobiography* (Cambridge, Mass.: The MIT Press, 1981), p. 76.

6.
Conversation between Cesar Pelli and Peter Eisenman, *Skyline* (May 1982), p. 24.

7.
Colin Rowe, "Chicago Frame," *The Mathematics of the Ideal Villa and Other Essays* (Cambridge, Mass.: The MIT Press, 1976), p. 99. First published in *Architectural Review* 120 (November 1956), pp. 285–89.

8.
Vincent Scully, "Louis Sullivan's Architectural Ornament, a Brief Note Concerning Humanist Design in the Age of Force," *Perspecta: The Yale Architectural Journal* 5 (1959), p. 77.

9.
Ibid., p. 80.

10.
See John Hejduk, "The Silent Witnesses," *Perspecta: The Yale Architectural Journal* 19 (1982), pp. 70–80.

THE NATURE OF THE NEW SUBLIME: PORTLAND PUBLIC SERVICE BUILDING

1.
Edmund Burke, *A Philosophical Enquiry Into the Origins of Our Ideas of the Sublime and Beautiful* (London, 1757).

2.
Ibid., p. 73.

3.
Ibid., p. 32.

4.
Ibid., p. 50.

5.
Ibid., p. 58.

6.
Christopher Hussey, *The Picturesque; Studies in a Point of View* (London: Frank Cass, 1967), p. 201, quoting Uvedale Price, *An Essay on the Picturesque* (London, 1794).

7.
Emil Kaufmann, *Architecture in the Age of Reason, Baroque and Post-Baroque in England, Italy and France* (Hamden, Conn.: Archon Books, 1955), p. 79.

8.
Ibid., p. 106.

9.
Emil Kaufmann, "Three Revolutionary Architects, Boullée, Ledoux, and Lequeu," *Transactions of the American Philosophical Society* 42, part 3 (1952), p. 504.

10.
See Alberto Pérez-Gómez, *Architecture and the Crisis of Modern Science* (Cambridge, Mass.: The MIT Press, 1983), pp. 130–61). Pérez-Gómez discusses the effect of Newtonian natural philosophy on the symbolic geometry of Boullée and Ledoux.

11.
Burke, *A Philosophical Enquiry*, p. 122.

12.
See Barbara Novak, *Nature and Culture, American Landscape and Painting 1825–1875* (New York: Oxford University Press, 1980), pp. 34–44. Novak discusses the change from the old, Burkean sublime to a nineteenth-century transcendental one.

13.
Immanuel Kant, *Critique of Judgement* (1790), quoted in Lorenz Eitner, ed., *Neo-Classicism and Romanticism 1750–1850, Sources and Documents* 1 (Englewood Cliffs, N.J.: Prentice-Hall, 1970), pp. 96–7.

14.
Ibid., p. 98.

15.
Henri Focillon, *The Life of Forms in Art* (New York: Wittenborn, Schultz, 1948).

16.
Le Corbusier, *Towards a New Architecture* (London: The Architectural Press, 1946), p. 188.

17.
See Vincent Scully, *The Earth, the Temple and the Gods; Greek Sacred Architecture* (New Haven: Yale University Press, 1969), pp. 176–79.

SCENOGRAPHY AND THE PICTURESQUE: BOZZI HOUSE

1.
Robert A. M. Stern, "One Hundred Years of Resort Architecture in East Hampton: The Power of the Provincial," *East Hampton's Heritage, An Illustrated Architectural Record* (New York: W. W. Norton and Co., 1982), p. 63.

2.
Henry-Russell Hitchcock, *Architecture: Nineteenth and Twentieth Centuries* (Harmondsworth: Penguin Books, 1971), p. 364.

3.
Vincent Scully, *The Shingle Style and the Stick Style. Architectural Theory and Design from Downing to the Origins of Wright* (New Haven: Yale University Press, 1971), p. 23. Originally published as *The Shingle Style,* 1955.

4.
Vincent Scully, *The Shingle Style Today, or the Historian's Revenge* (New York: George Braziller, 1974), p. 8.

5.
Ibid.

6.
Ibid., p. 9.

7.
Ibid., p. 34.

8.
The *modus operandi* of Stern's office makes attribution of authorship in work coming from it a complex matter. Stern is the first to point out that he is "not original." By this he means wittily to imply the importance of tradition and the absurdity of pretending to be outside one. However, Stern's is essentially a critical mind, and while all projects from the office fit a certain loose bundle of themes, which Stern has long championed, often against the heaviest odds, individual designs frequently emanate from those designers who are in charge of a particular project in the office. Stern is the master critic in this situation, sifting through alternate schemes, picking winners. The spirit behind many individual projects varies considerably because they are often the work of different people. Stern's interventions sometimes alter much, and usually for the better, but often leave the deepest meanings little changed. The Bozzi house, however, is almost pure Stern in its conception, although in detail it shows the hand of Terry Brown, the project architect. For this reason, among others, it is treated in this chapter, while other, sometimes better-known projects from Stern's office

will not be mentioned. Perhaps the emotional ties of the context resulted in this purity (see note 10); in any event, the design was worked out with great speed and fluidity and accepted by the client with exceptionally few problems, and this makes it an excellent building for the examination of the essential Stern.

9.
Caroll Meeks, "Picturesque Eclecticism," *Art Bulletin* 32 (1950), p. 233.

10.
There is a more specific genesis to the tower than its generally Richardsonian descent. When in 1968 Stern added a screened porch to what was then his summer residence three doors down the street from the Bozzi house, he did so by turning the elevation of his Wiseman house of 1965–67 into a plan, thereby following Venturi's manipulation of the same shape in elevation plan and section in the Vanna Venturi house of 1962–64 and maintaining the same geometry as the arched window of Venturi's 1960–63 Guild house. As a mass, the double-height volume of the 1968 porch addition is detached from the house and back lit, accessible from the house by two panels of a screen folded back from the faceted curve, as in the plan of the Bozzi house tower. With the tower grown in height, and the roof conical and spiky, rather than flat, the Bozzi house seems more assertive than its predecessor, as indeed the whole house does. Perhaps ultimately the house is a gesture to the gentler curves of the earlier project, acknowledging time and change.

11.
Scully, *The Shingle Style,* p. 85.

12.
Ibid., pp. xxiii–lix.

13.
Andrew Jackson Downing, *Cottage Residences; or a series of designs for rural cottages and cottage villas. And their gardens and grounds* (New York, 1842), p. ix.

14.
See Donald Pilcher, *The Regency Style 1800–1830* (London, 1948), p. 43.

15.
See Scully, *The Shingle Style*.

16.
Ibid., pp. xlvii–xlix.

17.
Downing, *Cottage Residences*, p. ix.

18.
Uvedale Price, *An Essay on the Picturesque as Compared with the Sublime and Beautiful and, on the Use of Studying Pictures for the Purpose of Improving Real Landscapes* (London, 1794).

19.
Archibald Alison, *Essays on the Nature and Principles of Taste* (Edinburgh, 1790).

20.
Ibid., p. 2.

21.
Ibid., p. 42.

22.
Ibid., p. 55.

23.
Richard Payne Knight, *Analytical Enquiry into the Principles of Taste* (London, 1805).

24.
See Nikolaus Pevsner, "Richard Payne Knight," *Art Bulletin* 31 (December 1949), pp. 293–320.

THE CONTINUITY OF THE CLASSICAL: MANCHESTER SUPERIOR COURT BUILDING

1.
William E. Buckley, *A New England Pattern, the History of Manchester, Connecticut* (Chester, Conn.: Pequot Press, 1973), p. 159.

2.
Andrea Palladio, *The Four Books of Architecture* (New York: Dover, 1965), p. 14. Originally published as *I Quattro Libri dell'Architettura* (Venice, 1570).

3.
Marc-Antoine Laugier, *An Essay on Architecture* (Los Angeles: Hennessey and Ingalls, 1977), p. 61. Originally published as *Essai sur L'Architecture* (Paris, 1753).

4.
Ibid., p. 66.

5.
John Locke, *The Second Treatise of Government*, section 57.

6.
Thomas Jefferson to William Johnson, June 12, 1823, in *Collected Letters of Thomas Jefferson*.

7.
See John Summerson, "The Lutyens Memorial Volumes Reviewed," *Royal Institute of British Architects Journal* (August 1951), p. 390.

8.
Allan Greenberg, "Lutyens's Architecture Restudied," *Perspecta: The Yale Architectural Journal* 12 (1969), p. 142.

9.
See Allan Greenberg, "A Sense of the Past: an Architectural Perspective," *The Chicago Architectural Journal* 1 (1981), pp. 42–8.

10.
Leland Roth, "McKim, Mead and White Reappraised," *A Monograph of the Works of McKim, Mead and White 1879–1915* (New York: Arno, 1977), p. 40.

THE IRONIES OF THE DIFFICULT WHOLE: GORDON WU HALL

1.
Ralph Adams Cram, *Holder Tower and the New Dining Halls* (Princeton: Princeton University Press, 1918), p. 7.

2.
Ibid., p. 6.

3.
Colin Rowe and Robert Slutzky, "Transparency: Literal and Phenomenal," *The Mathematics of the Ideal Villa and Other Essays* (Cambridge, Mass.: The MIT Press, 1976), p. 161, quoting Gyorgy Kepes, *Language of Vision* (Chicago, 1944).

4.
Ibid.

5.
Colin Rowe, "The Mathematics of the Ideal Villa" in ibid., p. 12, discussing the Villa Stein.

6.
Vincent Scully, *The Shingle Style Today, or the Historian's Revenge* (New York: George Braziller, 1974), p. 30.

7.
Rowe, "The Mathematics of the Ideal Villa," p. 15.

8.
Fillipo Tomaso Marinetti, "Futurist Manifesto," *Le Figaro* (20 February 1909). Quoted in Reyner Banham, *Theory and Design in the First Machine Age* (London: The Architectural Press, 1960), p. 103.

9.
Robert Venturi, *Complexity and Contradiction in Architecture* (New York: Museum of Modern Art, 1977), p. 101.

10.
Robert Venturi, Denise Scott Brown, and Steven Izenour *Learning from Las Vegas* (Cambridge, Mass.: The MIT Press, 1977), p. 129.

11.
Le Corbusier, *Towards A New Architecture* (London: The Architectural Press, 1946), p. 123.

12.
Ibid., p. 251.

13.
Venturi, Scott Brown, and Izenour, *Learning from Las Vegas*, p. 130.

14.
Vincent Scully, "Introduction," to Venturi, *Complexity and Contradiction*, p. 11.

15.
Venturi, *Complexity and Contradiction*, p. 13.

16.
See John Shearman, *Mannerism* (Harmondsworth: Penguin Books, 1967), p. 21.

17.
Venturi, Scott Brown, and Izenour, *Learning from Las Vegas*, p. 50.

THE CITY: A MACHINE FOR THINKING IN

1.
Letter to Wilhelm Fleiss, June 12, 1900. Freud is describing a visit to Bellevue, the house where, five years before, he had dreamed "Irma's Dream," which forms the heart of the crucial second chapter of *The Interpretation of Dreams.*

2.
Henry-Russell Hitchcock and Philip Johnson, *The International Style* (New York: W. W. Norton and Co., 1966), p. 18.

3.
See Juan Pablo Bonta, *Architecture and Its Interpretation, A Study of Expressive Systems in Architecture* (Cambridge, Mass.: The MIT Press, 1979). Chapters 4 and 5 examine changing interpretations of Mies van der Rohe's German Pavilion at the Barcelona Exhibition of 1927.

4.
See Aldo Rossi, *The Architecture of the City* (Cambridge, Mass.: The MIT Press, 1982), especially chapter 1, "The Individuality of Urban Artifacts," and "The Critique of Naive Functionalism."

5.
See Reyner Banham, *Theory and Design in the First Machine Age* (London: The Architectural Press, 1960), especially pp. 320–30.

6.
See Sigfried Giedion, *The Eternal Present: The Beginnings of Architecture, A Contribution on Constancy and Change* (New York: Pantheon, 1964).

7.
See Nikolaus Pevsner, "Modern Architecture and the Historian or the Return of Historicism," *RIBA Journal* 68, no. 6 (April 1961), pp. 230–37.

8.
Geoffrey Scott, *The Architecture of Humanism, A Study in the History of Taste* (London: The Architectural Press, 1980) pp. 63–4.

9.

While the qualitative aspects of Aldo Rossi's theory in *The Architecture of the City* are powerful, its qualitative aspects are more tentative. The qualitative dimension of Rossi's analysis of the city arises from the idea that the individuality of urban artifacts is a result of "the event and the sign that has marked the event" (p. 106). The ensuing proposition that architectural symbolism may be the restatement of such events at later periods of a city's evolution (pp. 114–15) is related to my sense of the term mythological content. It seems to me, however, that Rossi ignores the lack of consensus concerning such restatements. The passage from nature to culture may have been conveyed by myth in the "normal childhood" of man which Rossi analyzes in relation to the founding of Athens (pp. 131–37), but it is the *differences* in the restatements of such a myth, rather than the simple fact of the myth's persistence, that I find interesting.

10.

The notable exceptions are Henry-Russell Hitchcock's *Modern Architecture, Romanticism and Reintegration* (1929) and his *Architecture: Nineteenth and Twentieth Centuries* (1958). These are unique among books by modernist writers in considering modern work in relation to traditional work. Even here, however, treatment is token. Fiske Kimball's *American Architecture* (1928) is the one book which consciously tries to find common ground between the new work and the then establishment's designs.

11.

Vladimir Nabokov, *Lectures on Literature* (New York: Harcourt Brace Jovanovich, 1980), pp. 316–20. James Joyce's *Ulysses*, published in 1922, is the description of a single day, Thursday June 16, 1904. Nabokov's *Lectures* are collected from his courses at Cornell University from 1948 to 1958.

12.

Scott, *The Architecture of Humanism*, p. 37.

BIBLIOGRAPHY

GENERAL REFERENCES

I was particularly influenced by three books not related to architecture:

Barthes, Roland.
Mythologies. First published in French by Editions du Seuil, Paris, 1957.

Freud, Sigmund.
The Interpretation of Dreams. First published in German by Franz Deauticke, Leipzig and Vienna, 1900.

Popper, Karl.
The Poverty of Historicism. First published in *Economica,* 1945.

Several books on architecture were especially significant to the development of my thinking:

Hitchcock, Henry-Russell.
Modern Architecture, Romanticism and Reintegration. New York: Payson and Clarke Ltd., 1929.

Rossi, Aldo.
The Architecture of the City. Cambridge, Mass.: The MIT Press, 1982. First published as *L'Architettura Della Citta.* Padua: Marsilio Editori, 1966.

Scott, Geoffrey.
The Architecture of Humanism, A Study in the History of Taste. London: The Architectural Press, 1980; Constable and Co., 1914.

Scully, Vincent.
American Architecture and Urbanism. New York: Praeger, 1969.

The following lists are by no means exhaustive. I include only material I found helpful in my research. While I group entries under chapter headings for ease of reference, these references often had wider influence in the book.

INTRODUCTION: A METHOD OF CRITICISM FOR MODERN ARCHITECTURE

On Utopian modernism:

Hitchcock, Henry-Russell
and Johnson, Philip.
The International Style. New York: W. W. Norton and Co., 1966. First published as *The International Style, Architecture since 1922.* New York: W. W. Norton and Co., 1932.

Le Corbusier.
Towards a New Architecture. London: The Architectural Press, 1946. First published in English by John Rodker, 1927, and in French as *Vers une architecture* by Editions Cres, 1923.

Pevsner, Nikolaus.
"Modern Architecture and the Historian or the Return of Historicism." *RIBA Journal* 68, no. 6 (April 1961): 230–37.

On the critque of Utopian modernism:

Argan, Giulio Carlo.
"On the Typology of Architecture." Translated by Joseph Rykwert. *Architectural Design* (December 1963): 564–65.

Collins, Peter.
Changing Ideals in Modern Architecture 1750–1950. London: Faber and Faber, 1965.

Colquhoun, Alan.
"Typology and Design Method." *Arena* 83 (June 1967).

Eisenman, Peter.
"The Houses of Memory: The Texts of Analogue." Editor's introduction to *The Architecture of the City.* Cambridge, Mass.: The MIT Press, 1982.

Greenberg, Allan.
"A Sense of the Past: An Architectural Perspective." *The Chicago Architectural Journal* 1 (1981): 42–48.

Johnson, Philip.
"House at New Canaan, Connecticut." *Architectural Review* 108 (September 1950): 152–59.

Pérez-Gómez, Alberto.
Architecture and the Crisis of Modern Science. Cambridge, Mass.: The MIT Press, 1983.

Rowe, Colin.
"The Mathematics of the Ideal Villa: Palladio and Le Corbusier compared." *Architectural Review* 101, no. 603 (March 1947): 101–4.

Summerson, John.
"The Mischievous Analogy." *Heavenly Mansions and Other Essays in Architecture.* New York: W. W. Norton and Co., 1963, pp. 195–218.

Venturi, Robert.
Complexity and Contradiction in Architecture. New York: Museum of Modern Art, 1966.

Vidler, Anthony.
"After Historicism." *Oppositions* 17 (Summer 1979): 1–5.

Watkin, David.
Morality and Architecture. The Development of a Theme in architectural history and theory from the Gothic Revival to the Modern Movement. New York: Oxford University Press, 1977.

THE CITY: A MACHINE FOR THINKING IN

Banham, Reyner.
Theory and Design in the First Machine Age. New York: Praeger, 1960; London: The Architectural Press, 1960.

Bonta, Juan Pablo.
Architecture and Its Interpretation, A Study of Expressive Systems in Architecture. Cambridge, Mass.: The MIT Press, 1979.

Colquhoun, Alan.
"Symbolic and Literal Aspects of Technology." *Architectural Design* (November 1962): 508–9.

Focillon, Henri.
The Life of Forms in Art. New Haven: Yale University Press, 1942. First published as *Vie des Formes.* Paris, 1933.

Gowans, Alan.
Images of American Living: Four Centuries of Architecture and Furniture as Cultural Expression. Philadelphia: Lippincott, 1964.

Jordy, William H.
American Buildings and their Architects, vols. 3 and 4. Garden City, New York: Doubleday and Co., Inc. 1972. Especially vol. 3, chapters 3 and 7 on the Robie House and the Boston Public Library, and vol. 4, chapters 2 and 4 on the Philadelphia Savings Fund Society Building and 860 Lake Shore Drive. This is one of the few books to deal in detail with single buildings only.

Kimball, Sidney Fiske.
American Architecture. Indianapolis: The Bobbs-Merrill Co., 1928.

Rossi, Aldo.
A Scientific Autobiography. Cambridge, Mass.: The MIT Press, 1981.

Schorske, Carl.
Fin-de-Siècle Vienna: Politics and Culture. New York: Knopf, 1980.

Scruton, Roger.
The Aesthetics of Architecture. Princeton: Princeton University Press, 1979. Especially chapters 7 and 8.

Scully, Vincent.
"Frank Lloyd Wright and the Stuff of Dreams." *Perspecta: The Yale Architectural Journal* 16 (1980): 8–28.

Wittkower, Rudolph.
Architectural Principles in the Age of Humanism. London: Warburg Institute, University of London, 1949.

THE REPRESENTATION OF PERCEPTION: GEHRY HOUSE

For Gehry's own thoughts see:

Gehry, Frank.
"Frank Gehry" Interview. *American Architecture Now.* Edited by Barbaralee Diamondstein. New York: Rizzoli, 1980.

Gehry, Frank.
"Interview." *Archetype* 1, no. 2 (Summer 1979).

Gehry, Frank.
Projects. *GA Houses* 6. Tokyo: A.D.A. Edita, 1979, pp. 56–83.

Nairn, Janet.
"Frank Gehry: The Search for a 'No Rules' Architecture." *Architectural Record* 159, no. 7 (June 1976): 95–102.

Gehry, Frank.
"Frank Gehry." *California Counterpoint: New West Coast Architecture 1982.* New York: IAUS and Rizzoli, 1982, pp. 50–62.

On various artists of interest in relation to Gehry's work:

Filler, Martin.
"Eccentric Space: Frank Gehry." *Art in America* (June 1980): 111–17.

Fried, Michael.
"Ronald Davis: Surface and Illusion." *Artforum* (April 1967): 37–41.

Matta-Clark, Gordon.
"Interview." *Gordon Matta-Clark.* Exhibition catalogue, International Cultureel Centrum. Antwerp, 1977.

Matta-Clark, Gordon.
Splitting. New York: 98 Greene Street Loft Press, 1974.

Schjeldahl, Peter.
"Review of the Avant-Garde in Russia 1910–1930: New Perspectives." *Art in America* (April 1981): 76–91.

On Malevich I found especially useful:

Douglas, Charlotte.
"0–10 Exhibition." *The Avant-Garde in Russia 1910–1930: New Perspectives.* Catalogue of the Los Angeles County Museum of Art show July 8-September 28, 1980. Cambridge, Mass.: The MIT Press, 1980, pp. 34–40.

Malevich, Kasimir.
The Non-Objective World. Chicago: Paul Theobald, 1959. First published as *Die Gegenstandslose Welt.* Munich, 1927.

Marcade, Jean-Claude.
"K.S. Malevich: From *Black Quadrilateral* (1913) to *White on White* (1917); From the Eclipse of Objects to the Liberation of Space." *The Avant-Garde in Russia 1910–1930: New Perspectives.* Cambridge, Mass.: The MIT Press, 1980, pp. 20–24.

Martin, Jean-Hubert.
"L'Art Suprematiste de la Volumo-Construction." *Oeuvres de Casimir Severinovitch Malevitch. 1878–1935.* Paris: Centre Georges Pompidou.

Gray, Camilla.
The Great Experiment: Russian Art 1863–1922. London: Thames and Hudson, 1962.

On the California architectural context:

Gebhard, David.
Architecture in California 1868–1968. Catalogue of an exhibition organized by David Gebhard and Harriette von Bretonn. Santa Barbara, Cal.: Standard Printing of Santa Barbara, Inc., 1968.

Gebhard, David.
Schindler. London: Thames and Hudson, 1971.

McCoy, Esther.
Five California Architects. New York: Reinhold, 1960.

McCoy, Esther.
Modern California Houses; Case Study Houses 1945–1962. New York: Reinhold, 1962.

THE ANXIETY OF THE SECOND FALL: HOUSE EL EVEN ODD

Eisenman's writings are opaque but reward intensive study. Of the available writings and interviews not already mentioned, the most interesting are:

Eisenman, Peter.
"House X." *Architecture and Urbanism* 112 (January 1980): 15–151.

Eisenman, Peter.
"Post-Functionalism." *Oppositions* 6 (1975): editorial pages.

Eisenman, Peter.
"Introduction." *Philip Johnson Writings.* New York: Oxford University Press, 1979.

Eisenman, Peter.
"Interview." *Archetype* 1, no. 4 (Winter 1980).

Eisenman, Peter.
"The End of the Classical: The End of the Beginning, the End of the End." *Perspecta: The Yale Architectural Journal* 21 (1984).

Few writings on Eisenman have grasped his message. Among the exceptions are:

Gandelsonas, Mario.
"From Structure to Subject: The Formation of an Architectural Language." *Oppositions* 17 (Summer 1979): 7–29.

Rowe, Colin.
"Introduction." *Five Architects*. New York: Oxford University Press, 1975.

Schneider, Bernhard.
"Perspective Refers to the Viewer, Axonometry refers to the object." *Daidalos* (1981): 81–95.

Tafuri, Manfredo.
"Peter Eisenman: The Meditations of Icarus." Unpublished manuscript.

Relevant to Eisenman but not specifically related to his work is:

Vidler, Anthony.
"The Third Typology." *Oppositions* 7 (Winter 1976): 1–4.

Of writings on the subject of perspective I found particularly useful:

Battisti, Eugenio.
Filippo Brunelleschi, The Complete Work. New York: Rizzoli, 1981.

Kitao, Timothy.
"Prejudice in Perspective: a Study of Vignola's Perspective Treatise." *Art Bulletin* (September 1962): 173–94.

Galli da Bibiena, Ferdinando.
L'Architettura Civile. Introduction by Diane Kelder. New York: Benjamin Blom, 1971. First published as *L'Architettura Civile Preparata Sulla Geometrica e Ridotta alle Prospettiva*, 1711.

Of the many writings on Piranesi's *Carceri* I found the best to be:

Huxley, Aldous.
Prisons. London: Trianon Press, 1949.

Lehmann, Karl.
"Piranesi as Interpreter of Roman Architecture." *Piranesi*. Northampton, Mass.: Smith College Museum of Art, 1961, pp. 88–98.

MacDonald, William L.
Piranesi's Carceri, Sources of Invention. The Katherine Asher Engel Lectures, 1978. Northampton, Mass.: Smith College, 1979.

Sekler, Patricia May.
"G.B. Piranesi's Carceri etchings and related drawings." *Art Quarterly* (Winter 1962): 331–63.

Wilton-Ely, John.
The Mind and Art of Giovanni Battista Piranesi. London: Thames and Hudson, 1978.

For a view of Piranesi's relation to the present I found helpful:

Scully, Vincent.
Modern Architecture: The Architecture of Democracy. New York: George Braziller, 1961.

THE SENSIBILITY OF SILENCE: FOUR LEAF TOWERS

Very seldom if ever have critics made sense of Pelli's work. For this work the most helpful references are:

Pastier, John.
Cesar Pelli. New York: Whitney Library of Design, 1980.

Pelli, Cesar.
"Interview" with Peter Eisenman. *Skyline* (May 1982).

Pelli, Cesar.
"Transparency: Literal and Perceptual." *Architecture and Urbanism* (November 1976): 80.

Tigerman, Stanley, ed.
Late Entries to the Chicago Tribune Tower Competition. New York: Rizzoli, 1980, p. 55.

See also:

Macrae-Gibson, Gavin.
"Four Leaf Towers: Icons of the Non-Ideal." *Architecture and Urbanism* (February 1983): 25–29.

Macrae-Gibson, Gavin.
"The Museum of Modern Art: Modernism for the Masses." *Architecture and Urbanism* (November 1984): 56–60.

On the question of the carved form and the static and dynamic tower:

Giedion, Sigfried.
Space, Time and Architecture; The Growth of a New Tradition. Cambridge, Mass.: Harvard University Press, 1941.

Ledoux, Claude-Nicolas.
Architecture Considerée Sous le Rapport de l'Art, des Moeurs et de la Legislation. Paris, 1804.

Taut, Bruno.
"Alpine Architecture." *Glass Architecture by Paul Scheerbart and Alpine Architecture by Bruno Taut.* Edited by Denis Sharp. Praeger, 1972. Taut's book first published as *Alpine Architektur.* Hagen, 1919.

On the question of the skin and "distancing":

Johnson, Philip.
Mies van der Rohe. New York: Museum of Modern Art, 1947.

Morrison, Hugh.
Louis Sullivan, Prophet of Modern Architecture. New York: W. W. Norton and Co., 1935.

Rowe, Colin.
"Chicago Frame: Chicago's Place in the Modern Movement." *Architectural Review* 120 (November 1956): 285–89.

Scully, Vincent.
"Louis Sullivan's Architectural Ornament, a Brief Note Concerning Humanist Design in the Age of Force." *Perspecta: The Yale Architectural Journal* 5 (1959): 73–80.

Tafuri, Manfredo and Dal Co, Francesco.
Modern Architecture. New York: Harry N. Abrams, 1976, especially pp. 151–57.

On the sensibility of silence:

Hejduk, John.
"The Silent Witnesses." *Perspecta: The Yale Architectural Journal* 19 (1982): 70–80.

Sontag, Susan.
"The Aesthetics of Silence." *Styles of Radical Will.* New York: Farrar, Straus and Giroux, 1967.

THE NATURE OF THE NEW SUBLIME: PORTLAND PUBLIC SERVICE BUILDING

For Graves's own work see especially:

Graves, Michael.
"Michael Graves" Interview. *American Architecture Now.* Edited by Barbaralee Diamondstein. New York: Rizzoli, 1980.

Wheeler, Karen; Arnell, Peter;
Bickford, Ted.
Michael Graves, Buildings and Projects 1966–1981. New York: Rizzoli, 1982.

On Romantic classicism:

Andrews, Stuart.
Eighteenth-Century Europe: The 1760s to 1815. Longmans, 1965.

Eitner, Lorenz.
Neo-Classicism and Romanticism 1750–1850; Sources and Documents. Englewood Cliffs, New Jersey: Prentice-Hall, 1970.

Honour, Hugh.
Neo-Classicism. Harmondsworth: Penguin Books, 1968.

Hope, Thomas.
Household Furniture and Interior Decoration. London, 1807.

Kaufmann, Emil.
Architecture in the Age of Reason; Baroque and Post-Baroque in England, Italy and France. Hamden, Conn.: Archon Books, 1955.

Kaufmann, Emil.
"Three Revolutionary Architects: Boullée, Ledoux, and Lequeu." *Transactions of the American Philosophical Society* 42, part 3 (1952).

Watkin, David.
Thomas Hope 1769–1831 and the Neo-Classical Idea. London: John Murray, 1968.

On the sublime:

Burke, Edmund.
A Philosophical Enquiry into the Origin of our Ideas of the Sublime and Beautiful. London, 1757.

Novak, Barbara.
Nature and Culture, American Landscape and Painting 1825–1875. New York: Oxford University Press, 1980.

Richardson, Albert E.
Monumental Classic Architecture in Great Britain and Ireland During the Eighteenth and Nineteenth Centuries. London: B. T. Batsford Ltd., 1914.

On the concept of architecture in relation to a landscape perceived as sacred:

Scully, Vincent.
The Earth, the Temple and the Gods; Greek Sacred Architecture. New Haven: Yale University Press, 1969, 1962.

SCENOGRAPHY AND THE PICTURESQUE: BOZZI HOUSE

Of Stern's writings see especially:

Stern, Robert.
"One Hundred Years of Resort Architecture in East Hampton: The Power of the Provincial." *East Hampton's Heritage, An Illustrated Architectural Record.* New York, W. W. Norton and Co., 1982, pp. 56–129.

Stern, Robert.
"The Doubles of Post-Modern." *Harvard Architectural Review* 1 (Spring 1980): 75–87.

Stern, Robert.
"Classicism in Context." *Post-Modern Classicism.* Edited by Charles Jencks. London: Academy Editions, 1980, pp. 35–39.

On the Shingle style:

Scully, Vincent.
The Shingle Style and the Stick Style. Architectural Theory and Design from Downing to the Origins of Wright. New Haven: Yale University Press, 1971. First published as *The Shingle Style.* New Haven: Yale University Press, 1955.

Scully, Vincent.
The Shingle Style Today, or the Historian's Revenge. New York: George Braziller, 1974.

Scully, Vincent.
"The Shingle Style." In *The Architectural Heritage of Newport, Rhode Island 1640–1915* by Vincent Scully and Antoinette F. Downing. Cambridge, Mass.: Harvard University Press, 1952, pp. 141–63; plates 186–230.

Sheldon, George William.
Artistic Country Seats: types of recent american villas and cottage architecture, with instances of country clubhouses. 2 vols., 5 parts. New York, 1886–87.

Zaitzevsky, Cynthia and Miller, Myron.
William Ralph Emerson 1833–1912. Catalogue of an exhibition presented by the Fogg Art Museum and the Carpenter Center, May 30–June 20, 1969.

The theorists of the picturesque make dreary reading because they write so long-windedly. Taken as a whole, however, the ideas put forward in the thirty years from 1790 to 1820 are extremely pertinent to certain aspects of the current situation. The most important source material is:

Alison, Archibald.
Essays on the Nature and Principles of Taste. Edinburgh, 1790.

Price, Uvedale.
An Essay on the Picturesque as Compared with the Sublime and Beautiful, and, on the Use of Studying Pictures for the Purpose of Improving Real Landscapes. London, 1794.

Knight, Richard Payne.
An Analytical Enquiry into the Principles of Taste. London, 1805.

Loudon, John Claudius.
Encyclopaedia of Cottage, Farm and Villa Architecture and Furniture. London, 1833.

For critical writing on the period I found helpful:

Bull, Duncan (ed.).
Classic Ground. New Haven: The Yale Center for British Art, 1981.

Hersey, George, L.
"J.C. Loudon and Architectural Associationalism." *Architectural Review* (August 1968): 89–92.

Hussey, Christopher.
The Picturesque; Studies in a Point of View. New York: G.P. Putnam's Sons, 1927.

Pevsner, Nikolaus.
"The Picturesque in Architecture." *RIBA Journal* 55 (1945): 55–61.

Pevsner, Nikolaus.
"The Genesis of the Picturesque." *Architectural Review* 96 (1944): 139–46.

Pevsner, Nikolaus.
"Richard Payne Knight." *Art Bulletin* 31 (December 1949): 293–320.

Pilcher, Donald.
The Regency Style 1800–1830. London, 1948.

Watkin, David.
The English Vision: The Picturesque in Architecture, Landscape and Garden Design. London: John Murray, 1982.

For the effect of the English theories on nineteenth-century American architecture:

Downing, Andrew Jackson.
Cottage Residences; or a series of designs for rural cottages and cottage villas. And their gardens and grounds. New York, 1842.

Meeks, Caroll.
"Picturesque Eclecticism." *Art Bulletin* 32 (1950).

Rowe, Colin.
"Character and Composition; or some vicissitudes of architectural vocabulary in the nineteenth century." *Oppositions* 2 (January 1974): 41–60.

Van Rensselaer, Mariana.
Henry Hobson Richardson, and his Works. Boston: Houghton, Mifflin and Co., 1888.

THE CONTINUITY OF THE CLASSICAL: MANCHESTER SUPERIOR COURT BUILDING

For Manchester's history see:

Buckley, William E.
A New England Pattern, the History of Manchester, Connecticut. Chester, Conn.: Pequot Press, 1973.

For Lutyens see:

Butler, Arthur Stanley George.
The Architecture of Sir Edwin Lutyens. 3 vols. London: Country Life; New York: Scribner's Sons, 1950.

Goodhart-Rendel, H.S.
"The Work of the late Sir Edwin Lutyens O.M." *RIBA Journal* (March 1945): 123–29.

Greenberg, Allan.
"Lutyens's Architecture Restudied." *Perspecta: The Yale Architectural Journal* 12 (1969): 129–52.

Inskip, Peter.
"Lutyens's Houses." *Edwin Lutyens.* Architectural Monographs 6. London: Academy Editions, 1979, pp. 9–29.

Summerson, John.
"The Lutyens Memorial Volumes Reviewed." *RIBA Journal* (August 1951): 390–91.

Weaver, Lawrence.
Houses and Gardens by E. L. Lutyens, described and criticised by Lawrence Weaver. London: Country Life, 1914.

For McKim, Mead and White see:

Granger, Alfred Hoyt.
Charles Follen McKim; a Study of his life and work. Boston: Houghton, Mifflin and Co., 1913, especially chapter 3.

Greenberg, Allan.
"Introduction." *A Monograph of the Work of McKim, Mead and White, 1879–1915, Student's Edition.* New York: Architectural Book Publishing Co., 1981.

Roth, Leland.
"McKim, Mead and White Reappraised." *A Monograph of the Work of McKim, Mead and White, 1879–1915.* New York: Arno, 1977; Benjamin Blom, 1973.

Wilson, Richard Guy.
Charles F. McKim and the Development of the American Renaissance: A Study in Architecture and Culture. Thesis, University of Michigan.

On Jefferson:

Adams, William Howard.
The Eye of Thomas Jefferson. Washington, D.C.: National Gallery of Art, 1976.

Lehmann, Karl.
Thomas Jefferson, American Humanist. New York: Macmillan Co., 1947.

O'Neal, William B.
Jefferson's Buildings at the University of Virginia. Charlottesville: University of Virginia Press, 1960.

For recent attitudes to the classical:

Searing, Helen.
"Speaking a New Classicism." *Speaking a New Classicism: American Architecture Now.* Northampton, Mass.: Smith College Museum of Art, 1981, pp. 9–22.

Summerson, John.
The Classical Language of Architecture. London: Methuen and Co., Ltd., 1964.

Terry, Quinlan.
"Seven Misunderstandings about Classical Architecture." *Quinlan Terry.* London: Academy Editions, 1981.

Two useful books on courthouses are:

Greenberg, Allan.
Courthouse design: a handbook for judges and court administrators. American Bar Association Commission on Standards of Judicial Administration, 1975.

Lambert, Phyllis.
Courthouse: A Photographic Document. New York: Horizon Press, 1978.

THE IRONIES OF THE DIFFICULT WHOLE: GORDON WU HALL

On the Princeton campus:

Cram, Ralph Adams.
Holder Tower and the New Dining Halls. Princeton: Princeton University Press, 1918.

van Zandt, Helen and Lilly, Jan.
The Princeton University Campus—a guide. Princeton: Princeton University Press, 1964.

On Venturi, Rauch and Scott Brown the indispensable books are:

Venturi, Robert.
Complexity and Contradiction in Architecture. New York: Museum of Modern Art, 1977; 1966.

Venturi, Robert; Scott Brown, Denise; and Izenour, Steven.
Learning from Las Vegas. Cambridge, Mass.: The MIT Press, 1977; 1972.

Other helpful references include:

Venturi, Robert.
"Diversity, relevance and representation in historicism, or plus ça change . . . plus a plea for pattern all over architecture . . . with a postscript on my mother's house." *Architectural Record* (June 1982): 114–19.

Venturi, Robert and Scott Brown, Denise.
"Interview." *Harvard Architectural Review* 1 (1980): 228–39.

On Jacobethan architecture:

Shaw, Henry.
Details of Elizabethan Architecture. London: William Pickering, 1839.

Summerson, John.
Architecture in Britain 1530–1830. Part 1. Harmondsworth: Penguin Books, 1953.

Whiffen, Marcus.
An Introduction to Elizabethan and Jacobean Architecture. London: Art and Technics, 1952.

References relating to the idea of the difficult whole:

van Moos, Stanislaus.
Le Corbusier: Elements of a Synthesis. Cambridge, Mass.: The MIT Press, 1979.

Rowe, Colin and Slutzky, Robert.
"Transparency: Literal and Phenomenal." *Perspecta: The Yale Architectural Journal* 8 (1963): 45–54.

Shearman, John.
Mannerism. Harmondsworth: Penguin Books, 1967.

Summerson, John.
"William Butterfield; or, The Glory of Ugliness." *Heavenly Mansions and Other Essays on Architecture.* New York, W. W. Norton and Co., 1963.

ILLUSTRATION
CREDITS

ILLUSTRATION CREDITS

Note: Complete citations for published works appear in the bibliography, unless otherwise indicated.

1.
Courtesy of Sterling Library map room, Yale University.

2.
Gavin Macrae-Gibson.

3.
Gavin Macrae-Gibson.

4.
Courtesy of Frank O. Gehry Associates.

5.
Courtesy of Frank O. Gehry Associates.

6.
Gavin Macrae-Gibson.

7.
Courtesy of Frank O. Gehry Associates.

8.
Photo by T. Kitajima, reprinted by permission of A.D.A. Edita, Tokyo.

9.
From *Gordon-Matta Clark,* by permission of International Cultureel Centrum, Antwerp.

10.
From *Gordon-Matta Clark,* by permission of International Cultureel Centrum, Antwerp.

11.
Photo by T. Kitajima, reprinted by permission of A.D.A. Edita, Tokyo.

12.
From *Gordon-Matta Clark,* by permission of International Cultureel Centrum, Antwerp.

13.
From *Gordon-Matta Clark,* by permission of International Cultureel Centrum, Antwerp.

14.
From *Domus,* October 1979, reprinted by permission.

15.
Courtesy of Frank O. Gehry Associates.

16.
Copyright Ronald Davis. Courtesy of Blum Helman Gallery, New York.

17.
Gavin Macrae-Gibson.

18.
Copyright Ronald Davis. Courtesy of Blum Helman Gallery, New York.

19.
From *Domus,* August 1979, reprinted by permission.

20.
Copyright Ronald Davis. Courtesy of Blum Helman Gallery, New York.

21.
Collection of Kunsthistorisches Museum, Vienna.

22.
Courtesy of Frank O. Gehry Associates.

23.
Courtesy of Frank O. Gehry Associates.

24.
From Camilla Gray, *The Great Experiment: Russian Art 1863–1922.*

25.
From Camilla Gray, *The Great Experiment: Russian Art 1863–1922.*

26.
Courtesy of Frank O. Gehry Associates.

27.
Collection of Stedelijk Museum, Amsterdam.

28.
Collection of Stedelijk Museum, Amsterdam.

29.
From *Malevitch, Oeuvres de Casimir Severinovitch Malevitch (1878–1935)* (Paris: Centre Georges Pompidou, 1978).

30.
From Frank Lloyd Wright, *An American Architecture* (New York: Bramhall House, 1955).

31.
From David Gebhard, *Schindler.*

32.
Courtesy of Frank O. Gehry Associates.

33.
Collection of the Museum of Modern Art,
New York.

34.
Courtesy of Frank O. Gehry Associates.

35.
From *Art in Revolution*, exhibition catalogue (February 26–April 18, 1971), by permission of Hayward Gallery, London.

36.
Courtesy of Frank O. Gehry Associates.

37.
Collection of Stedelijk Museum,
Amsterdam.

38.
Courtesy of Frank O. Gehry Associates.

39.
From *Malevich: The Graphic Work 1913–
1930*, exhibition catalogue (November
1975–January 1976), by permission of The
Israel Museum, Jerusalem.

40.
Courtesy of Frank O. Gehry Associates.

41.
Gavin Macrae-Gibson.

42.
Courtesy of Peter Eisenman.

43.
Courtesy of Peter Eisenman.

44.
Courtesy of Peter Eisenman.

45.
Courtesy of Peter Eisenman.

46.
Courtesy of Peter Eisenman.

47.
Courtesy of Peter Eisenman.

48.
Courtesy of Peter Eisenman.

49.
Gavin Macrae-Gibson.

50.
Courtesy of Peter Eisenman.

51.
Courtesy of Peter Eisenman.

52.
Courtesy of Peter Eisenman.

53.
Courtesy of Peter Eisenman.

54.
From Eugenio Battisti, *Filippo Brunelles-
chi: The Complete Work*, by permission of
Electa Editrice, Milan.

55.
T. K. Kitao.

56.
T. K. Kitao.

57.
From Ferdinando Galli da Bibiena,
Architettura Civile, 1711.

58.
From Giuseppe Galli Bibiena, *Architectural and Perspective Designs dedicated to
his majesty Charles VI, Holy Roman Em-
peror* (New York: Dover Publications, Inc.,
1964), by permission.

59.
The British Architectural Library, RIBA,
London.

60.
By permission of Centro Internazionale di
Studi Architettura "Andrea Palladio" di
Vicenza.

61.
From Claude-Nicolas Ledoux, *Architecture
Considerée . . . .*

62.
From Le Corbusier, *Oeuvre Complète*, by
permission of Artemis Publishers, Zurich.

63.
Photo by Yukio Futagawa, reprinted by
permission of A.D.A. Edita, Tokyo.

64.
Courtesy of the Cooper-Hewitt Museum,
The Smithsonian Institution's National
Museum of Design.

65.
Gavin Macrae-Gibson.

66.
Courtesy of Peter Eisenman.

67.
Gavin Macrae-Gibson.

68.
Photo by Adams Aerial Survey, Inc., copyright Gavin Macrae-Gibson.

69.
Drawing by Mark Yoes, copyright Gavin Macrae-Gibson.

70.
From Philip Johnson, *Mies van der Rohe*, by permission of Hedrich-Blessing.

71.
From Philip Johnson, *Mies van der Rohe*, by permission of Hedrich-Blessing.

72.
Gavin Macrae-Gibson.

73.
Courtesy of Cesar Pelli and Associates.

74.
Gavin Macrae-Gibson.

75.
Gavin Macrae-Gibson.

76.
Drawing by Turon Duda, courtesy of Cesar Pelli and Associates.

77.
From Jean-Nicolas-Louis Durand, *Précis des Leçons d'Architecture*, first published 1802; this illustration was added in the 1840 edition.

78.
From Claude-Nicolas Ledoux, *Architecture Considerée . . . .*

79.
Courtesy of Cesar Pelli and Associates.

80.
Courtesy of Cesar Pelli and Associates.

81.
Courtesy of Colin St. John Wilson.

82.
Courtesy of Cesar Pelli and Associates.

83.
Gavin Macrae-Gibson.

84.
From Bruno Taut, *Alpine Architecture.*

85.
From Charles Jencks, *The Language of Post-Modern Architecture* (New York: Rizzoli, 1977), by permission.

86.
Collection of the Museum of Modern Art, New York.

87.
Gavin Macrae-Gibson.

88.
Gavin Macrae-Gibson.

89.
From Le Corbusier, *Oeuvre Complète*, by permission of Artemis Publishers, Zurich.

90.
Collection of the Museum of Modern Art, New York.

91.
Photo by Mitsuo Matsuoka, reprinted by permission of Schinkenchiku-sha Co., Ltd.

92.
Photo by Richard Wurts, Litchfield, Connecticut.

93.
Courtesy of Sterling Library map room, Yale University.

94.
Gavin Macrae-Gibson.

95.
Gavin Macrae-Gibson.

96.
From W. J. Hawkins, *The Grand Era of Cast-Iron Architecture in Portland*, by permission of Binford and Mort.

97.
Gavin Macrae-Gibson.

98.
Courtesy of Michael Graves.

99.
Gavin Macrae-Gibson.

100.
Gavin Macrae-Gibson.

101.
Gavin Macrae-Gibson.

102.
Gavin Macrae-Gibson.

103.
Gavin Macrae-Gibson.

104.
Courtesy of Michael Graves.

105.
Courtesy of Michael Graves.

106.
Courtesy of Michael Graves.

107.
By permission of Dover Publications, Inc.

108.
From Genevieve Levallet-Haug, *Claude-Nicolas Ledoux 1736–1806* (Paris and Strasbourg: Librairie Istra, 1934)

109.
From P. O. Rave, *Karl Friedrich Schinkel Lebenswerk: Berlin III*, by permission of Deutscher Kunstverlag.

110.
From Albert E. Richardson, *Monumental and Classic Architecture in Great Britain and Ireland*, by permission of W. W. Norton and Co., Inc.

111.
From Hugh Honour, *Neo-Classicism.*

112.
Courtesy of Michael Graves.

113.
Collection of Osterreichische Galerie, Vienna.

114.
From *Art in Revolution*, exhibition catalogue (February 26–April 18, 1971), by permission of Hayward Gallery.

115.
From Le Corbusier, *Towards a New Architecture*, p. 206.

116.
Gavin Macrae-Gibson.

117.
Courtesy of Michael Graves.

118.
Gavin Macrae-Gibson.

119.
Courtesy of Michael Graves.

120.
Gavin Macrae-Gibson.

121.
Courtesy of Michael Graves.

122.
Courtesy of Sterling Library map room, Yale University.

123.
Gavin Macrae-Gibson.

124.
Courtesy of Robert A. M. Stern, Architects.

125.
From Vincent Scully, *The Shingle Style*, by permission of Yale University Press.

126.
Courtesy of Robert A. M. Stern, Architects.

127.
Courtesy of Robert A. M. Stern, Architects.

128.
Gavin Macrae-Gibson.

129.
From George Sheldon, *Artistic Country Seats*, by permission of Da Capo Press.

130.
From *American Architect*, 1879.

131.
Courtesy of Robert A. M. Stern, Architects.

132.
From George Sheldon, *Artistic Country Seats*, by permission of Da Capo Press.

133.
Gavin Macrae-Gibson.

134.
From George Sheldon, *Artistic Country Seats*, by permission of Da Capo Press.

135.
From Mariana van Rensselaer, *Henry Hobson Richardson*, by permission of Dover Publications, Inc.

136.
From Mariana van Rensselaer, *Henry Hobson Richardson*, by permission of Dover Publications, Inc.

137.
Gavin Macrae-Gibson.

138.
From George Sheldon, *Artistic Country Seats,* by permission of Da Capo Press.

139.
Courtesy of Robert A. M. Stern, Architects.

140.
Gavin Macrae-Gibson.

141.
Courtesy of Robert A. M. Stern, Architects.

142.
Photo by Roberto Schezen, courtesy of Robert A. M. Stern, Architects.

143.
From George Sheldon, *Artistic Country Seats,* by permission of Da Capo Press.

144.
From Vincent Scully, *The Shingle Style,* by permission of Yale University Press.

145.
From Cynthia Zaitzevsky and Myron Miller, *William Ralph Emerson 1833–1912,* by permission of Fogg Art Museum, Harvard University. Photo by Myron Miller.

146.
From Henry-Russell Hitchcock, *Rhode Island Architecture* (Providence: Rhode Island Museum Press, 1939).

147.
Courtesy of Robert A. M. Stern, Architects.

148.
From Vincent Scully, *The Shingle Style,* by permission of Yale University Press.

149.
From George Sheldon, *Artistic Country Seats,* by permission of Da Capo Press.

150.
Gavin Macrae-Gibson.

151.
Gavin Macrae-Gibson.

152.
Courtesy of Allan Greenberg.

153.
Gavin Macrae-Gibson.

154.
Courtesy of Allan Greenberg.

155.
Gavin Macrae-Gibson.

156.
Courtesy of Allan Greenberg.

157.
Courtesy of Allan Greenberg.

158.
Gavin Macrae-Gibson.

159.
Gavin Macrae-Gibson.

160.
Gavin Macrae-Gibson.

161.
Courtesy of Allan Greenberg.

162.
Gavin Macrae-Gibson.

163.
Gavin Macrae-Gibson.

164.
From Phyllis Lambert, *Courthouse: A Photographic Document.*

165.
From *The Works in Architecture of Robert and James Adams,* edited with an introduction by Robert Oresko (New York: St. Martin's Press, Inc., 1975), by permission. Revised and enlarged version of 1902 edition published by E. Thecard Fils, Dourdan, France.

166.
From Desmond Guiness and Julius Trousdale Sadler, *Mr. Jefferson, Architect* (New York: Viking Press, 1973), p. 33, by permission.

167.
From Emile Esperandieu, *La Maison Carrée à Nîmes* (Paris: Laurens, 1929).

168.
From I. T. Frary, *Thomas Jefferson, Architect and Builder* (Richmond, Va.: Garrett and Massie, 1939), plate LIX.

169.
Courtesy of University of Virginia Rare
Book Department.

170.
From William B. O'Neal, *Jefferson's Buildings at the University of Virginia*, by permission of the University of Virginia.

171.
From *The Architecture of Sir Edwin
Lutyens*, vol. 3.

172.
From *The Architecture of Sir Edwin
Lutyens*, vol. 3.

173.
From *A Monograph of the Works of
McKim, Mead and White 1879–1915*, by
permission of The Ayer Company.

174.
From *A Monograph of the Works of
McKim, Mead and White 1879–1915*, by
permission of The Ayer Company.

175.
From *A Monograph of the Works of
McKim, Mead and White 1879–1915*, by
permission of The Ayer Company.

176.
From Michel Fleury, Arlain Erlande-Bran-
denburg, and Jean-Pierre Babelon, *Paris
Monumental* (Paris: Flammarion, 1974), by
permission of Hirmer Verlag, Munich.

177.
From F. Borsi, *Leon Battista Alberti* (Mi-
lan: Electa Editrice, 1975). Photo by Sergio
Anelli, courtesy of Electa Editrice, Milan.

178.
From Bernhard Berenson, *The Arch of
Constantine; or, the Decline of Form* (Lon-
don: Chapman and Hall, 1954).

179.
Gavin Macrae-Gibson.

180.
Gavin Macrae-Gibson.

181.
Gavin Macrae-Gibson.

182.
Gavin Macrae-Gibson.

183.
Courtesy of Venturi, Rauch and Scott
Brown, Architects.

184.
Gavin Macrae-Gibson.

185.
Gavin Macrae-Gibson.

186.
From Marcus Whiffen, *Elizabethan and
Jacobean Architecture.*

187.
Gavin Macrae-Gibson.

188.
Courtesy of Venturi, Rauch and Scott
Brown, Architects.

189.
Courtesy of Venturi, Rauch and Scott
Brown, Architects.

190.
Courtesy of Venturi, Rauch and Scott
Brown, Architects.

191.
Gavin Macrae-Gibson.

192.
Courtesy of Venturi, Rauch and Scott
Brown, Architects.

193.
From John Summerson, *Architecture in
Britain 1530–1830.*

194.
From Henry Shaw, *Details of Elizabethan
Architecture.*

195.
Gavin Macrae-Gibson.

196.
Gavin Macrae-Gibson.

197.
From Le Corbusier, *Oeuvre Complète*, vol.
1, by permission of Artemis Publishers,
Zurich.

198.
From Le Corbusier, *Oeuvre Complète*, vol.
1, by permission of Artemis Publishers,
Zurich.

199.
Gavin Macrae-Gibson.

200.
Courtesy of Venturi, Rauch, and Scott
Brown, Architects.

201.
From *Edwin Lutyens*, Architectural Mono-
graphs 6, by permission of Academy
Editions.

202.
Gavin Macrae-Gibson.

203.
From Sir Lawrence Weaver, *Houses and
Gardens by E. L. Lutyens.*

204.
From Hussey and Cornforth, *English
Country Houses open to the Public* (London: Country Life; New York: Scribners,
1950).

205.
Gavin Macrae-Gibson.

206.
From Cynthia Zaitzevsky and Myron Miller, *William Ralph Emerson 1833–1912*,
by permission of Fogg Art Museum, Harvard University.

207.
From Henry Shaw, *Details of Elizabethan
Architecture.*

208.
Gavin Macrae-Gibson.

209.
From Fernando Rigon, *Palladio* (Bologna:
Capitol, 1980), by permission of Centro
Internazionale di Studi di Architettura
"Andrea Palladio" di Vicenza.

210.
Gavin Macrae-Gibson.

211.
Gavin Macrae-Gibson.

212.
From Le Corbusier, *Towards a New
Architecture.*

213.
From Venturi, Scott Brown and Izenour,
Learning from Las Vegas, by permission of
The MIT Press.

214.
Courtesy of Venturi, Rauch and Scott
Brown.

p. 169.
Gavin Macrae-Gibson.

INDEX